THE NEW YORK KID'S BOOK

167
Children's Writers and Artists
Celebrate New York City

THE NEW YORK KID'S BOOK

Doubleday & Company, Inc.
Garden City, New York

LIBRARY OF CONGRESS CATALOGING IN PUBLICATION DATA
Children's Writers and Artists Collaborative.
The New York Kid's Book.
Includes index.
SUMMARY: Stories, articles, poetry, amusements,
illustrations, and photographs by well-known writers
and illustrators in celebration of New York City.
1. New York (City)—Literary collections.
2. Children's literature, American.
[1. New York (City)—Literary collections.
2. Literature—Collections] I. Title.
PZ5.C4383   810'.8'032

ISBN 0-385-12918-1
Library of Congress Catalog Card Number 77–15171
Copyright © 1979 by The New York Kid's Catalog, a New York Partnership
All Rights Reserved
Printed in the United States of America

First Edition

BOOK DESIGN BY BENTE HAMANN

"At Work on the Statue of Liberty" reprinted from *The Tallest Lady in the World* © 1967 by
Norah Smaridge. "Caving In," by Pyke Johnson, Jr. © 1977 by *The New York Times* Com-
pany. Reprinted by permission. "The Delicatessen-loving Dog" © 1979 X. J. Kennedy.
"Flubs & Fluffs" cartoons, by Jerry Robinson, © 1975, 1976, 1977 by News Syndicate Co.
Inc. Reprinted by permission of the author. "Pleased to Meet You" reprinted from *Scary
Things*, by Norah Smaridge, © 1974 by Abingdon Press. Photograph for "A Special Star and
New York City" © 1975 by Helmut K. Wimmer. "Wraith" by Edna St. Vincent Millay, first
and last stanzas, reprinted from *Collected Poems*, Harper & Row. © 1921, 1948 by Edna
St. Vincent Millay. The title page illustration and the chapter openings were adapted from
"Type City," by Dorothy Yule, a print that first appeared as part of a portfolio of fourteen
prints entitled *William Alan Yule*, privately printed at St. Martin's School of Art in London in
1975 in a limited edition of ten, with two artist's proofs.

EDITORS

CATHARINE EDMONDS

JOAN GROSS

OLGA LITOWINSKY

STEPHEN MOOSER

PAMELA MORTON

BARBARA BEASLEY MURPHY

BARBARA SEULING

BEBE WILLOUGHBY

CONTRIBUTORS TO THE NEW YORK KID'S BOOK

Adrienne Adams
Joan Aiken
Lloyd Alexander
Sue Alexander
Aliki
Gerald Ames
Berthe Amoss
Mary Anderson
Louise Armstrong
Frank Asch
Philip H. Ault
Thomas G. Aylesworth

Norman Baker
Richard Meran Barsam
Bill Basso
Nathaniel Benchley
Marvin Bileck
Mary Bloom
Judy Blume
Betty Boegehold
Don Bolognese
Demetre Bove
Franklyn M. Branley
Stanlee Brimberg
Ashley Bryan
Barbara Bullock
Robert Burch
Barbara Burn

Malcolm Carrick
Pamela Carroll
Ida Chittum
Joe Ciardiello
Daniel Cohen
Chris Conover
Barbara Cooney
Scott Corbett
Rachel Cowan
Julia Cunningham

Roald Dahl
Martina D'Alton
Beatrice Schenck de Regniers
Jorge Diaz
Emil P. Dolensek
Judy Donnelly
Michael Dorman
Roger Duvoisin

Ed Edelson
Catharine Edmonds
Marc Edmonds
Eleanor Estes

Norma Farber
Margo Feiden
Edith Bing Firestone
Don Freeman

Jean Fritz
Burton Frye

Rachel Gallagher
Nancy Garden
May Garelick
James Cross Giblin
Winnette Glasgow
Shirley Glubok
A. D. Goldstein
Constance C. Greene
Sheila Greenwald
Joan Gross

Irene Haas
Marylin Hafner
Paul Hagerman
Suzanne Haldane
Beverly Hall
Ole Hamann
James Haskins
Esther Hautzig
Barbara Shook Hazen
Barbara Hennessy
Tom Huffman
Bernice Kohn Hunt
Johanna Hurwitz

Pyke Johnson, Jr.

X. J. Kennedy
M. E. Kerr
Barrie Klaits
Fernando Krahn
Ruth Krauss

Nancy Larrick
Madeleine L'Engle
Elizabeth Levine
Joan Lexau
Howard Liss
Olga Litowinsky
Jean Little
Myra Cohn Livingston
Joseph Low
Francesca Lyman

David Macaulay
Ann McGovern
Georgess McHargue
Robert Makla
Eve Merriam
Sheila Moon
Stephen Mooser
Gisela Moriarty
Lillian Morrison
Pamela Morton
Barbara Murphy
Walter Myers

Laurie Norris
Andre Norton

Margaret O'Connell

Sidney Offitt

Richard Peck
Gloria Perry
Daniel Manus Pinkwater
Mariana B. Prieto
Penelope Proddow

Robert Quackenbush

Elaine Raphael
Sam Reavin
Johanna Reiss
Ken Rinciari
Jerry Robinson
Barbara Rollock
Richard Rosenblum
Lavinia Russ

Alice Schick
Joel Schick
George Selden
Steve Senn
Barbara Seuling
Dennis Seuling
Phil Seuling
Ann Zane Shanks
Dorothy Shuttlesworth
Alvin Silverstein
Virginia Silverstein
Walter Simonson
Alfred Slote
Norah Smaridge
William Jay Smith

Hannah Solomon
Joe Staton
Edward Stevensen
Tal Stubis
Susan Suba
George Sullivan
Lowell Swortzell

Charlene Joy Talbot
Alfred Tamarin
Sydney Taylor
Tobi Tobias
Margot Tomes
P. L. Travers
Susan Trentacoste
Judith Turner

Stuart Whyte
Karen Shaw Widman
Jay Williams
Jennifer Brown Williams
Bebe Willoughby
Helmut Wimmer
Lauren L. Wohl
Judie Wolkoff
Rose Wyler

Jane Yolen
Dorothy Yule

Georg Zappler
Margot Zemach
Charlotte Zolotow

CONTENTS

*This book is for all
New York kids,
past, present, and future*

LIST OF ILLUSTRATIONS

New York Kid's Book

INTRODUCTION

Dear Readers,

If you're wondering what *The New York Kid's Book* is, it's a celebration of New York in every shape and form. It came about when CWAC, a small group of writers and illustrators, learned that children's rooms in public libraries across the city were being forced to cut their hours and curtail services to the children. New York City was in trouble. Our feeling was that since New York had been good to us, we wanted to return something of our talents to the city. The inevitable result was a book.

So we drew up a proposal for the book, including a plan to donate two years of royalties to the children's rooms of the circulation branches of the New York Public Library. Doubleday liked the idea, then handsomely offered to give each of these rooms a copy of the book.

We invited children's writers and illustrators from across the country to contribute a written piece, an illustration, a photograph on the city to the book. And you can see by the size of the book how generously colleagues have responded.

We hope this book will inspire you who live in the city and you who come to visit . . . to explore this wonderful town, this big apple, this concrete and earth encyclopedia of knowledge, adventure, science and art. For it is your passion for New York City that will keep it alive and well for the next generation of children. We believe it is in well-loved cities that the greatest strides of civilization are often made.

We thank our many talented contributors, and our editors, Janet Chenery and Mary Jones.

With appreciation for the courage of our city's librarians,

With hope for our great city's future

And love for the children here,

The Children's Writers and Artists Collaborative, CWAC:

Catharine Edmonds

Joan Gross

Olga Litowinsky

Stephen Mooser

Pamela Morton

Barbara Beasley Murphy

Barbara Seuling

Bebe Willoughby

Kid City

PAUL HAGERMAN

Do you know that if all the grown-ups in New York were thrown out of the city, New York would still be the sixth largest metropolis in the United States!

New York's public school system has over 1,100,000 students. That's more than the entire population of Dallas, Boston, or San Francisco. Only Los Angeles, Chicago, Philadelphia, Detroit, and Houston have more people than New York has students.

What would New York be like without grown-ups? How would the kids run the city all by themselves? They'd probably do a better job than the grown-ups, don't you think?

NEW YORK
IN THE BEGINNING

EXCERPT FROM *DIARY* *OF A LITTLE GIRL IN OLD NEW YORK,* 1849–50, BY CATHERINE ELIZABETH HAVENS

(FROM THE COLLECTION OF ANDRE NORTON)

August 6, 1849

I am ten years old today, and I am going to begin to keep a diary . . .

I remember . . . going with my nurse to the Vauxhall Gardens, and riding in a merry-go-round. These Gardens were in Lafayette Place, near our house . . .

Back of our house was an alley that ran through to the Bowery, and there was a livery stable on the Bowery, and one time my brother, who was full of fun and mischief, got a pony from the stable and rode it right down into our kitchen and galloped it around the table and frightened our cook almost to death . . .

We moved from Lafayette Place to Brooklyn when I was four years old . . . My brother liked Brooklyn because he could go crabbing on the river, but I was afraid of the goats, which chased one of my friends one day. So we came back to New York, and my father bought a house on Ninth Street. He bought it of a gentleman who lived next door to us, and who had but one lung, and he lived on raw turnips and sugar. Perhaps that is why he had only one lung . . .

I am still living in our Ninth Street house. It is a beautiful house and has glass sliding doors with birds of Paradise sitting on palm trees painted on them. And back of our dining room is a piazza, and a grape vine, and we have lots of Isabella grapes every fall. It has a parlor in front and the library in the middle and the dining room at the back. On the mantel piece in the library is a very old clock that my father brought from France in one of his ships . . .

[My cousin Anna] and I are together in school, but now they have moved way up to Fifteenth Street; but I walk up every morning to meet her and we walk down to school together . . .

Saturdays I go up to Anna's, and on Irving Place, between Fourteenth and Fifteenth streets, there is a rope walk, and we like to watch the men walk back and forth making the rope . . .

New York is getting very big and building up. I walk some mornings with my nurse before breakfast . . . up Fifth Avenue to Twenty-third Street, and down Broadway home. An officer stands in front of the House of Refuge on Madison Square, ready to arrest bad people, and he looks as if he would like to find some.

Fifth Avenue is very muddy above Eighteenth Street, and there are no blocks of houses as there are downtown, but only two or three on a block. Last Saturday we had a picnic on the grounds of Mr. Waddell's country seat way up Fifth Avenue [ed. note: corner of Thirty-seventh Street], and it was so muddy I spoiled my new light cloth gaiter boots. I have a beautiful green and black changeable silk visite [ed. note: "a loose fitting, unlined coat"], but my mother said it looked like rain and I could not wear it, and it never rained a drop after all. It has a pink ruffle all around it and a sash behind.

Miss Carew makes my things. She is an old maid, and very fussy, and [my niece] Ellen and I don't like her. She wears little bunches of curls behind her ears, and when she is cutting out [cloth] she screws up her mouth, and we try not to laugh . . .

t' Fort nieuw Amsterdam op de Manhatans

Manhattan Streams

NATHANIEL BENCHLEY

Between three and four hundred years ago, when the Dutch first settled on Manhattan, it was a hunting and fishing ground for the Indians. Streams, creeks, and ponds, fed by underground springs, kept the earth moist and helped the foliage grow, and the rocky spine of the island was covered with a heavy stand of trees. The streams and rivers teemed with fish and shellfish, and the wildlife included deer, bears, wolves, and foxes, not to mention porcupines, muskrats, bobcats, and an occasional errant moose.

From what is now Yonkers, to the north, and present-day Brooklyn and Long Island, in the east, the Indians came to hunt and fish, and also to train their young men in wilderness survival. When a youth was considered old enough to be alone in the forest he was sent to Manhattan, where he would make a shelter for the nighttime, catch what fish or game he could, and cook it for his meals. When he had proved he could fend for himself, he was deemed ready to become a hunter.

In 1626, a Dutchman named Peter Minuit came to buy land for a settlement. He found some Indians fishing at a pond, and offered them a bargain: in return for the rights to the island, he gave them merchandise and trinkets worth about twenty-four dollars. (Nobody can be sure what the exact value was at the time.) The Indians, who came from Canarsee (Brooklyn) and had no claim to Manhattan in the first place, were astounded at their good luck, and they hurried back across the river before Minuit might change his mind. When the real Manhattan Indians found out what had happened, it was too late; the Dutch had settled in, and eventually took over the island.

Nowadays, all that remains of the old Manhattan are some of the trees in the parks and the streams that flow beneath the city streets. Time and again people have tried to dam up these steams, but they continue to flow, fed by the same springs that fed them hundreds of years ago. Minetta Brook was once tapped and made into an indoor fountain by a hotel that rose above it, and in one corner of the basement of a hospital uptown you can, if you listen carefully, hear the gurgling of one of the many streams that couldn't be stopped.

Harlem Gets Its Name

Before the arrival of the Dutch on Manhattan, present-day Harlem was known by its Indian name as Muscoota, in honor of the Muscoota River which ran through its fields. By the middle of the seventeenth century Dutch settlers began establishing farms in Muscoota. The farmers thought the area deserved a Dutch name, but they couldn't decide which one to pick. Each

settler wanted the spot named after his own hometown back in Holland. Governor Stuyvesant finally stepped into the dispute. He asked each settler for the name of his hometown. When he noticed that none of them had come from Haarlem, he once again displayed the wisdom for which he was famous by promptly christening the place Nieuw Haarlem.

Adriaen Block, a Dutchman, built the first houses on Manhattan Island and was the first resident of the island.

Farmer Quackenbush in New Amsterdam

THE REAL STORY
OF THE FIRST QUACKENBUSH
TO ARRIVE IN AMERICA

ROBERT QUACKENBUSH

There was once a farmer in Holland who raised ducks. He was named Quackenbush because he was always seen chasing his ducks out from their hiding places in the bushes.

Farmer Quackenbush had a very successful duck business. On every holiday, people came from all over to buy his ducks for their festive dinners. Then, suddenly, people stopped buying his ducks. Roast goose had become the rage for holiday feasting. This was a disaster for Farmer Quackenbush because he was stuck with a farm full of hundreds of quacking ducks, with new ones hatching every day. What could he do with all those ducks?

The year was 1660, and many people were leaving Holland to seek opportunities in the New World.

"I have an answer," Farmer Quackenbush said to his wife one morning. "We'll move to New Amsterdam and take our ducks with us. We'll sell the ducks to all the settlers in America."

"Good idea," said his wife. "And the sooner we get rid of all of those ducks the better I'll like it."

So Farmer Quackenbush sold his farm in Holland and boarded a ship to New Amsterdam with his wife and baby and ducks. For two months they traveled across the sea. It was a miserable voyage. The ducks quacked the whole time. The sailors on board had to be restrained from tossing Farmer Quackenbush and his ducks overboard.

At last the ship reached New Amsterdam, and Farmer Quackenbush waddled all of his ducks directly to the market square. But no one would buy his ducks.

"Haven't you heard?" the people in the market told him. "Roast turkey is the popular thing here in America."

Farmer Quackenbush left with his wife and baby and ducks to find a room at the inn. But the innkeeper would not let them stay.

"Ducks are not allowed here," he said. "This is a quiet and respectable place."

As they went down the street, townspeople hollered and jeered at them.

"Noise polluters!" they shouted. "Get those ducks out of town!"

So Farmer Quackenbush and his little family had to spend their first night in America in an open field on the outskirts of New Amsterdam. The ducks quacked all night and the ground was cold, making sleep impossible.

"There's only one thing to do," Farmer Quackenbush said to his wife. "Let's leave the ducks behind and go elsewhere. But we must make a fast getaway!"

With that they gathered up their belongings and ran down the road. A wagon came along and the driver asked where they were going so late at night.

"Same place you are," Farmer Quackenbush told the driver, who agreed to take them with him—all the way to Albany.

Once in Albany, Farmer Quackenbush had to decide what he would do for a living, since he had had it with ducks. He decided a quieter profession was the answer and became a brickmaker.

As soon as he could, Farmer Quackenbush built a brick road all the way to Washington, D.C., that still exists today. It would give him a way to escape, he figured—just in case someone discovered he was the one who left the people of New Amsterdam with all those quacking ducks on their hands.

Old New York Cole Slaw

MARIANA B. PRIETO

When the Dutch West Indies company settled in Manhattan in 1624 they planted their favorite vegetables—cabbage, onions, and potatoes.

Today, people still enjoy the foods that Dutch housewives introduced here long ago.

Quite often when you order a hot dog or a hamburger, cole slaw is served with it. Had it not been for the early Dutch settlers we might not have had this delicious dish. They called it "Kool slaa," meaning cabbage salad. The original slaw was not made with mayonnaise. It was made with a dressing of vinegar, oil, salt and pepper.

On the Trail of the Manhattan Indians

GISELA MORIARTY

Imagine real Indians living in caves right on Manhattan Island! A good way to explore New York's Indian heritage is to start at the Museum of the American Indian, the world's largest Native American museum. A miniature scene of Inwood Hill Park there shows what Indian life was like in Manhattan during the 1500s. The museum excavated Inwood Hill Park in 1920 and recovered many ornaments, tools, and other objects now on display. The finds also made it possible to re-create, in miniature, the caves, bark wigwams, and lodges in which many people could live together, as well as common activities such as drying fish and digging out a canoe. Notice the heaps of shells on the ground—shellfish were an important part of the Indian diet here.

Inwood Hill, at the northern end of Manhattan, offered shelter in its rocky overhangs and caves, as well as fresh spring water, good fishing, and easy access from the rivers. The Indians at Inwood were a branch of the Algonquians, who date back as far as 9000 B.C.

Taking your modern wampum to a bus stop near the museum, or to the 157th Street Broadway subway station, you can go uptown to explore Inwood Hill Park itself. There you'll still find the caves and the level land that was Shorakapkok, home of the Indians long after 1626, when Manhattan was "sold" to the white man downtown. (Up at Inwood Hill, the Indians didn't even know about that deal and stayed around for nearly a hundred years more.)

Then, traveling down to Fifth Avenue and 103rd Street, you can visit the Museum of the City of New York. Here, a miniature scene shows Indian life at Inwood the way Henry Hudson might have found it in 1609, when he sailed up the river. Another miniature shows the Dutch West India Company buying Manhattan Island from the Canarsie Indians in 1626 for goods worth sixty guilders, about twenty-four dollars. Other exhibits describe how the Indians got along with the early Dutch settlers of New York, who established New Amsterdam here in 1624 with just thirty families.

In 1620 there were about 25,000 Algonquian-speaking Indians in the Northeast. By 1676 most of them had been killed by wars and by new kinds of diseases brought by European settlers. Manhattan, which means "island surrounded by hills," is actually an Algonquian name.

If you want to know still more about Manhattan Indians, there is a special book published by the Museum of the American Indian called *New York City in Indian Possession*, by R. P. Bolton.

To reach Inwood Hill Park, take the Eighth Avenue express subway to 207th Street and Broadway, then walk west, or take the No. 4 bus to the Cloisters and walk north, all the way across Dyckman Street and through the woods. The caves are along the northern cliffs just before the Spuyten Duyvil Creek, which marks the end of Manhattan Island.

Dig This

PAUL HAGERMAN

You would learn a lot about what New York used to be like just by digging down a few feet. If you found a place that hadn't been disturbed much, it's possible that you might find an arrowhead or a farm tool. It wasn't that long ago that there were farms in midtown Manhattan. The Manhattan Indian tribe lived here for centuries. (As a matter of fact, there are still 3,262 Indians living in New York City. There are two pow-wows and Indian dances held each month in Manhattan.)

You might also find a human skull. There once were many more graveyards in Manhattan than there are now. Some, such as Washington Square, have been turned into parks and others now have buildings on top of them. You probably know that there are over seven million people living above the ground in New York, but did you know that there are an estimated 31,125,000 dead people buried beneath it?

If you dug down in certain places between lower Manhattan and Thirty-fourth Street, you might find sea shells. Much of the land between the financial district and the midtown area was once swampy or entirely under water. Because of landfill projects Manhattan is now 25 per cent larger than it was when it was first settled. You'd have to dig down very far before you hit bedrock in this area of the city. That's the reason why there aren't many skycrapers between lower Manhattan and the midtown area.

Copper Mine

One of the world's largest deposits of copper lies under the streets of New York, in over 380 million pounds of pure copper electric cables.

New York, How You've Changed!

Watch NIEUW AMSTERDAM change to NEW YORK right before your eyes! If you follow the directions very carefully, you will change the name of the Dutch settlement of 1624 to the true name of the Big Apple today. (SOLUTION, PG. 367.)

1. Write down the words NIEUW AMSTERDAM.

2. Take out all of the M's, replace them with A's, and close up the space between the words.

3. Exchange the positions of the I and the D.

4. Add a K in the exact middle of the word.

5. Move the second consonant after the first double letter to the end. Reverse the order of the second and third letters.

6. Add an O after each 7th letter.

7. Wherever a double letter appears, remove both letters.

8. Add a Y after every second vowel.

9. Drop the second consonant; exchange the positions of the R and the K.

10. Reverse the positions of the fourth and fifth letters.

11. Wherever a letter appears for the second time, omit it.

12. Drop the U; move the T three spaces ahead.

13. Replace the S with a C and move it back 4 places; add spaces between the Y and the W and between the K and the C.

The first people who settled in New York were Dutch. They built houses and a fort at the lowest tip of Manhattan Island and called it New Amsterdam, after their home village of Amsterdam. That was in 1624.

The second people to arrive were blacks, starting in 1626. At first they were slaves, but later they became free and worked as farmers and tradesmen.

Jews arrived in 1654. The population "exploded" to a thousand a couple of years later. The colony looked interesting to the British. They quietly invaded New Amsterdam and renamed it after the Duke of York, New York.

Dig This Ditch

The largest garnet crystal found in North America came out of a ditch on Thirty-fifth Street.

The Singing Subway Man and the Buried Ship

BARBARA BEASLEY MURPHY

It takes centuries to create a city. Beginning with shacks and dusty footpaths, New York City has evolved into a mass of concrete, steel, and glass. And the transformation goes on.

Someone once said, "New York would be a nice place to live, if they ever finished it." But the changes are what make a city alive. There is a constant process of decay and renewal. As it changes, the city leaves part of its past in the earth. Layer upon layer, the city builds upon the past. There is always someone to mourn what has been lost or left behind. And there is always someone to burn with curiosity when a remnant of that past is discovered in some unlikely place.

Such a man was James Kelly, foreman of the construction crew who began building the Seventh Avenue Line of the New York Subway System in 1913. By 1918 he had led his crew of Italian immigrants thirteen miles under New York from the southern tip of Manhattan to the Bronx. The crew called Kelly the singing subway man because he belted out tunes to them as they worked. His favorite was: "They're Going to Dig a Subway to Ireland."

In May 1916, when the crew had reached Cortland Street, less than a mile from the beginning, their pickaxes struck something more solid than the soft earth. As they shoveled the soil away, they could see the partial outline of an ancient ship. The dim yellow light in the damp tunnel revealed a ship's bow, keel, and ribs protruding waist high from the western wall of the tunnel on the Hudson River side. The oak was badly charred. A cannonball, a clay pipe, and shattered bits of pottery rested on nearby timbers.

"Hey," James Kelly said, "let's find out about this! It's bound to be important to the history of this town."

He called up various museums and asked if their historians would be interested in examining it. "Perhaps you'll want to excavate it," he said.

One historian said, "It might be the remains of the *Tijger*. That was a Dutch ship who sailed here early in 1600 to trade beads for beaver pelts. One day she burned in the harbor and we don't know what became of her."

"Well, man, don't you want to come and see her? We could sure try to excavate her."

"No, I don't believe so."

And nothing Kelly could do could coax anyone into it. So he tried on his own to free the ship from the tunnel. He lined his crew up along the ten-foot section of tunnel wall and ordered them to pull the timbers out. But they wouldn't budge. Next he got a mule team and hitched them up to the one-foot-square keel. They strained but could not move it. Kelly thought then that a considerable length of the ship was still buried.

The construction company pressed Kelly to move ahead in the digging of the tunnel. "We've got to keep to our schedules. Can't lose money over this old hulk."

So Kelly cut off the keel and bow at the point where it disappeared into the tunnel wall. The section had three ribs attached and he took it to the New York Aquarium. It was put in a tank for the seals to play on.

All through his lifetime Kelly kept his dream of excavating the *Tijger*, one of the first European boats to anchor in what is now New York Harbor. In 1966, when the seventy-foot-deep cellar hole was dug for the World Trade Center, it was just opposite the spot where Kelly had cut off the *Tijger*'s bow. In the center of the hole an anchor with a ten-foot shank and a rudder were found. Today they're stowed away someplace in the World Trade Center. No one is making any effort to preserve them. The rest of the bits of wood which were found were hauled to a dump without any archaeologist's looking at them. Thus James Kelly's wish to resurrect the ancient ship never came true. He died in 1972.

—◆◆◆—

Uranium Mine

If you ride over the West Side Highway with a Geiger counter, it will click, because there is uranium underneath. The real estate value of these locations is far higher than any wealth under the ground, therefore it is not mined.

The Rocks Beneath Our Feet

STEPHEN MOOSER

If you think the Fordham Gneiss, the Inwood Dolomite, and the Manhattan Schist are rock groups soon to be appearing at Madison Square Garden you are only partly right. They are not rock groups, but rather groups of rocks. Manhattan schist, as a matter of fact, is a rock that appears not in Madison Square Garden, but under it. Gneiss, dolomite, and schist are the geological names of the types of stone upon which most of New York is built.

Fordham gneiss is a hard rock which can be found in the Bronx around Fordham University. In Upper Manhattan the gneiss gives way to what is known as Inwood Dolomite. This is a much softer rock, which is visible around Inwood Park, Fort Tryon, and Fort George. It also appears as the whitish stone which gives Marble Hill its name.

The gray rocks which are seen scattered over much of Manhattan and are especially visible in Central Park are examples of Manhattan schist. This is the hardest of the three. During the last great ice age the massive sheet of ice which covered Manhattan pounded, pressed, and polished the schist to an unbelievable hardness. It is this solid layer of rock which provides the strong base for New York's skyscrapers. The schist first rises near Fort Tryon. It slants slightly as it travels through Upper

Manhattan, but straightens out just in time to support the tall buildings at Rockefeller Center. It dips down sharply at Washington Square, but reappears at the tip of the island where it firmly supports the tall buildings in the Wall Street area, including the tallest building of them all, the twin towers of the World Trade Center.

Rock Hunting in the City

BARRIE KLAITS

You can collect rocks all over the city. But some of them are too big to take home. They are attached to buildings and streets. To find them, you have to walk and look.

Look at curbstones. Beneath the grime there is granite. Walk down Sixth Avenue, Fifth Avenue, Fourth Avenue and look for buildings made of pure, sugar-white marble. Walk up Third Avenue and Second Avenue and find buildings like tan Swiss cheese. The rock is travertine, and it formed in a hot spring in Italy. Walk crosstown and see brownstones. Dinosaurs were alive when the brown sandstone used in these buildings was forming in Connecticut and New Jersey.

Step inside the lobbies of grand office buildings and look up and around you. The walls may be marble, stained purple, brown, yellow, and pink by minerals like iron. The colors spread out in all directions and remind you of birds, butterflies, fish, or whatever you want them to be. Other marble walls have real fossils in them. Look at the gray marble in public bathrooms. You might find the outlines of sea shells. The wall was once the bottom of an ocean, and the sea shells belonged to living animals. The ocean has dried up. The animals are long gone. But they hardened into limestone rock together. Then the limestone was pressed and squeezed into gray marble.

Visit the lobbies of hospitals and apartment houses to collect red or green serpentine marbles. White streaks of calcite cut through the Christmas colors. The streaks are called "gash veins."

Look at stone window sills on school buildings, the ones that look like concrete. Up close there are teeny, tiny "bugs." The "bugs" are fossil shells of foraminifers. The forams once floated on an ocean or crawled on its floor.

Blackboards and black stone steps are made of slate, a rock that formed when mud dried up and hardened into shale. Shale gets pressed and squeezed deep down in the earth until it turns into slate.

Make friends with statues, especially with their granite or gabbro stones. Cool off in the Washington Square fountain while you lean on its granite walls. When you are tired, relax on a bench made of smooth granite or white marble.

Keep your collection locked in your memory. Then no one can ever take it from you.

POTPOURRI

theblimp
theblimp
floats

I went to see the Mayor at City Hall... *(typographic cityscape composed of repeated words: tree, bush, shrubs, bushes, grassandsomeleavesgreen, grassgreengrassgreengra, tinthemiddlecentralpark, iceinwonderlandstatues, seafountainandnippless, meadowandemonstrators, espeareinthesummernight, nahmemorialschaeffertoo, aroselcalliopemerrygoup, mayarchesncheckers, tersaterdarkarethere, arswhoseillyouaworld, akefrozenandskatedtronn, adgreenwalksandtalking, tinthemiddlecentralpark, tinthemiddlecentralpark, zoozoozoozoozoozoozoozo, znzarzl gzruznt, repeated numerals 7777 8888 9999 1111 2222 3333 4444 5555 6666, madisonsquarecircusrowsnoflowers, circuscircuscircuscir, big big big big big, tall tall tall, macysmacysmacys, busybusybusy)*

A Visit to the Mayor

WILLIAM JAY SMITH

I went to see the Mayor at City Hall,
And he said, "Hello," but that wasn't all.

He said, "Good morning!" and "How do
                  you do?
Did you ride on the ferry? Have you
                been to the zoo?

Do you have a pet dog? Or a bird? Or a
                    cat?
And what will you be—have you thought
                about that?

Have you thought when you grow up one
                day what you
Will want to be then? What you'll want
                to do?

Will you fly an airplane, sail an ocean
                liner,
Be a taxi-driver, a dress-designer?

Will you dress up in white and look after
                the sick,
Or work at a switchboard: 'Number,
              please—click!'

Be a butcher, a baker, dog-trainer, or
                farmer,
A tight-rope walker or a snake charmer?

An architect, a builder of bridges,
A gardener's assistant, a trimmer of
hedges?

A detective who solves a terrible crime
In the Case of the Lazy Man who killed
Time?

There are so many things in the world to
do;
Which of them all will appeal to you?"

He looked at me then in a very nice way;
I smiled, but I didn't know what to say.
So I said, "When I'm twenty or
twenty-nine,
I'll come back and tell you." And he said,
"That's fine."

New Amsterdam's first city hall, built in 1642.

Then he picked up his gloves and put on
his hat,
And he said, "Good-bye, I've enjoyed our
chat."

I went to see the Mayor at City Hall,
And he said, "Hello," but that wasn't all.

Bicycling in New York

CATHARINE EDMONDS

New York is a beautiful city to be seen on a bicycle—an endlessly changing series of panoramas for which you are the camera, to film as fast or as slowly as you want.

In Manhattan, the Central Park Drive is a tree-lined, three-lane road, closed to cars from the end of May to early September every weekday, Tuesday and Wednesday evenings, and weekends sunrise to sunset. The weekend schedule is year-round. (This all goes for other city parks too.)

Bike clubs race early in the morning on weekends. As for renting bikes, you need a parent if you're under age: like all other bike rental shops, the one at the Central Park Boathouse, near East Seventy-second Street, requires a deposit and a credit card or driver's license. For more information, call 472-1003, or 861-6800 10–5 weekdays and 9–5 weekends. P.S. Bikes aren't allowed on walkways, which are narrow and full of pedestrians.

The best times for riding the city streets

are before and after rush hours and Sundays, though Saturdays are good too. The lighter the traffic, the more room you have, and the less fumes you breathe. Park and Fifth avenues are beautiful runs and less bumpy than the other avenues. Sixth Avenue now has an official bike lane. (Potholes and manhole covers are hazardous to your health.) Broadway is long and fascinating, and can take you all the way downtown. It does have some confusing twists and turns when it intersects with other avenues, especially above Forty-second Street, so if you miss it, it's better to head down the other avenue and take a cross-street back. The Wall Street area is another good place for bicycling. A totally different New York, it's full of nooks and crannies to explore.

Other Manhattan treasures include Riverside Drive, the Columbia University area, Carl Schurz Park (Gracie Mansion and along the East River), Beekman Place and Sutton Place, Washington Square and Greenwich Village, and anywhere else that strikes your fancy.

To get from Manhattan to the other boroughs by bicycle, take the Brooklyn Bridge bikeway to Brooklyn (it's the only one you can ride), the Queensboro Bridge walkway to Queens, the Henry Hudson Bridge walkway to Riverdale and the Bronx, the ferry to Staten Island. You can also take the Triborough Bridge walkway to Randall's Island, the 102nd Street footbridge to Ward's Island, and the Roosevelt Island Bridge walkway from Queens Plaza South to Roosevelt Island. Bikes aren't allowed on parkways, highways, subways, buses, or in tunnels. Call regular train and bus information about taking your bike out of the city.

A special place for bicycling is the bicycle race track in Kissena Park (south end), 158th Street and Booth Memorial Avenue, Flushing, Queens. A quarter-mile asphalt banked track, it's the only public track in the state, and it's free from 8 A.M. to 5 P.M. on weekdays (weekends are reserved for bike clubs). Morning is the best time in hot weather. There are bike races every evening starting at 6:30 P.M. If you're eight years or older, you can join a bike club and race too! For more information, call the Century Road Club Association, FI 3-8888, preferably between 6 and 9 P.M., and ask for Mr. Louis Maltese.

For more tours and information on bikes, repairs, equipment, clubs, and so on, see *The New York Bicycler,* by Rafael Macia (paperback $2.50) and *Bicycle Tours in and around New York,* by Dan Carlinsky and David Heim (paperback $2.95). These have valuable information and ideas and are handy to take with you.

Happy wheeling!

If you're not familiar with bike riding in New York traffic, it is important to remember that motorists expect and depend on you to follow the same rules they do: ride *with* the traffic, stop on the red, give pedestrians right of way, don't tailgate (on your life), use hand signals always and reflectors and lights at night. Bicycles and cars are like cats and dogs: if they don't grow up together, they have a hard time understanding each other. This is especially true in New York's fast, un-predictable traffic, where bicycles are relatively new. If you ride *against* the traffic, as a number of careless people do, drivers get very confused, can't judge your position, and can just as easily head right for you as pass you, particularly if there's another car coming up on his other side. In any case, you might as well be a Martian cat to some dogged drivers. They honk when they needn't and don't when they should, jam on the brakes—zap! whip up on your left and turn right DIRECTLY in front of you—no horn, no blinker . . . Most drivers have *no idea* how long it takes a bicycle to stop and start. As a bicyclist, you are the small, fragile David using your wits, competing with an army of awkward two-ton Goliaths. One more word from the unscathed to the alert and wise: always keep to the right, being particularly careful of taxis and double-parked cars, unless you're on a one-way Bus Route. Then it is best to stay on the left: there is *nothing* like having a mammoth bus looming up behind you and flattening you against a parked car as it zeroes in on the bus stop!

Blind Justice?

PAUL HAGERMAN

New York City has a rather unpleasant history of dishonest politicians and judicial corruption. For this reason, the statue of Blind Justice on top of City Hall is appropriate.

Statues of Blind Justice traditionally depict a woman holding the scales of justice. She is always blindfolded to show that she will weigh the evidence in the case and ignore the political or social prominence of the person on trial.

The statue on top of City Hall is exactly like all the other statues of Blind Justice throughout the world, except for one thing. It's the only statue in the entire world in which "Blind" Justice is *not* blindfolded.

In New York City, Blind Justice sometimes peeks.

Riddle-Around-New York

ROSE WYLER AND GERALD AMES

Why did Peter Stuyvesant pay the Indians twenty-four dollars for Manhattan Island?

He couldn't get it for less.

•

Why was General Grant buried in New York City?

Because he was dead.

•

Why does the Statue of Liberty stand in New York Harbor?

She can't sit down.

•

Why is Staten Island like the letter T?

Because it's in the midst of waTer.

•

The largest ship ever to come into New York Harbor is the *Queen Elizabeth II*. What does she weigh?

Anchor.

•

What is the largest gem in town?

The baseball diamond at Shea Stadium.

•

What building has the most stories?

The New York Public Library on Fifth Avenue has the most stories for adults. The branch with the largest number of kids' stories is the Donnell Library on West Fifty-third Street. It has over eighty thousand books in the Children's Room.

•

Why is a teen-ager who's in trouble at school like the Brooklyn Bridge?

Both are suspended.

•

Why do so many New Yorkers look down in the mouth when they start to work?

They're dentists. New York has more dentists than any city in the world—over two thousand in Manhattan alone.

•

How do people raise strawberries in city apartments?

With a spoon.

•

What can the people of New York City do that no one else can do?

Vote for the Mayor of New York.

•

Our TV weathermen never look out the window to see if it's raining. Why not?

TV studios don't have windows.

•

What New Yorker earns his pay,
Traveling fifty miles a day,
Not on foot, not by plane,
Not by auto, not by train?

The operator in the World Trade Center who runs the elevator going to the observation deck. The deck is on the 107th floor, about a quarter of a mile above sea level. The operator makes more than a hundred round trips in a six-hour shift. So each day he travels over fifty miles—by elevator.

•

How many big men were born in Harlem?

None. Although many famous people were born in Harlem, they all started life as babies.

•

How can a New Yorker make an honest living from crooked dough?

By baking pretzels. The city has five pretzel factories.

•

Why does New York City keep paying salaries to people who never do a day's work?

The people work at night. Watchmen patrol city buildings; scrub women clean offices after they close; operators keep the subways running; policemen and firemen protect the city after dark. Life in New York City goes on around the clock.

•

What did one light bulb on the big Broadway sign say to another?

I'm not going out tonight. How about you?

•

I LOVE NEW YORK I LOVE NEW YORK

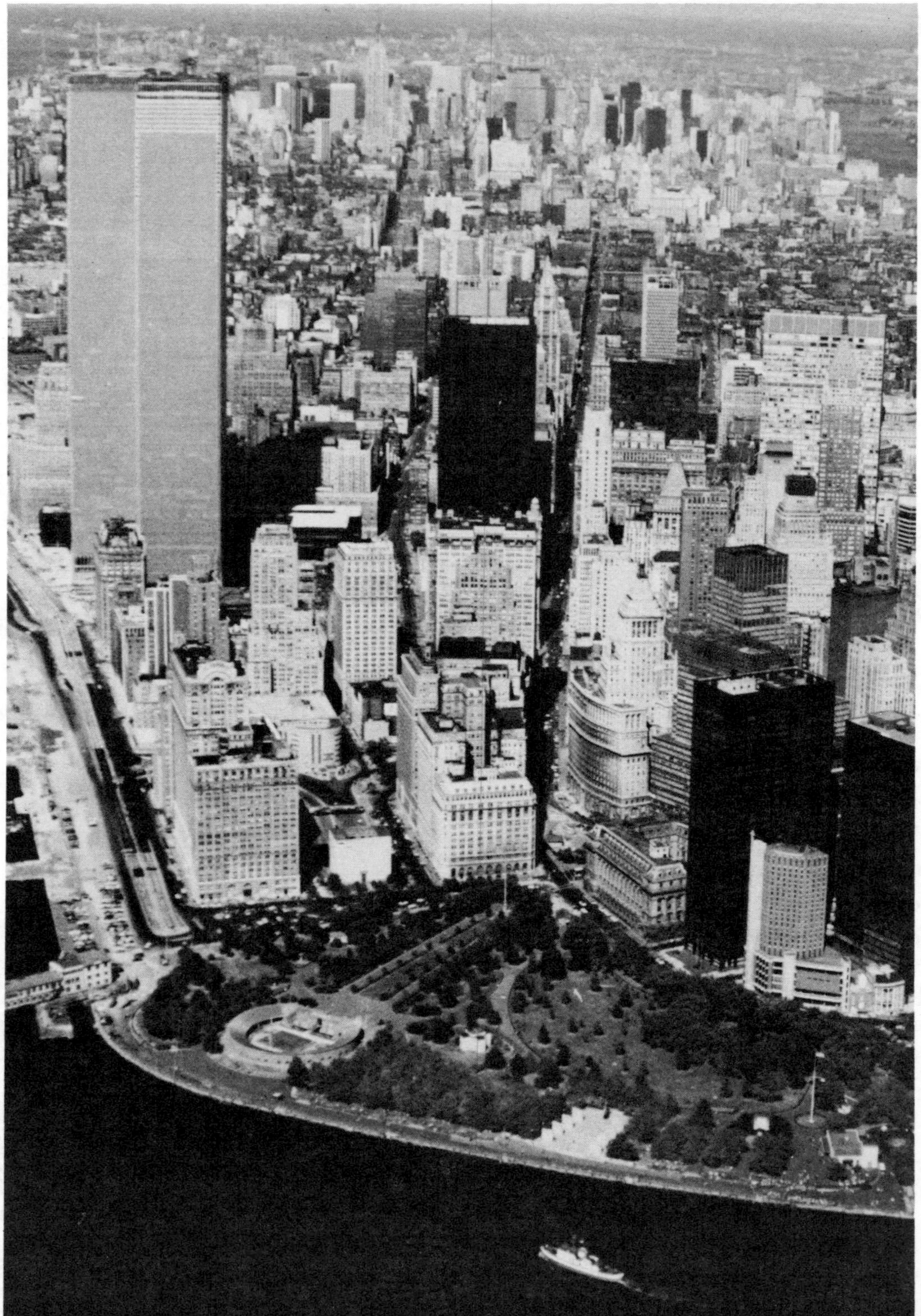

I LOVE NEW YORK I LOVE NEW YORK

Address Finder

Here is a neat way to find street numbers
in Manhattan from Fourteenth Street to Fifty-ninth Street.

WEST SIDE STREETS

Buildings numbered	1 to 99 are between	5th & 6th Avenues
"	"	100 to 199 " "	6th & 7th "
"	"	200 to 299 " "	7th & 8th "
"	"	300 to 399 " "	8th & 9th "
"	"	400 to 499 " "	9th & 10th "
"	"	500 to 599 " "	10th & 11th "
"	"	600 to 699 " "	11th & 12th "

EAST SIDE STREETS

Buildings numbered	1 to 99 are between	5th & Park Avenues
"	"	100 to 199 " "	Park & 3rd "
"	"	200 to 299 " "	3rd & 2nd "
"	"	300 to 399 " "	2nd & 1st "
"	"	400 and higher " "	1st & East River

Remember, streets run east and west. Avenues run north and south.

To find the nearest street when you have only an avenue address, drop the last digit of the number, divide it by 2, and follow these instructions:

Avenue A, B, C, D	add 3
1st & 2nd Avenue	add 3
3rd Avenue	add 9 or 10
4th Avenue/Park Avenue South	add 8
5th Avenue up to 200	add 13
5th Avenue up to 400	add 16
5th Avenue up to 600	add 18
5th Avenue up to 775	add 20
5th Avenue above 2000	add 24
Avenue of the Americas (6th Avenue)	subtract 12 or 13
7th Avenue	add 12

7th Avenue above 110th Street	add 20
8th Avenue	add 9 or 10
9th Avenue	add 13
10th Avenue	add 14
11th Avenue	add 15
Amsterdam Avenue	add 59 or 60
Audubon Avenue	add 165
Broadway, up to 750	is below 8th Street
Broadway, 756 to 846	subtract 29
Broadway, 847 to 953	subtract 25
Broadway, above 953	subtract 31
Columbus Avenue	add 59 or 60
Convent Avenue	add 127
Fort Washington Avenue	add 158
Lenox Avenue	add 110
Lexington Avenue	add 22
Madison Avenue	add 26
Manhattan Avenue	add 100
Park Avenue	add 34 or 35
St. Nicholas Avenue	add 110
West End Avenue	add 59 or 60

THESE TWO AVENUES ARE SLIGHTLY DIFFERENT:

Central Park West	divide house number by 10 and add 60
Riverside Drive, up to 165th Street	divide by 10 and add 72

NEWYORKNEWYORKNEWYORK

Ellen is all alone in her Latin class, so in her report she is always marked head, *and that pleased her father very much until he found out she was the only one in it . . .*

FROM *Diary of a Little Girl in Old New York,* 1849–50

Far-out Figures

PAUL HAGERMAN

Along the curbs of New York you can see 65,000 parking meters, 91,000 fire hydrants, and 17,800 traffic lights. Out in the center of the street you'll see white lines marking the traffic lanes. If you took a long tape measure, you'd find out that there are 18,500,000 feet of white lines on the city streets—enough to paint a solid white line all the way to California.

THE SEAL OF THE CITY OF NEW YORK

The Seal of the City of New York was adopted in 1664. Its features represent different aspects of life in New York during the early days of the city.

The man on the left is a Dutch sailor. He is holding a sound line, which was used to measure the depth of the sea. Next to him is another navigation instrument called a cross staff. The Indian holding a bow across from him is a Coastal Algonquian and a member of the local Manhattan tribe.

Between them, the Indian and the sailor hold a shield on which the sails of a windmill, two barrels, and two beavers are shown. These represent the flour and fur trades which were very important to the early settlers.

The eagle perched above the shield is taken from the New York State shield and symbolizes courage and majesty. The laurel leaf bar beneath the shield and the laurel wreath surrounding the seal stand for victory and truce.

The Latin words at the bottom of the seal mean "Seal of the City of New York." The last word, *Eboraci*, means "place at the water," and refers to New York.

In 1625, the date on the seal, there were almost two hundred people living on Manhattan with the first governing council.

Sightseeing

A CROSTIC
(SOLUTION, PG. 368.)

4-letter word
  JETS

5-letter words
  BRONX
  FERRY
  MACYS
  PLAZA

6-letter words
  GIANTS
  BOWERY
  SUBWAY

7-letter words
  BATTERY
  YANKEES
  SKYLINE

8-letter words
  BROADWAY
  CITY HALL
  BRONX ZOO

10-letter words
PARK AVENUE
SKYSCRAPER

11-letter word
CONEY ISLAND

12-letter word
CARNEGIE HALL

13-letter word
LINCOLN CENTER

14-letter words
BROOKLYN BRIDGE
FRAUNCES TAVERN

15-letter word
STATUE OF LIBERTY

16-letter word
GREENWICH VILLAGE

17-letter word
ROCKEFELLER CENTER

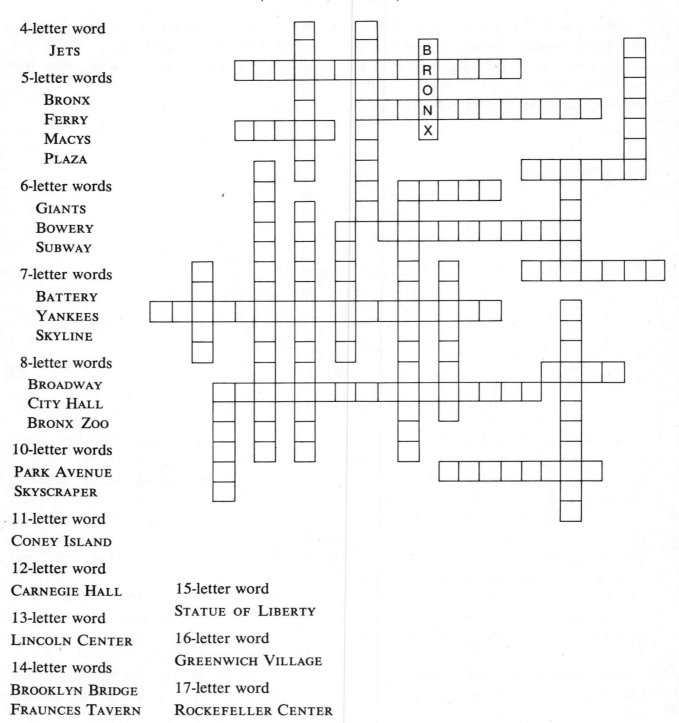

Pigeon English

OLGA LITOWINSKY

"Boy, do I have news for you, Chris," said the Pigeon one day.

"You mean they're going to put me somewhere without any traffic?"

"Nope. Remember when you told me that your last name is really Colombo?"

"Of course."

"And then you said that *colombo* means 'pigeon' in Italian?"

"Right. *Colomba* means 'dove.'"

"Yes, yes, I know. That's what the news is about."

"Doves?"

"No, pigeons. Everyone is always talking about doves—they get all the publicity. You know, dove of peace, the dove that flew off Noah's ark to look for land, lovey-dovey, and all that. I'm sick of it. Now we pigeons are getting our chance."

"You mean free handouts of food aren't enough? You want more? Think how I feel, stuck on this pedestal in the middle of Columbus Circle. Nobody even knows I'm here except you pigeons."

"Well, I was just talking to the Mayor, and he said . . ."

"Yes?"

"To honor the New York City pigeon, henceforth all things named after Christopher Columbus will be translated into Pigeon English!"

"You mean . . ."

"That's right. From now on it's Pigeon Circle, Pigeon Avenue, Pigeon University, the Pigeon Broadcasting System. And wait until the Pigeon Day Parade—Chris, come back. Don't leave me. I was only joking! Chris, Chris . . ."

CENSUS

New York City's pigeon population is twice as big as Vermont's people population.

Service with a Smile

Ike is a New York City tour guide for a popular bus tour company. In his daily adventures with out-of-towners, he gives out some fascinating information about New York; not all of it is found in the tour guide training manual. The billboard in Times Square, for example, which blows smoke, works something like a gigantic steam iron, explains Ike. He points out (with a smile) that the Empire State Building has been under attack two times in its history—once by an Army Air Corps plane which flew into its 78th and 79th floors, and another time on the movie screen by a giant gorilla. He'll tell you (and I'll bet you didn't know) that one of the chief engineers on the Brooklyn Bridge was a woman, Emily Roebling.

"Where are all the gas stations?" an out-of-town kid wants to know, not recognizing our subtle versions of these traditional American landmarks.

"There are none," replies Ike, with a twinkle in his eye. "We use the subways."

"What's all that smoke coming out of the streets?" asks a woman.

"Dragons," answers Ike.

More Far-out Figures

New York City is 300 square miles, 40° north latitude, 74° west longitude, and has eight million inhabitants, nearly two million of which live in the borough of Manhattan alone.

YELLOW PAGES

The Manhattan Yellow Pages of the New York Telephone Company for 1977 were 2⅜ inches thick. The white pages were 2½ inches thick.

Radio Stations
Who Plays What in New York

AM RADIO

WMCA	570	Talk, Sports (Mets, Islanders, Nets, NFL Monday Night Football)
WVNJ	620	Contemporary Pop ("Beautiful Music")
WNBC	660	Contemporary Pop
WOR	710	Talk, Drama, Sports (Jets)
WABC	770	Contemporary Pop
WNYC	830	Classical, Talk, Civic Reports
WCBS	880	All News, Sports (Yankees)
WPAT	930	Contemporary Pop ("Beautiful Music")
WINS	1010	All News
WHN	1050	Country
WNEW	1130	Contemporary Pop, Sports (Knicks, Giants, Rangers)
WLIB	1190	Caribbean, Soul
WEVD	1330	Nostalgia, Foreign, Jazz, Talk
WQXR	1560	Classical

FM RADIO

WPAT	93.1	Contemporary Pop ("Beautiful Music")
WNYC	93.9	Classical
WPLJ	95.5	Rock (Album-oriented)
WQXR	96.3	Classical
WYNY	97.1	Soft Rock
WEVD	97.9	Nostalgia, Foreign, Jazz, Talk
WOR	98.7	Rock (Top 40)
WXLO	99.0	Rock, Disco
WBAI	99.5	Free-form programming
WVNJ	100.3	Contemporary Pop ("Beautiful Music")
WCBS	101.1	Rock, Pop, Oldies
WPIX	101.9	Contemporary Pop
WNEW	102.7	Progressive Rock
WNCN	104.3	Classical
WRVR	106.7	Jazz
WBLS	107.5	Rhythm and blues, Soul, Rock, Latin

BROOKLYN BRIDGE

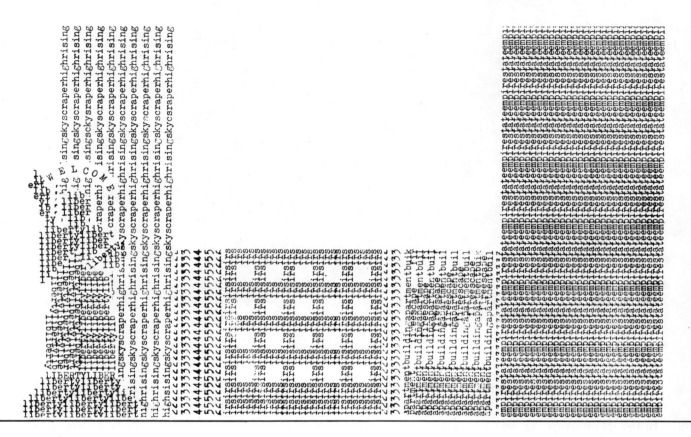

Before the Bridge

OLGA LITOWINSKY

It was in 1812. Fire swept through Brooklyn. Volunteer firemen rushed to the blaze, where they fought to control the flames. Anxiously they prayed for help from New York City, across the East River. It arrived at last: a "floating engine" so large it took between thirty and forty men to crank it. But because none of the small ferries on the East River had the capacity to transport this engine, its arrival was delayed until the captain of a fishing boat offered to take the machine across. Meanwhile, the fire destroyed a number of buildings, and property damage was extensive.

After this disaster the citizens of Brooklyn realized that the small boats that ferried them across the river were inadequate for the needs of a growing town, and so in 1814 the first steamboat ferry, the *Nassau*, was put into service. The steamer could carry five hundred people at a time. It quickly became popular and well patronized by all the citizens of Brooklyn.

As Brooklyn grew, the ferry boat traffic

A BROOKLYN FERRYBOAT OF ABOUT 1820

grew with it. But steam ferry service, too, was found to be unsatisfactory and sometimes dangerous. It was pleasant on a summer day to disembark at the Fulton Ferry station on the Brooklyn side of the river, stop off for some fresh oysters from the East River, and then walk home up the hill. But fog, ice, and storms were another matter. Complaints about the service grew more frequent, and some visionaries, like John A. Roebling, began to dream about building a bridge across the East River. It is said that he began to work out ideas for a bridge in February 1853, while he was trapped aboard a drifting ferryboat in the ice-choked river.

But there were others, like a writer from the *Long Island Star*, who had dismissed the idea of a bridge. In an article written

three years earlier, "Bridging the East River—Can It Be Done?" the writer thought it "was possible," but his arguments against the bridge ran this way: 1. "The boats are good enough"; 2. "It will not be used after it is built"; 3. "It will cost too much"; 4. "The people of Brooklyn don't want it"; and 5. "It will afford too good a chance for the Russians and Austrians to march into Brooklyn by way of New York [should war break out]."

Seventeen years later Roebling's dream won out against such arguments. His son, Washington, was appointed chief engineer of the East River Suspension Bridge. The bridge opened on May 23, 1883, and the ferry service suffered as cable cars and pedestrians eagerly crossed over high above the river. The last ferry to Brooklyn vanished in 1964 when the Verrazano Bridge linking Brooklyn and Staten Island was opened.

Today, another group of dreamers would like to see a Brooklyn ferry in operation again. Plans are under way to develop the area under the Brooklyn Bridge—using many of the buildings still there from the ferry's golden days. A short distance from the river, on Cadman Plaza West, is the old Fulton Ferry Bank, complete with its original sign. Around the corner is a former oyster market and what were once the offices of many of Brooklyn's most prestigious lawyers. Near the old ferry landing is a new restaurant—on a nonfloating barge! By 1980, this area should be flourishing once again, and a commercially operated "ferry" may be carrying passengers from Manhattan to Brooklyn.

While waiting for the next ferry to arrive, why not stand on a bit of wharf and gaze over the river at South Street Seaport. If you block out the skyscrapers on the Manhattan skyline, close your ears to the traffic roaring overhead on the Bridge, and use your imagination, you may have a vision of your own—the East River shrouded with sail and steam as it was more than a century ago. Foghorns, bells, mist . . . *"Oysters, mister? Fresh from the river. Get 'em here."*

Brooklyn Bridge

(A JUMP-ROPE RHYME)

WILLIAM JAY SMITH

Brooklyn Bridge, Brooklyn Bridge,
I walked to the middle, jumped over the
edge,

The water was greasy, the water was
brown
Like cold chop suey in Chinatown,

And I gobbled it up as I sank down,—
Down—
Down—
Down—
Down—

Brooklyn Bridge, Brooklyn Bridge,
I walked to the middle, looked over the
edge.

But I didn't jump off, what I said's
not true—
I just made it up so I could scare you:
Watch me jump!—
Watch me jump!—
Watch me jump!—
BOO!

Under the Brooklyn Bridge

OR IT'S WHAT YOU DON'T SEE THAT COUNTS

NANCY GARDEN

ave you ever wondered what holds up Brooklyn Bridge? A couple of big boxes, that's what!

Actually, they're called *caissons*, but they looked like boxes when they were towed into place before being sunk in the East River. Back in the late 1860s when Brooklyn Bridge was designed, the caissons and the steel wire intended for its four main cables were such new ideas in American bridge building that people said, "Impossible!" But Chief Engineer John Roebling went ahead anyway.

John Roebling never saw the caissons he designed, much less his new-fangled cables or the finished bridge. He died in 1869 following an accident at the site. But his son Washington took over and set to work getting the caissons built.

The principle was simple. Each caisson, one on the Manhattan side and one at Brooklyn, would do double duty. First, as a giant wooden box, with its open end down, it would be filled with compressed air to keep out water, thus forming a protective shield for workers digging out the river bottom. Later, deep under water and filled with concrete, it would become the foundation for the bridge's two huge masonry towers.

A simple idea—but there were problems. Early one Sunday, air burst out of the Brooklyn caisson, throwing debris 500 feet high. There were fires, too, one so bad the damage took months to repair. Roebling himself helped the firefighters. Two weeks later, there was another air explosion.

But it was the Manhattan caisson that brought more sinister tragedy: caisson disease.

Caisson disease—"the bends"—is caused by nitrogen bubbles in body tissues and in the bloodstream. The bubbles form when a person who works at higher than normal air pressure returns to normal pressure too quickly. But no one knew this then, and no one really knew how to treat the disease. They only knew that it caused terrible pain, dizziness, nausea, and other symptoms —and that it could lead to death.

No one knows exactly how many Brooklyn Bridge workers suffered from the bends by the time the Manhattan caisson was finished, but it was more than a hun-

dred; several men died. Not even Washington Roebling was spared. After months of fighting pain and weakness he had to give up going to the site. But that didn't stop him any more than cries of "Impossible!" had stopped his father. By mail and through his wife Emily he continued to direct construction, including the spinning of the cables, each of which contained about 5,500 steel wires. Roebling was not well enough to attend the gala opening on May 24, 1883—but the President of the United States, Chester A. Arthur, went to his house to pay his respects.

The Roeblings' bridge, the longest suspension bridge in the world until 1903, was the model for later bridges, including the George Washington and the Verrazano-Narrows in New York. In 1964 it was declared a national historic landmark.

It still arches magnificently above those two unseen but vital concrete-filled boxes —all because the Roeblings didn't let pain or cries of "Impossible!" stop them.

I Bought the Brooklyn Bridge

ALFRED SLOTE

Last winter when I was visiting New York City, a gentleman down at the Battery asked me if I was looking to buy anything in the city.

"What do you have for sale?" I asked him.

"That bridge over there," he said. "It's called the Brooklyn Bridge."

"That's beyond my means," I told him. "I thought maybe a tie from Macy's or a baseball undershirt from Paragon. Besides, what could I do with a bridge?"

"You could make your money back charging tolls," the gentleman said. "And since I've been trying to unload this bridge for a long time, I'll let you have it for the cut-rate price of ten dollars."

"Ten dollars? Why the scrap value of that bridge alone is worth a thousand," I said.

"It would cost me a fortune to scrap it," said my new friend. "But you could charge the first ten cars that cross it a dollar apiece and you'd have your money back in minutes."

"Why don't *you* charge them?" I said, for although I am from Michigan, I am not stupid.

"I don't have the time. Look, don't do me any favors. If you don't want a bargain for ten bucks, forget it. I'm only trying to do you a favor."

"I'll take that bridge," I said, and gave the gentleman a ten-dollar bill.

The next morning I got out to my bridge nice and early and decided to set up my toll booth on the Brooklyn side since more cars seemed to be coming from that direction. The first car I stopped was driven by an old woman.

"Sonny," she said, "you could get killed out here. What's your problem?"

"I'm sorry, madam, but it now costs a dollar to cross the Brooklyn Bridge."

"Does it? I tell you," she said, forking over a dollar, "this city is getting worse and worse."

Right behind her was a big yellow truck. "Get out of my way," the driver shouted down at me.

"It'll cost you a buck to cross, sir."

"It'll cost you a hospital bill if you don't get out of my way."

"Sorry, the bridge is privately owned as of this morning. One dollar."

The truck driver was furious, but cars behind him were honking even more furiously so he gave me a dollar and said he'd run me over on his way home.

A taxi driver said I was crazy. "This bridge belongs to the people of the city," he hollered at me.

"I bought it yesterday from one of them. One dollar," I said.

"They'll put you in Bellevue," he screamed, "and if I give you a buck they'll put me there too."

But he gave me a buck because there was now a line of cars and trucks a mile long behind him, all honking.

Well, to make a long story short, that winter morning I collected over fifty dollars in tolls from drivers who couldn't stand the honking. After that I had to quit because I couldn't stand the cold.

Now I'm in the market to buy a nice warm tunnel. Do you know of one?

Storage Space

The space inside the great stone arches of the Brooklyn Bridge were originally used as wine cellars. The choicest wines imported from Europe were aged there. After Prohibition, they were used for the storage of fish from the Fulton Fish Market, and now they are used for miscellaneous storage.

OLD NEW YORK

The Nasty Stamp Act

CATHARINE EDMONDS

In 1765, Britain announced that it had decided to support its troops here by taxing the American colonists. They would be required to buy large blue stamps to affix to all kinds of papers, documents, playing cards, and innumerable other pleasures and necessities. You even had to buy one to get an ale at the tavern. And the stamps could cost up to £10, a *lot* of money.

New York City was in an uproar. The first stamp collector resigned after two months in fear for his life. Newspapers urged people not to buy the stamps.

When the first shipload of stamps arrived, New Yorkers threatened to destroy both ship and paper. The stamps were moved to Fort George in Bowling Green for safekeeping.

The Stamp Act was passed by Parliament on November 11, 1765; city bells tolled mournfully, shops were closed, flags flew at half-mast. People dressed in black. That evening a mob demonstrated outside the fort, hanging and burning effigies of the British Governor and the devil. The Governor and his family fled to safety on a British warship.

The boycott against British goods was maintained by lawyers, merchants, mechanics, and tradesmen alike. The city

OR THE FUNERAL OF MISS AME-STAMP

suffered badly—there were no court sessions, no marriage licenses, no land deeds; debts went unpaid, no ships left harbor, business dwindled, farm products declined, people wore coarse, homespun clothing—but New Yorkers stuck to the pact. They were the only ones in the colonies who did.

In January of 1766, another ship full of stamps docked. The boxes of hated paper were seized and burned. Little attempt was made to catch the offenders.

The persistent protest by New York City began to spread to the surrounding countryside. Tenants rioted and refused to pay rent, and took every chance to disobey British authority. Nine years before the Battle of Lexington, New York was on the verge of a civil war over the Stamp Act.

Already twenty-four people had died or been injured in the hostilities.

Finally in the spring of 1766 the Stamp Act was repealed. Up until the Revolution, March 18 was celebrated every year as the great victory day against the evil stamps. A statue of King George III was raised in Bowling Green in appreciation.

Unfortunately, however, King and Parliament sought other ways to control the colonies and obtain funds for their depleted treasury. Little did they realize that the New York uprising was but a prelude to a war that would be fought by all the colonies together.

Only six years after its joyous installation, the grand statue of the King was toppled, to be melted down for colonial bullets.

Patriots pull down the statue of King George III at Bowling Green, 1776.

REVOLUTIONARY NEW YORK

CATHARINE EDMONDS

From September 1776 until the Treaty of Paris in September 1783, New York City was occupied by the British. After a valiant attempt to save this strategic prize, the colonists could not hold it against British General Howe's massive, well-trained forces. Ninety-five percent of the population had fled the city, but thousands of Loyalists (to England) returned, along with swarms of Loyalist refugees from the colonist-held countryside.

Shortly after the British took over, a terrible fire swept the city, burning about seventeen hundred buildings, including Trinity Church and Peter Stuyvesant's old home, the Bouwerie. There was another devastating fire in 1778.

The British did little to rebuild. Normal trade ceased, wharves and homes rotted, monuments crumbled, weeds overtook gardens. Loyalists took over abandoned Whig (colonist) homes, and troops were quartered everywhere. Many churches were vandalized and left in ruins or used as barracks, stables, and military hospitals and prisons. King's College (now Columbia University) was also used as a hospital. Classes were suspended, the faculty dispersed, and books were used by British soldiers in exchange for tavern fare. There was much looting and pilfering, and free use of patriots' property and merchandise. City life was a shambles. Even though seventeen thousand prisoners were paroled during the war, at least fifty died every week under terrible prison conditions.

Nevertheless, New York partook of that strange prosperity that sometimes comes with war. As the Continental army starved and froze, New Yorkers enjoyed the influx of British luxuries. And there was drastic inflation. Rents quadrupled, food prices octupled. The city still had a mayor, though all his power belonged to the British commandant. Three newspapers went on printing, the theater remained open (mostly British officers acted), and there were cricket matches and bear-baiting for entertainment. Royal birthdays were celebrated, and the city was even honored by a visit from Prince William Henry, son of the English King, in 1781!

British surrender in October of that year came as a shock to the city's Loyalists.

The last of the British troops finally embarked for England at the end of November 1783. General Washington and the Continental army returned in triumph. They marched down into the city from Harlem, and celebrated victory in good old Fraunces' Tavern.

IN THE SHADE OF THE OLD APPLE TREES

City Hall Park was a commons covered with apple trees when the Declaration of Independence was read there in July 1776 in the presence of George Washington. A few weeks later, the English overran the area, and the same apple trees were used as a gallows. Nathan Hale, a patriot spy, was captured by the British and hanged there. A statue of Hale commemorates him in the park today.

The Inauguration of George Washington

CATHARINE EDMONDS

On the corner of Wall and Nassau streets stands George Washington's statue in front of the old U. S. Customs House. There are statues aplenty of him, but this one is special, for it stands right where the man himself stood and took the first presidential oath.

In March 1789, New York City, already a thriving port and international center, was named the first capital of the nation. (Washington, D.C., was still a swamp.) Red-brick City Hall was proudly renamed Federal Hall and renovated to accommodate the first Congress under the new Constitution. On April 6, Congress elected George Washington President.

Days before the inauguration, citizens began pouring into city taverns, inns, and homes with tales of Washington's progress from his Virginia home and of all the celebrations along his path.

At last he arrived by ceremonial barge from New Jersey, followed by crowds of boats, military salutes, and thousands of people roaring from every harbor shore. Washington was a tall, quiet man; he was impressive yet modest and sincere, the wise soldier who had led his people through a bloody war to independence; and they loved him. He had wanted to grow old on his farm, but the nation had called him to lead it again.

The morning of April 30 arrived with the crack and boom of a salute from Fort George in Bowling Green. Thousands more streamed into the city. In the Senate chamber upstairs in Federal Hall, John Adams spearheaded the noisy debate over what title the nation's leader should have —Highness, Excellency, Mightiness? The temporary decision: Mr. President.

At half past noon, the President-elect entered his coach-and-four awaiting him outside his Cherry Street mansion, and a splendid parade proceeded to Federal Hall: first the grand marshal riding alone, then dragoons on horseback, then artillery, grenadiers, Highlanders playing bagpipes, the light infantry, the Sheriff of New York County and City, the Senate committee in their carriages. Guarded by footmen and mounted attendants, Washington followed in his coach. In a simple brown suit with silver buttons, he bowed to the crowds that cheered and waved. Then came more officials, diplomats, and carriages. Washington and the Senate committee walked up Broad Street into Federal Hall. He reappeared on the second-floor balcony, Senate and House members assembled around him. Then, overcome by the sight of the thrilled and waiting throng, Washington had to sit a moment.

As close as possible to the balcony's edge, between Samuel Otis, Secretary of the Senate, and Robert Livingston, Chancellor of New York State, Washington stood by a lectern with an open Bible on a red pillow. He placed his hand on a passage of Genesis, and Livingston read the oath, "Do you solemnly swear . . . ?"

Washington answered after him, "I solemnly swear that I will faithfully execute the office of President of the United States, and will, to the best of my ability, preserve, protect, and defend the Constitution of the United States," and, as Otis held up the Bible, humbly kissed the page, saying, "So help me God."

"It is done," Livingston said and, facing the crowd, shouted, "Long live George Washington, President of the United States!" The people broke into enthusiastic cheering, and the flag rose and billowed out. Cannons boomed from ship and fort alike and church bells rang wild.

In 1821, the crumbling Federal Hall was sold for salvage. Washington, D.C., had been the capital for over ten years, and New York, the largest city in the nation, had built a new City Hall at Broadway and the Brooklyn Bridge. The old Customs House still stands as a national historic site called the Federal Hall National Memorial. The statue of George Washington above the lunch-hour soap-box orators stands as a reminder of a historical moment filled with emotion and new spirit.

The Inauguration of General George Washington as the first President of the United States.

New York, the First Capital of the United States

CATHARINE EDMONDS

One of the grandest moments in the city's history was its brief term as first capital of the United States. Very brief it was —fifteen months, from the beginning of 1789 to April 1790.

Although there were no bathrooms, few paved streets, no street lamps except on darkest nights, and dogs, goats, and pigs had the run of the streets, New York was a lively and glamorous place to be. Over a thousand ships entered the harbor that year, and commerce flourished.

The bustling city was peopled with congressmen, dignitaries, and government officials—not to mention President George Washington himself! Wall Street and Broadway were the main social and business thoroughfares. (Broadway was also the path for the cows to and from the Lispenard Meadows, west of today's Canal Street, where they grazed.)

Samuel Otis, Secretary of the Senate, lived at No. 5 Wall, and Alexander Hamilton, Secretary of the Treasury, at No. 58. The Spanish and French ambassadors and General Knox, Secretary of War, lived on Broadway; John Jay, Chief Justice, at No. 133 Broadway. Thomas Jefferson, Secretary of State, lived on Maiden Lane—while he looked for something better. Vice-President Adams lived on Richmond Hill, a beautiful estate where part of Greenwich Village is now.

• At first George Washington lived on Cherry Street in the gracious Franklin mansion (see the plaque on the Brooklyn Bridge), but it was too far away from Congress at Federal Hall. It was also too small for the Washington family, its household staff of twenty-two, and the streams of visitors. (Washington's steward was the famous Samuel Fraunces, the West Indian who ran Fraunces' Tavern.)

In February 1790, Washington moved to the McComb mansion at 39 Broadway, the largest and most elegant in the city. Even there he had to build a large stable to house the cumbersome, fancy state coach, his horses, carriages and wagons. He was still bemoaning the $12,317 in household expenses for the smaller house.

Social events abounded. In May 1789 the Inauguration Ball took place, attended by three hundred guests who danced and celebrated till 2 A.M. The next week the French ambassador gave another ball in honor of Washington, and soon after, the President gave a grand dinner in honor of Mrs. Washington's arrival. Then the city's social routine began. On Sunday there were services at fashionable St. Paul's Church, and then a promenade on the Battery and tea with friends. Monday was the night for a private dinner with friends. Tuesday from 3 to 4 P.M. the President's levee was able to chat with him a few moments. Wednesday was reserved for dinner at the Alexander Hamiltons, and on Thursday, it was dinner at the John Jays. On Friday, Mr. and Mrs. Washington gave their formal evening reception, and on Saturday there was an extravagant dinner at General Knox's lavish house. Governor Clinton also gave dinners occasionally, as did the foreign diplomats. Then of course there were holidays to celebrate and the President's special dinners, Dancing Assembly meetings, and plays at the John Street Theatre, three times a week, which Washington enjoyed.

With the abundance of elegance, from imported silver, china, silks and satins to the latest London and Paris fashions (ladies' coiffures were trussed up so high they sometimes caught fire from the chandeliers), there were many who complained about the regal pomp and extravagance, including Mrs. Washington. She would have much preferred to do as she pleased than continually attend endless social occasions. Others thought that such foolishness gave reason for the hated Loyalists to ridicule Washington and the new government.

Washington felt far from pompous about it. He also liked to travel in the city unofficially. Once a maid with a little boy trailed him into a shop and told him the boy was named after him. Washington fondly put his hand on the boy's head, blessed him, and went on his way. The boy was Washington Irving.

Alas, the party didn't last. The other cities kept up the competition and, bolstered by a ghastly winter and steaming summer, caused Congress to pass an act naming Philadelphia the interim capital until 1800, when a new site on the Potomac River would be ready.

On August 30, 1790, Washington bade farewell to New York, and all the excitement and glamour of that first year went with him.

Erasmus Hall in 1824.

The Oldest High School

KAREN SHAW WIDMAN

The oldest high school in New York State and the second oldest in the entire nation, Erasmus Hall Academy was originally intended to educate and house a handful of boys. The school was built in 1787 by the Dutch Reformed Church and named for Desiderius Erasmus (1466–1536), the Dutch scholar, humanist, and teacher. A statue of Erasmus has stood on the school campus since the early 1930s, and anxious students throw coins into his open book, just for good luck, before exams.

In 1801, girls were admitted to Erasmus for the first time and the school offered co-educational instruction to 75 students. When the school was 109 years old the City of New York took over its control and renamed it Erasmus Hall High School. Between 1911 and 1940, four large buildings were constructed around the original wooden schoolhouse, which was preserved intact. With its crenelated towers, arches, and stained-glass windows, Erasmus Hall stands today like a castle on Flatbush Avenue in Brooklyn.

A Working Boy in 1818

WILLIAM E. DODGE

From *Old New York*, a lecture by William E. Dodge delivered at Association Hall, April 27, 1880, upon the invitation of merchants and other citizens of New York. Published by Dodd, Mead & Company.

Eighteen hundred and eighteen found me a boy in a wholesale dry-goods store, No. 304 Pearl Street, near Peck Slip. My employers were two most worthy Quakers. A promise made by my father to the junior partner, that when he went into business I was to be with him, will account for my leaving school so early.

My father lived at that time at 98 William Street. William Street was then the fashionable retail dry-goods centre.

I had to go every morning to Vandewater Street for the keys, as my employers must have them in case of fire in the night. There was much competition as to who should have his store opened first, and I used to be up soon after light, walk to Vandewater Street and then to the store very early. It had to be sprinkled with water, which I brought the evening before from the old pump at the corner of Peck Slip and Pearl Street, then carefully swept and dusted. Then came sprinkling the sidewalk and street, and sweeping to the centre a heap for the dirt-cart to remove. This done, one of the older clerks would come, and I would be permitted to go

home for breakfast. In winter the wood had to be carried and piled in the cellar, fires made, and lamps trimmed. That first year my salary was $50 for the year.

The dry-goods auction-stores were mostly on the corners, and on the blocks from Wall to Pine Streets. When our employer would purchase a lot of goods at auction, it was our business to go and compare them with the bill, and if two of us could carry them home we did so, as it would save the shilling porterage.

I remember that while in this store I carried bundles of goods up Broadway to Greenwich Village, near what are now Seventh and Eighth Avenues and Fourth to Tenth Streets, crossing the old Stone Bridge at Canal Street. This had long square timbers on either side in place of railing, to prevent a fall into the sluggish stream—some fifteen feet below—which came from the low lands where Centre Street and the Tombs now are. It was called the Colic (though its true name was Collect, as it took the drainage of a large district), and was the great skating place in winter. Turning in at the left of the bridge I took a path through the meadows, often crossing on two timbers laid over the ditches where the tide ebbed and flowed from the East River.

I remember well the old Fly Market,

which commenced at Pearl Street where Maiden Lane crosses. There was a very large arched drain, over which the market was built, extending from Pearl Street to the dock. Maiden Lane then was narrow at Pearl Street, only about fifteen feet wide. In the winter, when the streets were running with the wash of melting snow and ice, the mouth of the sewer at Pearl Street would often clog up, and then the water would set back as far as Gold Street. The sidewalk was some two feet above the roadway to provide for the great flow of water that came down from Broadway, Nassau, William and Liberty Streets. At that time there was no system of sewerage.

The boys used to get old boots, and, placing them on a pole, would make in the slush of snow and ice footprints all across Pearl Street as if persons had been passing, and then would run around the corners to see some poor stranger step into the trap and sink above his knees in water and slush.

Silk Tea Bags

The tea bag was invented in 1904 by a New York merchant, Thomas Sullivan, who sent his customers samples of tea in small silk bags. Happy customers found they could brew the tea right in the bags.

Sad Days

In April 1865, assassinated President Abraham Lincoln's body was brought to New York City on its way to Springfield, Illinois, to lie in state for a few days in City Hall. Approximately 120,000 New Yorkers filed past the bier. On April 25, twelve black horses pulled a hearse bearing the body up Broadway to the Hudson River Railroad, where the coffin was placed on a train.

Somebody Else's Head ☞

PAUL HAGERMAN

This statue in Madison Square was originally intended as a memorial to Abraham Lincoln. When the sculptor discovered that no one was interested in buying it, he cut off Lincoln's head and welded on the head of Secretary of State William Seward.

The problem is, the statue depicts a man who is tall and lanky, and Seward was barely five feet four inches. Also, the sculptor made the head the wrong size—it is too small for the rest of the statue. Rather than cast a new, larger head; however, the sculptor simply welded on the little head and sold the statue "as is."

Street Vendors' Cries

My clams I want to sell today
The best of clams from Rockaway

And if you don't believe it's true
Come buy my clams and then you'll know

Come you that have money
(and I that have none)

Come buy my fine clams, and let me go home.

Hot corn, hot corn
Here's your lily white corn

All you that's got money
(Poor me that's got none)

Come buy my hot corn
and let me go home.

"Brooms! Brooms! Any brooms or brushes today?"

"Cherries! Cherries! Here's cherries!"

"Milk below, Maids! Milk from the Cow!"

48

New York in the Eighties: An Author's Notes

JOAN AIKEN

Silk-stockinged footmen in grander houses

everybody changed for dinner

Broughams — cutters — victorias — dog carts — the grooms would take the carriage round to the stable

Basketwork pony-carriages — landaus — "vis-à-vis" — polished dark-blue brougham

Writers: Scott & Irving were gentlemen: Poe, Melville, & Harriet B. Stowe were not

Magazines — contributed to by Poe & Washington Irving — women's weeklies: fashion plates and paper patterns — New England love stories — small ads

Writing with a stylographic pen

Going for a spin on the Hudson in the ice-boat

Steam yachts fitted with tiled bathrooms — costing half a million

Gentlemen in patent-leather shoes, white waistcoats, ulsters

A plush-lined cab was called a "herdie"

Old ladies in caps and shawls and black brocade — silk mittens

Rice griddle cakes and syrup for breakfast

strawberry shortcake and vanilla ice

broiled mackerel, mayonnaise of celery, ham cooked in champagne, lima beans in cream,

corn soufflé

champagne, madeira, burgundy

Dining at 6 instead of 2

Madison Avenue was unfashionable — had to be within stone's throw of Washington Square

grey cashmere dress — dinner dress of whaleboned silk, lace neck-ruffles, tight sleeves with a flounce, gold bracelet, velvet wrist-band, satin shoes

fur cap with a bird's wing for walking in The Central Park

velvet hat — grey velvet bonnet trimmed with frosted grapes

49

summer wear: lace veil, white silk dress with broad black satin stripe, huge hat wreathed with crimson roses and green veil

Dinner parties: roses, maidenhair ferns, bonbons in silver baskets

elegance: feuille-morte taffeta, black-lace bonnet with a tea-rose

The elite went to dances in the ballroom at Delmonico's — Assembly balls — subscription

Middle-aged elegance: black velvet polonaise, jet buttons, tiny green muff

Governess: black merino and plum silk with crochet lace collar

Widow: white crape cap — lace-edged cambric handkerchief

At the opera: tall hat, pearl-grey trousers, opera cloak

Wallack's Theatre — Ibsen — opera on Mondays and Fridays — Wednesday you lend your box to poor relations

Debutantes in white tulle — poor ones in tarlatan

Chaperones in purple poplin trimmed with velvet bands — beaded dolman — cluny lace

Embroidered India mull — patterns taken from Butterick's magazine

Houses had striped awnings in summer

Older ladies in old-fashioned roomy barouches — powdered footman — carriage on big C-springs

Coach with fringed hammercloth

Interiors: dark-green velvet walls — occasional tables — albums with views of European rivers

Dark shiny hotel sitting rooms with colored lithographs

Domed front hall, red Turkey carpet, new hot-air furnaces, gas chandeliers, yellow oak glass-fronted bookcases

Houses in Gramercy Park, Irving Place, Union Square

Nottingham lace curtains, gilt cornices, marble tables, mahogany armchairs, empire sofas, new French damask wallpaper, Turner's *Rivers of France*, black marble fireplaces, inlaid wood worktables, French lamps with fringed shades

Violets in The Central Park — the Ramble — the Dell

Children: boys in plaid velvet bonnet — plaid alpaca dress

Cabriolet bonnet of white velvet plumed with crystal-spangled feathers

Ermine-tippet-crossed beaver bonnet

Black-and-white hackney carriages with blue curtains

Lunch at Fifth Avenue Hotel — oyster soup, stuffed goose, broiled bass

How the Cops Got Their Name

STEPHEN MOOSER

Back in the early 1800s the Bowery was a tough and wild place. The area around the Bowery was ruled by gangs with names like The True Blue Americans, The Atlantic Guards, The Dead Rabbits, and the toughest and most famous of them all, The Bowery Boys. They made their own laws and had little respect for the police or other forms of authority. Up to this time the police in New York hadn't worn special uniforms. New York's Mayor, a man named Harper, thought that maybe his police would command more respect if they wore fancy uniforms. So, in about 1840, Mayor Harper dressed the police in flashy uniforms complete with rows of shiny brass buttons. Shortly thereafter the police were summoned to the Bowery. They were needed to help clear the way for some firemen who had been called to extinguish a blaze in the old Bowery Theater.

The gangs were not at all impressed with the fancy uniforms. In fact, they thought they were rather silly. They laughed at the policemen and refused to obey their commands. Other similar events followed until, finally, the embarrassed police gave up their uniforms. For years afterward the only way you could identify a policeman was by the large star-shaped copper badge he wore. It was because of this badge that police came to be called "cops" and "coppers."

Paradise Park

STANLEE BRIMBERG

If you had wanted to see it, you would've had to saturate your handkerchief with camphor to endure the horrid stench. There was not the slightest sign of

Broad Street Canal in 1659.

cleanliness or comfort. You might have heard the groans of the dying and the fiendish yell of the drunken rioters. Many of the rooms of the dingy lodging houses were without windows. The wretched dwellings were connected by secret underground tunnels. You would have been sure not to venture down Murderer's Alley unarmed. For there, of all places, it may truly have been said that he who entered left hope behind.

Murderer's Alley, the Den of Thieves, home of the gangster members of the Plug Uglies, the Shirt Tails, the Forty Thieves, and the Dead Rabbits—that was Five Points, Paradise Park, in the year 1850.

In colonial days, a peaceful fresh-water pond called the Collect provided swimming in summer and skating in winter for the citizens of New York City. But as the city grew, the still water became putrid. A canal was dug along what is today Canal Street in the hope that the moving water from the rivers would relieve and revive the pond, but it did not.

The poor dumped refuse into the Collect, watered their animals from it, and built their shacks around the pond, which became known as Cow Bay. On the south side of the pond, five streets met in an open space. That intersection became known as The Five Points, but its real name was Paradise Park.

It was a far cry from paradise. The cramped living conditions of the poor immigrants who settled there bred crime, sickness, and desperation. The police force considered the area unmanageable.

Things continued to worsen until the Reverend and Mrs. Pease arrived from Connecticut. They began to tackle the problem by working with the children of the neighborhood. At first they had to pass out sweets and play marbles with the children to earn their confidence. Later, the Peases cared for their health, provided food and shelter for them, and taught them more constructive ways of living.

At the end of the century, The Five Points was torn down and the neighborhood was rebuilt. But Paradise Park is still there. It is the parking lot at the corner of Worth, Baxter, and Park streets, just a few blocks north of City Hall. The entrance of 155 Worth Street was the mouth of Murderer's Alley.

Walk a short block up Baxter Street to Leonard and you will be on the edge of Cow Bay. The pond is gone now. In its place stands the new Criminal Courts Building, where until very recently the infamous Tombs prison was located.

New York Gangs

JAMES HASKINS

We think that street gangs are a twentieth-century phenomenon. We assume that the Savage Nomads, the Young Sinners, the Reapers, the wars over "turf," and the activities that terrorize people in neighborhoods are something new to our society. But there have been gangs in New York almost as long as there has been a New York.

Up until the early 1800s, gangs were just loosely knit groups. It was not until the 1820s that they became really organized with names and leaders and rules. The first

organized gang, the Forty Thieves, arose in the Five Points-Paradise Square district, and soon other thieves and pickpockets and thugs were forming gangs of their own. Some of these called themselves the Roach Guards, the Plug Uglies, the Shirt Tails, and the Dead Rabbits.

The Roach Guards started in the back room of a liquor store owned by a man named Roach. The Plug Uglies were huge —much larger than the men of other gangs. Their name came from their large plug hats, which they stuffed with wool and leather to serve as protective helmets in battle. The Shirt Tails always wore their shirts outside their trousers. The Dead Rabbits branched off from the Roach Guards. Once during a stormy meeting of the Guards, someone had thrown a dead rabbit into the center of the room, and the dissenting group had seen this as a sign. In those days, among the gangs, a rabbit was a tough guy, and a dead rabbit was a super tough guy. The dissenting members split from the Roach Guards and took the name Dead Rabbits. Their battle standard was a dead rabbit stuck on a pike.

The gangs' weapons were many and varied. Some were fortunate enough to own pistols and muskets, but the usual weapons were knives and brickbats and bludgeons. For close work there were brass knuckles, ice picks, pikes, and other interesting paraphernalia.

Like twentieth-century gangs, these gangs included women. During battles, most of them stayed on the sidelines, ready to supply ammunition or to give medical aid. But some fought right alongside the men. The most notable female fighter was Hell-Cat Maggie, who was with the Dead Rabbits in the 1840s. Legend has it that her teeth were filed to sharp points and that she wore long, false fingernails made of brass.

And, like today's gangs, the gangs of the last century were conscious of publicity and very concerned with their image. Once, in 1857, the New York *Times* reported on a street brawl, describing the gangs involved—among them the Dead Rabbits—as groups of thieves and criminals. A few days later, the *Times* carried this item:

We are requested by the Dead Rabbits to state that the Dead Rabbit club members are not thieves, [and] that they did not participate in the riot . . . The Dead Rabbits are sensitive on points of honor, we are assured, and wouldn't allow a thief to live on their beat, much less to be a member of their club.

Graves and Burial Grounds

MARY ANDERSON

Graveyards in Greenwich Village? A cemetery under the Forty-second Street library? It's hard to believe! Yet in the 1700s, Union Square, Madison Square, Washington Square, and Bryant Park were all Potter's Fields.

Before the city had grown past lower Manhattan, Forty-second Street was considered country. And so it was. As late as 1680, bears were still roaming the upper part of the island, through the dense forests inhabited by deer and wolves.

Secluded places such as this were often set aside as Potter's Fields. In them were buried not only strangers and paupers, but citizens whose families were unable to afford the cost of a lot in church cemeteries. Later, when interment in churchyards of those who had died of yellow fever was forbidden by law, these bodies too were buried here.

So as the city grew up from the Battery, Potter's Fields were gradually moved farther and farther uptown. Even today, a Potter's Field can still be found on the outskirts of the city. In 1868 Hart's Island, a piece of land off the east coast of the Bronx, was purchased as a permanent home for Potter's Field. It cost $75,000, and since then more than 700,000 strangers have been buried there.

The public is not allowed on Hart's Island. The only way to get there is on a creaking ferry which carries the inmates from Riker's Island who bury the bodies. Prisoners have always tended the unknown and forgotten of Potter's Field.

There are also famous figures buried in historic sites around Manhattan, just a subway or bus ride from many of us.

St. Mark's-in-the-Bowery on Tenth Street and Second Avenue (the oldest church site still occupied by a house of worship in New York) is the burial place of Peter Stuyvesant, former Governor of New Amsterdam. His black granite tombstone is set directly into the outer wall of the church.

Trinity Cemetery near 155th Street and Amsterdam Avenue is the resting place of James Audubon. The cemetery itself is part of the farmland he once owned. Also buried there, in the older section between Broadway and Riverside Drive, is Clement C. Moore, who wrote "The Night Before Christmas." The older section also holds the mausoleum of Madame Jumel, who was once married to Aaron Burr. The Jumel Mansion on 160th Street hosted such guests as Washington, Franklin, Jefferson, Hamilton, and Nathan Hale.

The largest single burial site in Manhattan is Grant's Tomb at 122nd Street and Riverside Drive. Almost directly opposite this huge landmark, commemorating one of our nation's Presidents, is a much smaller gravesite which often goes unnoticed. Yet it too is historic and noteworthy.

This simple granite urn mounted on a pedestal is the burial ground of St. Clair Pollock, who, on July 15, 1797, fell to his death in the Hudson River at the age of five. His father, a Dublin merchant, owned the land, then known as Strawberry Hill.

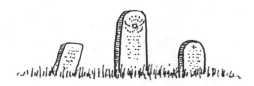

He sold the property soon after his son's death, with the stipulation that whoever bought it must keep up the grave. Long afterward, the city purchased the property, making it the only private grave on public land. School children from Riverside Church nearby still commemorate St. Clair's passing, with bunches of daisies placed on his grave.

The Ghost of Peter Stuyvesant

STEPHEN MOOSER

The last Dutch Governor of New York was a colorful one-legged man by the name of Peter Stuyvesant, a feisty man in life and, some contend, just as ornery after death.

Shortly after he died in 1672 some people reported that they had seen the Gover-

The arrival of Peter Stuyvesant.

nor's ghost walking around his old house. Then, in 1774, the old house burned to the ground and his ghost was reported again. Witnesses said they saw a one-legged ghost hobbling about the ruins, inspecting the damage to the house.

Early in the 1880s some roads were cut near the church where Stuyvesant was buried. Apparently this didn't suit the Governor at all. Strange rappings, like those made by a one-legged man walking around, were heard coming from within the church. One man even claimed to have seen the ghost walking wild-eyed inside the church. In addition, the church bell began to ring from time to time without anyone being near the bell rope.

Then, the strangest event of all occurred near the end of the nineteenth century. The city began to extend Second Avenue right through the church graveyard. One night, during the construction, the church bell began to toll. The sexton and some others ran to the church and unlocked it. When they got inside the empty church the ringing stopped. Under the belfry they noticed that the bell rope had been broken, as if someone had snapped it off with a powerful jerk. The next day, according to the sexton, the remainder of the rope was found at the spot where Peter Stuyvesant had been buried over a hundred years before!

Something's Missing

Most of Peter Stuyvesant is buried in New York City, but his leg—lost in a battle in the Dutch West Indies years before he became Governor of Nieuw Amsterdam —is buried on the Dutch island of Curaçao, in the Caribbean.

I have three little sisters who died before I was born and they are buried in the Marble Cemetery . . . The oldest child . . . was seven years old . . . and she was taken sick in school . . . and she died in forty-eight hours of scarlet fever . . .

FROM *Diary of a Little Girl in Old New York,* 1849–50

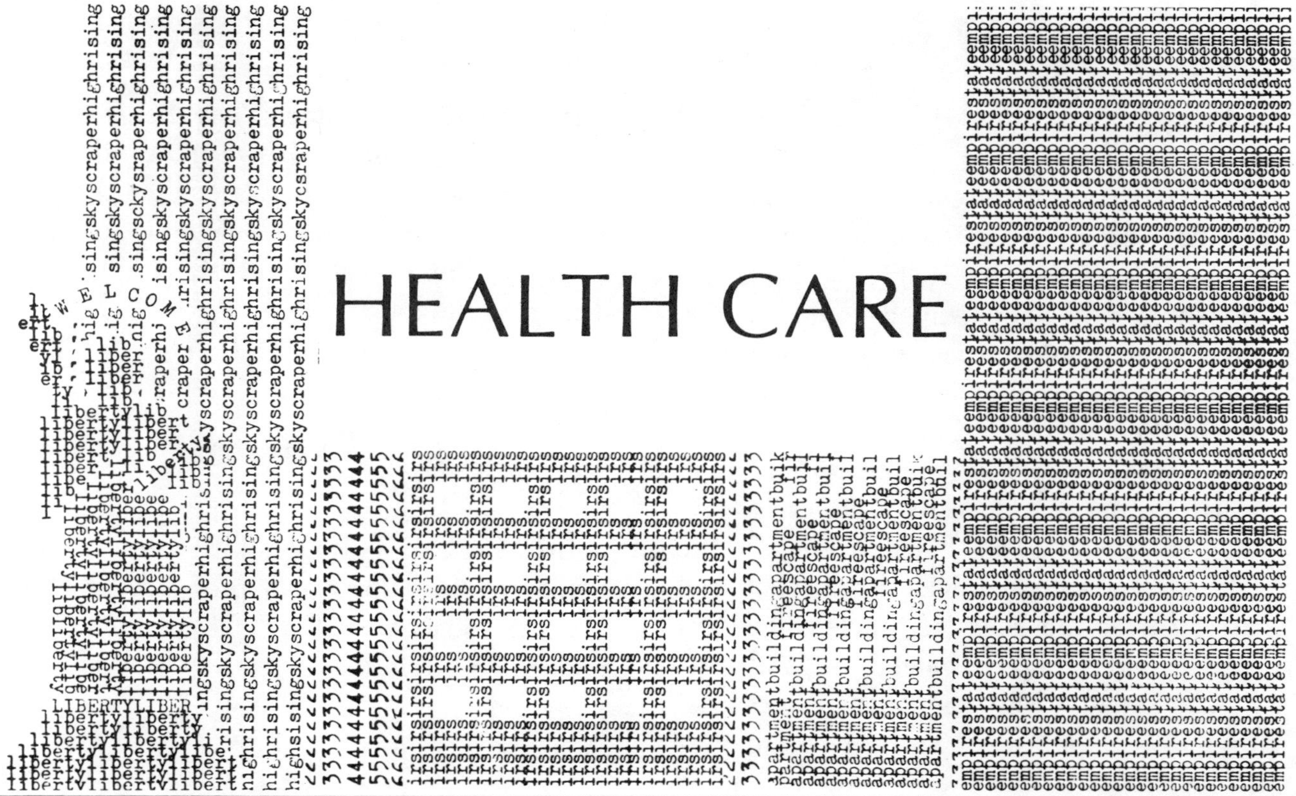

HEALTH CARE

The Doctors' Riot

BARBARA BEASLEY MURPHY

On April 13, 1788, John Hicks, Jr., a young medical student, did a silly thing. He picked up an arm he'd just dissected and shook it out the window at a bunch of kids peering in.

"This is your mother's hand," he shouted. "I just dug it up. Watch out or I'll smack you with it."

The children hollered and ran away. But one very scared boy believed Hicks. By coincidence his own mother had died recently so he hurried home to tell his father what Hicks had said. The man was furious and called his friends to go with him to the nearby cemetery. When they reached his wife's grave, by a worse coincidence, they found it empty. Whoever had robbed

it hadn't even bothered to refill the gaping hole to hide the broken coffin. Naturally the man believed the robber was the doctor who'd teased the children that day.

"Someone will pay for this desecration!" he shouted (and worse) as he led his friends through the streets of lower Manhattan. Others joined them, and the gang grew and grew until there were hundreds who stormed the hospital and its unsuspecting staff.

"We've heard stories for too long about young interns stealing bodies! Now we have proof!" they cried.

Holding brickbats and torches the mob encircled the building. They screamed, "Come out! Come out! And take *your* medicine!" They blocked all the doors and waited.

With no time to lose the entire medical staff fled through the back windows. Everyone except for Dr. Post and three students escaped. They stayed to guard the valuable anatomical specimens which provided students with much of their knowledge of the human body.

The enraged and misunderstanding mob rushed inside and destroyed almost everything in their path. The inside of the building was a shambles with shattered glass all over the floor, and surgical instruments twisted and damaged beyond use. All the anatomical specimens were destroyed or taken away. To protect Dr. Post and his students, the sheriff locked them in jail.

But the mob wasn't finished. They surged back into the streets, searching for doctors, hungering for revenge. They destroyed the home of Sir John Temple, who was not even a doctor. They believed *Sir John* meant surgeon. It wasn't until early in the morning two days later that the first riot in New York was quelled. Governor George Clinton called out the militia and dispersed the mob.

The Bone Bill

In 1854, the "Bone Bill" was passed, thanks to the efforts of a professor at NYU Medical School, making the dissection of unclaimed bodies legal.

POLIO VACCINE DISCOVERED

The first polio vaccine was discovered at the NYU Medical Center by Jonas Salk and Robert Sabin.

One New Yorker's answer to air pollution.

[There] is always someone coming to visit us, and now we have a cousin who has consumption and she is trying a cure called galvanism. Her doctor makes her wear a pair of soles in her shoes, and one is copper and the other is zinc, and it makes some kind of current that may help her. Ellen and I tried to squeeze them into our shoes and pretend we had consumption and cough, but they were too big . . .

FROM *Diary of a Little Girl in Old New York, 1849–50*

The Day Everyone Left New York

STEPHEN MOOSER

In 1822 a terrible epidemic of yellow fever struck New York City. In desperation the authorities decided to evacuate the entire city in order to fight the plague. On August 24 everyone, save for the sick and the doctors who were tending them, packed up and left town.

Once the city had been cleared, workmen moved in sprinkling lime over everything in an effort to control the disease. These same people stayed in the abandoned city guarding the homes of those who had fled. The city erected a fence along Chambers Street and forbade people to enter. A garden was planted down the middle of Broadway, and later that summer a fine crop of beans was harvested.

The tens of thousands of people who left the city settled out in the country on the site of what is now Greenwich Village. A makeshift city sprang up in the fields. So many financial institutions opened up along one path that the road was named Bank Street, a name that persists to this day.

Finally the fever vanished and when winter came many people moved back to their homes, but many others stayed on to create one of old New York's largest and most prosperous suburbs, Greenwich Village.

October 15, 1859

My eyes are so bad that I could not write in my diary, and Maggy takes me to Dr. Samuel Elliott's, corner of Amity Street and Broadway, and he puts something in that smarts awfully. He has two rooms, and all the people sit in the front room, waiting, and his office is in the back room; and they have black patches over their eyes—some of them—and sit very quiet and solemn. On each side of the folding doors are glass cases filled with stuffed birds and I know them all by heart now and wish he would get some new ones.

When I was four years old I had my tonsils cut out by Dr. Horace Green, who lives on Clinton Place. My nurse asked him to give them to her, so he put them in a little bottle of alcohol and sealed it up, and she keeps it in the nursery closet, and sometimes she shows it to me to amuse me, but it doesn't, only I don't like to hurt her feelings. My grandmother gave me a five-dollar gold piece for sitting so still when they were cut out . . .

FROM *Diary of a Little Girl in Old New York, 1849–50*

Who Cares?

Have you ever wondered as you walked along the street in New York and saw men or women sad and hungry, or sleeping in doorways, "Who will care for these people? Who will give them some food and a warm place to sleep? Who will love them? Who will hear their story and try to help them find a way to live in this big city?"

There *is* a group in New York whose whole life is given to receiving and serving food to people who have fallen on hard times and given up. The group is called The Catholic Worker, and it was founded nearly fifty years ago by Dorothy Day and Peter Maurin. Young and old volunteers run two houses of hospitality on the Lower East Side.

They never have a fund drive. They don't even have a public relations department. They do publish a monthly newspaper called *The Catholic Worker* which is sold for one cent a copy. They are just a group of people in the city who care, and who never cease hoping that people can start to live again.

Waiting at Bellevue

SIDNEY OFFITT

When my wife, Avodah, returned to school to study medicine at New York University, our sons, Ken and Mike, were eight and six years old. Medical school was a demanding grind which often made it necessary for Avy to remain overnight while she trained at Bellevue, a complex of buildings on Thirty-fourth Street which Dr. Lewis Thomas, the Dean, described as serving "the poor, the friendless, the unlucky, maimed and marred."

On days when the urge to visit their mother was strong enough, Ken and Mike would make their way downtown on the IRT subway to Thirty-fourth Street and then hike crosstown to Bellevue.

It was not unusual for the boys to sit in the waiting room of the emergency service. There they waited their turn to see their mother while priority was given to more pressing needs—a broken leg, superficial knife wounds, stomach cramps.

One early spring evening the boys sat beside an elderly gentleman who appeared not to have shaved in days. He wore a tattered Chesterfield coat, a crushed felt hat, and black ankle-high shoes with string substituting for shoelaces.

As the evening wore on, the man recounted to the boys the tale of his woes. "Nothing seems to go right anymore," they remember his saying. "Everything in New York City is going to pot. Subway fares are up, rents are out of reach. You can't walk the streets or the parks without fear of attack."

The boys sat quietly listening and nodding. Their smallest efforts to reply seemed only to distract the man. He continued his recitation. "Besides, I have pains in my back, aches in my shoulders, agonies in every finger and toe."

"I'm sorry for you," said Ken.

"I hope you feel better," agreed Mike.

When at last only the old man and the boys were left in the waiting room, the old gentleman asked what they were there for.

"We're waiting to see our mother. She works here," was the reply.

The old man stood up suddenly. "Well, it's been good talking to you," he said. "God bless you both." With that he tipped the worn fedora, smiled and departed.

Later, when the emergency room had slowed up, the boys recounted the experience to their mother. They were disquieted by the thought that somehow they had discouraged the old gentleman from receiving proper attention.

"You were speaking to Mr. Gonzaga," their mother told them. "He received medication from us earlier this week. But he returns every evening just to tell us his troubles. You listened. That was as good as any doctor could do."

CITY MAGIC

A Secret Language

BERNICE KOHN HUNT

Would you like to pass your best friend a note the other kids in class (and your teacher) can't read? Keep a diary your brother can't snoop in? Get letters your mother can't understand? You can, if you learn NEW YORK CIPHER.

All you have to do is memorize this diagram. It's a nine-box tick-tacktoe with the letters of the alphabet written in it like this:

A B C	D E F	G H I
J K L	M N O	P Q R
S T U	V W X	Y Z

Notice that every box in the diagram has a different shape. To write in cipher, draw the shape of the box each letter is in. If your letter is the first one, leave the box blank. If it's the second letter, put one dot in the box. If it's the third letter, put two dots in the box.

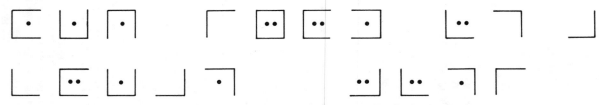

Now see if you can read this secret message. Then write one of your own. (SOLUTION, PG. 369.)

The High Priestess in New York

DANIEL COHEN

A lot of strange people have lived in New York but none stranger than Madame Helena Petrovna Blavatsky. H.P.B., as she was often called, was born August 12, 1831, the daughter of a Russian nobleman. At the age of sixteen she married a general in the Russian Army. A few months later she ran off with an English sea captain and spent the next twenty-five years roaming the world.

She was a circus performer in Constantinople and a spirit medium in Cairo. She said she went to Tibet, and slept inside the Great Pyramid in Egypt. H.P.B. told a million stories about her past, all different.

On July 7, 1873, her wanderings brought her, flat broke, to New York City, where she began attending spiritualist séances, calling up not ordinary spirits, but Kurdish warriors, black Africans, a Persian magician named Hassan Agha, and a host of others.

H.P.B. was no beauty. Indeed, most people described her as fat and loud. She was always sloppy, spending most of her days lounging around in a dirty bathrobe scattering cigarette ashes over everything and everybody. When she got dressed up her costumes were so bizarre that people would stop and stare. But she had the power to fascinate people and make them believe the most outrageous things. She made people believe that her servant Michalko, who had been dead for years, returned to give her a cross that had been buried with her grandfather.

By 1875 H.P.B. moved again, to a large apartment at 302 West 47 Street. At about this time her followers began receiving letters from a mysterious and invisible "Egyptian Brotherhood." The letters were written with gold ink on green paper. The Brotherhood claimed to be heir to the "wisdom of the ages" and advised people to follow Madame Blavatsky. People believed in the letters.

In 1876, when one of her followers died, H.P.B. decided to stage what she called the first cremation in America. Rites were held in the huge Masonic Temple on Sixth Avenue, and fifteen hundred tickets were sold to the spectacle. H.P.B. was there in full Egyptian regalia. Police had to hold back the crowds.

Out of all her dabblings with the occult Madame Blavatsky created—with her friend Colonel H. S. Olcott—a philosophical movement known as Theosophy that attracted hundreds of thousands of members. This movement still exists today.

H.P.B. could have become rich and successful in America. But she couldn't settle down. She developed an interest in the Hindu religion. So on December 17, 1878, she set sail for India. Her aim was to teach her brand of Hinduism to the Hindus. At this task she was remarkably successful, and her movement prospered in India.

Madame Blavatsky.

Madame Blavatsky was an audacious faker, a monumental egotist, and probably more than a little crazy. She was also one of the most colorful, remarkable people who ever lived. *I would love* to have met her.

The Magic Card

BARBARA ROLLOCK

Children's services in the New York Public Library introduced the "magic" of books to thousands of New York City children in 1908. Since then, books have become just one part of a vast collection of materials—records, cassettes, posters—available to young readers free of charge.

In addition, free activities for children take place monthly in almost all the eighty-one neighborhood branches that attract children from pre-school to seventh grade. These may be puppet shows performed by professional puppeteers, librarians, or the children themselves, after they have completed a puppet workshop or, in the spring, when the circus is in town, a local branch may feature a clown. There are special film showings for pre-schoolers in several branches as well as films for older children and their parents.

Librarians go out into the city to talk about children's books to school classes or assemblies and read picture books to the youngest children.

Magic Stores

BEBE WILLOUGHBY

Would you like to be a magician? It's not difficult, but it does require practice and patience. The first time you do a trick, don't expect it to come off perfectly. The stores listed below offer a wide selection of tricks and illusions, but demonstrators won't reveal any secrets about how they are done until you make your purchases.

Magic Center at 739 Broadway sells souvenirs of New York, joke items, and magic tricks. Its display of masks—of old men and women, monsters and apes—hang from the rafters, and provide much fun and interest.

Located at 304 West 34 Street is *Flosso Hornmann Magic Co.*, the oldest magic store in America. This store has always been owned by magicians and the famed Harry Houdini even owned it at one time. His handcuffs are on exhibit. Part of this store is a museum with many old interesting effects displayed in a glass case. There are old puppets and posters on display and puppets and posters which you can buy. One of their best buys, says the owner, is a magic set for about $10 which gives you about thirteen tricks and a good book of instruction. The general range of tricks in this store is from $1 to $10.

A carnival atmosphere permeates *Circle Magic* at 1661 Broadway. When you walk into this store you really think you've landed in another part of the world. There is a love quotient machine, a happy horse for kids, an auto driver machine to help you learn how to drive, a rifle range and Zolten, a machine that gives a message when you press the button of your astrological sign. One side of the store is devoted to magic and here the atmosphere is a little more serious. The cane that appears in your hand from nowhere is $25. One favorite trick is filling up a pitcher with milk, then lifting up the pitcher to find that the milk has vanished. There are many tricks and illusions offered in this store, running from $1 to $2,000.

Tannen's is tucked away on the seventeenth floor of 1540 Broadway, in Times Square. Tannen's is the largest magic store in the world. There is something for everyone in this store—from the beginning magician to the professional. Tricks and illusions run from $1 to $5,000. (A girl who goes into a cage and turns into a lioness is an illusion that costs $5,000.) This is a colorful place filled with many books and neatly arranged glass cases. The psychic spoon, the phantom flame, and the china change are a few recommended tricks that are not expensive and are fun to try. The Jiffy Coin Trick is only $1 and Mr. Tannen says it's the best dollar trick on the market. It works like this: a borrowed coin that is marked disappears under a handkerchief held by a volunteer and then is found in a series of boxes. Mr. Tannen says, "Magic is for everyone. It takes people away from what is happening around them for a little while."

FOOD FOOD FOOD

What's Cooking

JOAN GROSS

When your feet complain, when fatigue creeps into your soul, when you're bored with the delights of the Big Apple, it just may be Time to Eat. And that means you must choose a restaurant from a list that seems endless. You can get a decent hot dog and accompaniments at any Sabrett cart or enjoy foods of various ethnic persuasions all over Manhattan, particularly in Central Park. This article may give you some ideas about restaurants to sample, many of them in the Midtown area of Manhattan, whose chief virtue is good value for money received. Decor comes second, but if it's unusual it will be mentioned. Here, in no particular order, is What's Cooking:

TRADER VIC'S at the Plaza is dark, mysterious, and vaguely Polynesian. A huge outrigger canoe lies majestically in the lobby, and the sound of native drumming is gently persistent. Food is mainly Chinese and expensive, entrees over $5. A good place for special treats. 150 West 57 Street. Phone: 265-0947.

NATHAN'S, founded in 1916 as a hot dog stand in Coney Island, still carries the persuasive aroma of honky-tonk. Self service upstairs—hot dogs, pizza, corn on the cob, and celery tonic—junk food heaven! Restaurant downstairs with clowns and balloons on the weekends. Very moderate entrees around $3. Highly recommended for general snacking and eating. 6 East 58 Street. Phone: 751-9060.

MOLFETA'S, in the theater district, is an unpretentious Greek restaurant with a small, self-service cafeteria in the back. Friendly waiters, freshly cooked food (including fish), a Greek-American juke box, and very reasonable prices—entrees from $3—make this place enjoyable. Highly recommended. 307 West 47 Street. Phone: 582-9278.

GENROKU SUSHI may be the only Japanese fast food restaurant in New York—certainly the only one with a conveyor belt! Dishes pass by and you just reach out for the ones you want. The empty plates are counted and—presto—the bill. Naturally, sushi is featured—raw fish beautifully arranged on top of delicately flavored rice. Very moderate—all dishes $1, with soup 50¢. Average lunch is $2. A good place if you're shopping at Altman's. 366 Fifth Avenue at Thirty-fourth Street. Phone: 947-7940.

RAJA-RANI has the cozy, intimate quality of an Indian tent. Colorful cotton fabric drapes the ceiling; votive candles stand in niches all around the pink stucco walls. An Indian-Pakistani restaurant, it offers a special daily luncheon of various curries for $2.50 and up. Pleasant, informal service. 32 East 22 Street. Phone: 475-9693.

One of the best bargains in town is the AMERICAN CAFETERIA in the Concourse of Rockefeller Center, calculated to make the weary Fifth Avenue shopper a little happier. Appetizing salads, hot food, sandwiches, and drinks are arranged attractively in a "cluster" pattern—no traffic problems. Prices are most reasonable with entrees averaging $1.50. Note: Open only for breakfast and lunch, 7:30 to 4. 630 Fifth Avenue at Fiftieth Street. Phone: LT 1-3580 (ask specifically for American Cafeteria).

THE AUTOPUB is both a restaurant and museum with automotive artifacts scattered over several rooms. In the Classic Car Lounge, chassis of old cars serve as seats and tables. A cozy hamburger can be enjoyed while gazing at an authentic 1911 Ford Torpedo or a 1929 Brookland Riley. Very expensive—hamburgers are $3.50—but the atmosphere is intriguing. Choose the cheapest item on the menu, then look around. Old movies shown on weekends. 767 Fifth Avenue at Fifty-ninth Street in the General Motors Building. Phone: 832-3232.

FRAUNCES TAVERN is not for those who want a casual ham sandwich—entrees are around $6—but it is well worth a visit. Manhattan's oldest building still has a flavor of the original tavern in which George Washington bade farewell to his troops. The museum on the upper floors is fascinating and the whole building has been declared a Historic Landmark. It's recommended that young people come after 2 P.M. Broad and Pearl Street. Phone: BO 9-0144.

Stuffed animals gaze serenely at the diners happily chomping away at LÜCHOW'S, a German eating establishment of mammoth proportions—it can accommodate a thousand at a time. Prices are moderate to expensive with entrees around $5, but the menu is gargantuan, and you're sure to find something you like. Wursts are featured of course, and a wonderful German pancake. This convivial restaurant particularly likes children—adults may split orders with them. There is an oompah band at night, and a general sense of well-being prevails at all times. 110 East 14 Street. Phone: 477-4860.

At BROWNIE'S CREATIVE COOKERY don't ask for a hamburger. This is a vegetarian restaurant and one of the best in the city. Try a homemade peanut butter and fruit jam sandwich on pumpernickel ($1.30). All the food is fresh and beautifully cooked. After your meal, shop in the retail store around the corner where you can get everything from honey almond granola to a Queen Helene Herbal mud pack. A real treat. 21 East 16 Street. Phone: AL 5-2838.

A waxy, yellow provolone cheese hangs on a hook next to a huge prosciutto ham at MANGANARO FOODS, an Italian grocery store and informal restaurant. In the rear of this pungent emporium are a few long, family-style tables. Sit down. Green peppers fry gently in a black iron skillet, the tomato sauce bubbles away, and the smells coming from the enormous old restaurant stove are tantalizing. Entrees are simple and very reasonable: mixed meat, cheese, and peppers ($2.50). No menu—prices are written on a blackboard behind the stove. A wonderful place. 488 Ninth Avenue at Thirty-eighth Street. Phone: LO 3-5331.

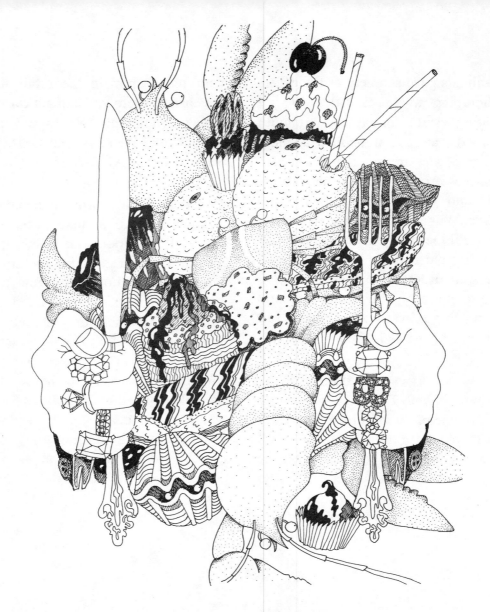

When Diamond Jim Had Had His Fill

STEPHEN MOOSER

Around the turn of the century Diamond Jim Brady, the financier and philanthropist, was the most famous eater in New York, or, for that matter, in the world. He loved to eat. At a typical meal he would begin with a gallon or two of orange juice. Then he would have three dozen oysters, followed by a dozen crabs. Finally, for the main course, he would consume six or seven large lobsters. Dessert was generally a platter full of French pastries and a two-pound box of chocolates.

A woman once asked Diamond Jim how he knew when he had had enough to eat.

Diamond Jim replied that when he sat down to a meal he always left four inches between his stomach and the table.

"When I can feel the two of 'em rubbing together pretty hard, then I know I've had enough," he said.

WHAT TO ORDER IN A SPANISH-CHINESE RESTAURANT
(and What You'll Be Missing if You Don't Go In)

RACHEL COWAN

You see many restaurants in New York which advertise both Spanish and Chinese food. They're usually small, and the people who run them came originally from China. They went first to Cuba or Santo Domingo, and now live in New York. They speak Chinese, Spanish, and English, and their food is a wonderful mixture of three styles of cooking. My family eats often at the Tacita de Oro (The Golden Cup) on the corner of Broadway and 100th Street. It doesn't look very special on the outside, but we're sure it's one of the best restaurants in the city. Sometimes the kids eat at the Dollar de Oro on Ninety-sixth Street near Broadway when they're tired of school lunches.

Here's what we've discovered to be the most delicious foods:

SPECIAL FRIED RICE—a big helping of white rice fried with shrimps, chunks of pork and beef and chicken, bean sprouts, lettuce, and onion. It's fluffy and filling.

ROPA VIEJA means "old clothes" in Spanish, because the slices of meat are shredded in a way that must have looked like rags to somebody. The meat is served with green peppers and olives in a mild sauce, and poured over white rice that's cooked exactly right. Each grain is separate and firm, not mushy.

PICADILLO means "chopped up" in Spanish, because it's a dish of chopped meat in a mildly spiced sauce that's also served with rice.

FRIED BANANAS—ask for "maduros" (ripe bananas), which are soft and sweet inside, crusty on the outside. "Tostones" are fried green bananas, which are good too but dry and slightly salty.

FLAN—a creamy molded custard drenched in caramel sauce.

BATIDO—a sweetish, cold, nourishing fruit milkshake. Try the slightly bland, subtle flavors of tropical fruits like papaya, mango, guanabana, or mamey if you're adventurous. The banana and pineapple batidos are sure bets.

CAFE CON LECHE for the grownups is not just "coffee with milk." It's strong espresso combined with hot milk to give a rich flavor.

These restaurants usually serve fresh Cuban bread and butter with the meal, and a dish of black beans to go with the white rice. We advise helping yourself to plenty of both. You'll also do well with steak and onions, Wonton soup, shrimps in spicy tomato sauce, oxtail stew, and a hearty caldo gallego (white bean soup). The prices are very reasonable, and the atmosphere is cheerful, often with Hispanic music in the background. You'll find families eating Sunday dinner there, working people getting a bargain lunch, and single men taking supper at the counter.

To Make Your Own Batido

Combine in a blender:

1 cup milk

1 tablespoon sugar

At least one large spoonful of fruit:

canned or fresh pineapple; or mango, mamey, papaya, or guanabana (which you can find in a corner *tienda* or *bodega*—small Hispanic grocery store—or fresh at a fruitstand in season); or a banana, or strawberries

As much ice as you'd like (several cubes at least)

Blend until ice is chopped up, pour and drink.

LIMERICK

JOAN GROSS

There once was a girl from New York
Who had an aversion to pork,
But she thought it was neat-o
To eat cuchifritos,
Believing they came from the stork.

Walkaway Foods

BARBARA SHOOK HAZEN

Variety is the spice of the Big Apple, a nice edible nickname for New York. The happy fact is that no city in the world offers a wider choice of inexpensive snacks. One reason—no city has a richer ethnic background of good cooks.

The following is a sampler of some of the unusual foods you may find sold on the streets and in the parks of New York or at counters.

All are delicious and actually good for you. So, the next time you feel like a treat, expand your taste buds. Even if you're not sure what it is, try it. Chances are you'll like it.

BAGEL: (Jewish) Unleavened hard roll in a doughnut shape. Comes plain or adorned with garlic, Kosher salt, onions, sesame, caraway or poppy seeds, raisins and cinnamon. Also pumpernickel. May be eaten plain, toasted, or topped with cream cheese and/or lox or any sandwich filling.

BAKLAVA: (Middle Eastern) Many-layered semi-transparent pastry enclosing crushed nuts and held together by a honey syrup. Very rich, very delicious.

BEANCURD: (Oriental) Thick custardlike substance made from soy beans. Used in main dishes and, sweetened, in desserts.

BURRITO: (Mexican) Flour tortilla rolled and filled with cubed beef in brown sauce.

CALPIS: (Japanese) Sweet, slightly fermented milk drink.

CALZONE: (Italian) Folded pizza dough deep-fried with cheese or sausage inside.

CHESTNUTS: (Italian) Roasted and sold by street vendors. Rich, deep-flavored.

CHILI: (Mexican) Thick, soupy dish made of chili peppers, chopped meat, green peppers, onions, and red beans. Varies with the maker.

CRÊPE: (French) Light, thin folded pancake. Dessert crêpes are filled with jams, sweet syrups, fruit, and ice cream. Main-dish crêpes may be filled with anything from creamed chicken to ham and eggs to sausage and green peppers.

CUCHIFRITOS: Pieces of pork and potato wrapped in dough and deep-fried.

DANISH: (Danish) Sweet, flaky pastries filled with honey, sweet cheese, or fruit jams. They are usually served at breakfast.

EGG ROLL: (Chinese) Also Spring Roll. Shredded pork, bean sprouts, mushrooms, and other Oriental vegetables in a special deep-fried dough crust. Served with soy sauce, mustard, and sweet sauce.

EMPANADA: (South American and Caribbean) Meat pie with mild to hot sauce.

ENCHILADA: (Mexican) Soft rolled tortilla (thin cornmeal pancake) filled with chicken, cheese, or beef and topped with melted cheese, shredded lettuce, and onion.

FALAFEL: (Middle Eastern) Fried vegetarian balls made of chick peas and spices. Usually served in pita bread.

FISH AND CHIPS: (British) Crisp, deep-fried mild fish chunks served (in England in a rolled newspaper) with french fries and vinegar.

GAUCHO PIE: See *Empanada*.

GORP: (Scandinavian) Healthy energizing mixture of dried fruits and nuts.

GYRO: (Greek) The word means literally to turn. A gyro sandwich is usually lamb roasted on a spit. Most often served on pita bread, a flat bread with a deep pocket.

HEROES: Also Submarines, Big-Boys, Grinders. Sandwiches most often served on a loaf of bread cut lengthwise. Sometimes a roll. Filled with hot foods, such as meatballs and peppers, or a variety of cold ingredients, such as salami, cold cuts, cheese, lettuce, tomato, onions, and pickles.

HOT DOGS: Try them with cheese, chili, relish, onions, or sauerkraut on top.

NAN: (Indian) Crisp, spicy unleavened bread cooked in a special tandoori (clay) oven.

PAKORA: (Indian) Deep-fried chicken or vegetable fritters. Flavored with special Indian spices and often served with yogurt-mint sauce.

PITA OR KHUBZ: (Middle Eastern) Flat bread which has a perfect pocket for all kinds of sandwich fillings.

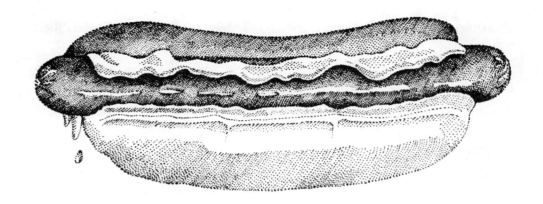

PIZZA: (Italian) Regular pizza is a round open pie. Made from special dough, it is topped with tomato sauce and cheese and may be garnished with many "extras"—anchovies, pepperoni, sausage, bacon bits, mushrooms, peppers, onions, or olives. Sicilian pizza is square and has a thicker crust.

QUICHE: (French) Main-dish custard pie, flavored with cheese, onion, ham, spinach, or seafood.

SAMOSA: (Indian) Spiced meat or vegetable (usually peas and potatoes) in a pastry turnover.

SEEDS: Sunflower seeds and soy beans (also seeds) make a crunchy treat when dry-roasted. Similar to roasted nuts. Found in health food stores.

SHISH KEBAB: (Middle Eastern) Meat, most often lamb or beef, chunks roasted on a skewer, often with onions, green peppers, tomatoes, and mushrooms. Also called shashlik.

SOUVLAKI: (Greek) Meat slow-cooked on a skewer. Most often lamb, which is sliced and served in pita bread.

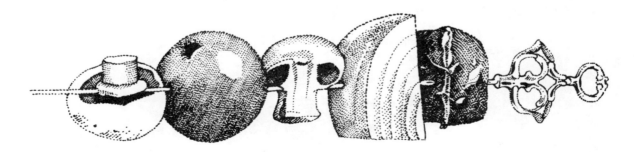

STRUDEL: (Viennese and German) Thin-crust fruit- or cheese-filled pastry.

SUSHI: (Japanese) Raw fish, vegetables, and beancurd embedded in seasoned rice and wrapped in seaweed.

TACO: (Mexican) Folded-over toasted tortilla filled with ground meat or chicken and topped with onion, cheese, and shredded lettuce. Meat may be piquant.

TORTILLA: (Mexican) Thin pancake usually made from corn flour. May be eaten buttered or used as basis of many dishes.

TOSTADA: (Mexican) Open toasted tortilla with chicken, cheese, or beef filling.

YAKITORI: (Japanese) Barbecued cubes of meat, fish, or vegetables served on thin skewers with soy sauce.

YOGURT: (Middle Eastern) Prepared food made from curdled milk. May be flavored, fruit topped, or frozen. Frozen yogurt is similar to ice cream.

ZEPPOLE: (Italian) Deep-fried dough similar to doughnuts (without the hole).

LIMERICK

WILLIAM JAY SMITH

A voluminous Person named Simpson
Continually ate curried shrimps on
Steaming mountains of rice,
Which was all very nice,
But increased the dimensions of Simpson.

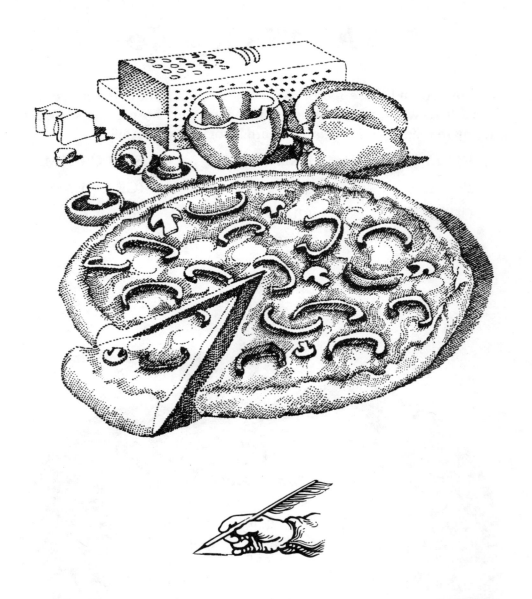

There is a bakery kept by a Mr. Walduck on the corner of Sixth Avenue and Eighth Street, and they make delicious cream puffs, and when I have three cents to spare, I run down there right after breakfast, before school begins, and buy one and eat it there. On the corner of Broadway and Ninth Street is a chocolate store kept by Felix Effray, and I love to stand at the window and watch the wheel go round. It has three white stone rollers and they grind the chocolate into paste all day long . . . Sometimes we go down to Wild's, to get his iceland moss drops, good for colds . . .

FROM *Diary of a Little Girl in Old New York*, 1849–50

The Big Apple

Can you find these foods in the Big Apple? Follow the letters forward, backward, up, down, or diagonally. You can use the same letter more than once in the same word. (SOLUTION, PG. 369.)

FALAFEL   HAMBURGER   EGG CREAM

PIZZA   MEAT PIE   ICE CREAM

CHESTNUTS   PRETZEL   SOUVLAKI

HOT DOG   KNISH   GUM

I Scream, You Scream, We All Scream for Ice Cream

BEBE WILLOUGHBY

What's new in New York City when it comes to ice cream? There really isn't much new about ice cream itself. The popular dessert is said to have made its debut in the royal courts of Europe in the 1500s, but ice cream, as we know it, is not like the European version. Good old-fashioned ice cream, and its side-kick, the cone, was introduced at the Chicago World's Fair in the late 1800s. Since then, it has swept the country as America's number one dessert.

Here in New York, ice cream lovers can visit many palaces where menus tempt the appetites of young and old alike. Open seven days a week, *Serendipity* is one such place. It has been an ice cream lover's haven for years, and the decor itself stimulates the appetite. Marble-top tables, bentwood chairs, and Tiffany lamps add a charm and warmth that sets the old sweet tooth dreaming. Serendipity is located at 225 East 60 Street. They serve various assortments of ice cream goodies. One scrumptious treat is their frozen hot chocolate ($2.25). Imagine a cup of delicious hot chocolate frozen icy cold whipped up like a big frothy mild shake topped with real whipped cream and chocolate shavings. Yummy! Giant banana splits ($3.75) served in old-fashioned pewter dishes and drug store sundaes ($2.75) are other menu delights. The frozen moccaccino ($2.25), a coffee-flavored drink mixed with hot chocolate and made into a shake, is a rare specialty. Apricot smush ($2.25), a concoction made from frozen apricot puree, is another menu headliner. Upstairs there is a party room which you may reserve for special occasions.

RUMPELMAYER'S at 50 Central Park South is the oldest ice cream parlor in New York. The lobby, decorated with stuffed animals, which are for sale, and the festive, party atmosphere make the stop here memorable. Birthday parties are their specialty, but please call for reservations in advance. Sundaes are $2.50, ice cream sodas $2.20, and sherbets $1.95. Rumplemayer's is also a restaurant with a wide choice of food.

THE FLICK at 1074 Second Avenue is a general family-style ice cream parlor. They serve a wide variety of ice cream dishes, drugstore style. A children's favorite there is the flambe. Charming, for kids of all ages. Ice cream sodas are $1.75, and a dish of ice cream is $1.75.

BASKIN-ROBBINS has an incredibly changing parade of thirty-one flavors. There are close to one hundred Baskin-Robbins in New York City. Periodically they run contests for ages two to sixteen. Some of the many prizes won from a poster contest commemorating their thirty-first birthday were: a Pacer auto, a trip around the country, a cruise, and a sailboat. Ice cream cones are $.45 a single scoop, sundaes are $1.10. Danger: a "Rocky Road" of calories awaits you.

YUM YUM'S has nutty o'grand—an ice cream cone with nuts on top—an ice cream sandwich shaped like a yo-yo, and a banana stick dipped in chocolate and coated with nuts. They offer take-out service only and have home catering service of ice cream, cakes, and specialties. Ice cream cones are 55¢, sundaes 75¢, and milk shakes 85¢.

CARVEL offers tours of their stores which show you how ice cream novelties are made. They suggest you make reservations in advance. You may reserve the entire store at Canal and Mulberry streets for a party of ten or more and the store will provide balloons and favors. One of their favorites is an ice cream cake made in the shape of a Raggedy Ann doll. They also have guitar cakes, Mickey Mouse cakes, and cakes made in the shape of your age number. Ice cream cones are 45¢, ice cream sundaes are 90¢.

HOWARD JOHNSON'S is a family ice cream store and the originator of multiflavored treats. Although they are specializing in only twenty-eight flavors at this time and their trade seems to be drifting to a light restaurant business, their ice cream has a unique homemade quality that still makes them a leading contender. Ice cream cones are 54¢, 81¢, 70¢. Sundaes are $1.30.

THOMFORD'S is located at 351 West 125 Street (corner of St. Nicholas Avenue). A long counter with stools and tables in the back decorate this old-fashioned ice cream parlor and restaurant, established in 1903. Ice cream cones are 27¢ and there is a candy counter here too.

MOTHER NATURE at 388 Amsterdam Avenue (Seventy-ninth Street) is an ice cream and frozen yogurt parlor serving Sedutto ice cream. Cones are 50¢ single and 80¢ double. Small sundaes are 65¢ and large sundaes are 95¢.

TREAT BOUTIQUE at Eighty-sixth Street and Third Avenue is a small shop filled with candies, dried fruits, nuts, licorice whips, and ice cream. This pure natural ice cream comes in sixteen flavors. A single scoop is 50¢.

PHILLY MIGNON ice cream counters are located around Manhattan. They serve Bassetts ice cream. A single cone is 65¢.

THE PEPPERMINT PARK stores, located at 1231 First Avenue and at 666 Fifth Avenue, sell 650 different candies. They are called the Candy Kings of New York. Frozen yogurt is another favorite. Cookies and cakes are handmade by Sicilian bakers at the First Avenue location and the ice cream is homemade too in thirty-two flavors, including sherbets. These are wonderful stores to visit. Ice cream cones are 45¢.

THE FOUNTAINHEAD is a friendly place for ice cream, located at Second Avenue between Twenty-third and Twenty-fourth streets. It's like a small-town ice cream parlor with wooden tables and chairs and there are sixteen flavors of ice cream at all times. Gourmet candies, nuts, and dried fruits are featured too. Cones are 45¢.

GERENSERS, in Greenwich Village at 407 Avenue of the Americas (Sixth Avenue, corner of West Eighth Street), offers all sorts of exotic ice cream flavors—English mincemeat, Polish plum brandy, and African violet to name only a few. There are forty-three ice cream flavors and four frozen yogurt flavors. Cones are 55¢; sundaes $1.10.

OSCAR'S, one of several stores carrying a wonderfully delicious ice cream called HÄA-GEN-DAZS, is located at 98 Christopher Street. Nine flavors and various health toppings will delight your taste buds. A single ice cream cone is 75¢. Oscar's Special Sundaes are $2.75 and $2.95 and frozen yogurt is 85¢. This is very special ice cream—many people's favorite.

HICKS is located at 16 East 49 Street. It is an attractive restaurant selling candy, confections, stuffed animals, and homemade ice cream. They claim to have the largest ice cream soda in the city at $2.25. One of their special creations is called Flaming Robin Rose Glow—a combination of fruits and different-flavored ice cream and sauces.

The Poor Man's Ice Cream Soda

OLGA LITOWINSKY

A popular New York specialty, the Egg Cream contains no egg, no cream. It is sweet and delicious, and you can buy one at soda fountains in drug stores, luncheonettes, and candy stores around the city. Alas, modern times, bottled Coke, and fast food have almost brought the New York Egg Cream to extinction. Help keep this endangered species, native to the Big Apple, alive. Order an egg cream whenever and wherever you can. Wake up, New York. Don't squander this municipal treasure.

Here's how to make it:

1 squirt of chocolate syrup (vanilla syrup if you like to be different). Fox's U-Bet is the closest you can come to perfect.
1 dash of cold milk
Enough seltzer. Stir until the drink spills.

Add more seltzer until the foam overflows.

Drink and enjoy. (Straw optional.)

You could add ice, but it wouldn't be the same. Whatever you do, don't forget *not* to add the egg and cream.

Sometimes my mother gives us a shilling to go and get some ice cream. We can get a half plate for sixpence, and once Ellen dared to ask for a half plate with two spoons, and they gave it to us, but they laughed at us, and then we each had three cents left. That was at Wagner's, on the other side of Broadway, just above Eighth Street.

FROM *Diary of a Little Girl in Old New York, 1849–50*

Your Birthday Should Be Special

BARBARA SEULING

Everybody has a birthday. Grown-ups may like to forget them, but kids seldom do. When you wake up and you know it's your birthday, you want the day to be different from all the rest. In spite of your family's and your friends' good intentions, maybe it's just not different enough. Here are a few things you can do to make your birthday truly memorable.

1. Call up your best friend and ask him (or her) to sing "Happy Birthday" to you.

2. Draw letters on all the eggs in the refrigerator:

   H A P P Y   B I R T H D A Y !

3. If it's a school day, sail a paper airplane over to the next lunch table, bearing the following message: IT IS MY BIRTHDAY. WHAT ARE YOU GOING TO DO ABOUT IT? Wait for an answer.

4. Write a note to yourself about something that is very important in your life, and put it away until next year, same time, for your birthday.

5. Run down to your nearest Baskin-Robbins ice cream store, fill out a special birthday card, and mail it in. Next year, you will get a birthday card and a coupon for a free ice cream cone. So your birthday will never be un-special again.

New York City Cookies

JOHANNA HURWITZ

BASEBALL COOKIES

New York City is the home of the Yankees and the Mets. Here are some cookies that don't require any baking. You roll them in your hands into the shape of balls. They are delicious to eat while watching a ball game, live or on TV.

½   cup wheat germ
1½   cups peanut butter
1½   cups honey
3   cups dried milk
¾   cup graham cracker crumbs

Mix all ingredients together thoroughly. Form into balls the size of large marbles. Roll in confectioners' sugar. This recipe makes about five dozen little balls.

AGGRESSION COOKIES

Everyone has a bad day sometimes. Instead of yelling at your sister or talking back to your teacher, after school ask your mother if you can make Aggression Cookies. Take your anger out on the dough

and by the time these cookies finish baking you will be happy again.

2 sticks of margarine at room temperature
1 cup light brown sugar
1 cup all-purpose flour
1 teaspoon baking soda
2 cups quick-cooking rolled oats

Mix all the ingredients together. Bang the dough with your fists—it will feel good. Then make one-inch balls out of the dough and place on an ungreased cookie pan. Press the balls flat with the bottom of a drinking glass that has been dipped in granulated sugar. Bake at 350° for 10 to 15 minutes. This recipe makes four dozen cookies.

TRAFFIC JAMS

The streets of New York City are filled with cars, trucks, and buses. Your kitchen will quickly be filled with a traffic jam of people wanting to sample these cookies when they smell them baking!

2 cups all-purpose flour
½ teaspoon baking powder
⅔ cup sugar
1½ sticks of margarine (at room temperature)
1 unbeaten egg
1 teaspoon vanilla

Mix all the ingredients together. Then place on a lightly floured board. (You can flour your whole kitchen table and use that if you don't have a special board.) Divide the dough into four parts. Shape each in a roll about 12 inches long and ¾ inch thick. Place on ungreased baking sheet about 4 inches apart and 2 inches from the edge.

Using the handle of a table knife, make a depression about ⅓ inch deep lengthwise down the center of each roll of dough. Fill the depression with any flavor of jam—it takes about ⅓ of a cup.

Bake at 350° for 10 to 15 minutes. Cut the jam-filled strips into bars on the diagonal.

ROCKS

Fordham gneiss, Inwood dolomite, and Manhattan schist are the three most important rock formations within New York City and the city's skyscrapers are built upon and anchored to these rocks.

You wouldn't care to eat true rocks, but these cookies which are also called rocks because of their bumpy, uneven appearance are not as hard as their name implies. They are not hard to make, either.

1 stick butter
1 stick margarine
1½ cups brown sugar

3 eggs
3 cups sifted all-purpose flour
1 teaspoon baking soda
½ teaspoon salt
2 teaspoons cinnamon
1 teaspoon ground cloves
1 cup raisins
1 cup chopped walnuts

Preheat oven to 375°. Cream the butter, margarine, and sugar together. Add eggs and beat well. Add sifted dry ingredients. Add raisins and nuts. Drop by rounded teaspoonfuls about two inches apart onto a greased baking sheet. Bake for 8 to 10 minutes. This recipe makes about five dozen "rocks."

MELTING POT COOKIE

For years New York City has been known as the melting pot because the city is made up of more foreign-born people and more national groups than any other city. Together all these people are New Yorkers.

These cookies are made up of many diverse ingredients which cook and melt together to make a delicious treat.

1 stick butter
1½ cups graham cracker crumbs
1 cup chopped walnuts
6 oz. chocolate chips
1½ cups grated coconut
   (you can buy it in a can)
1 can condensed milk

Preheat oven to 350°. Melt the stick of butter in a 9 inch by 13 inch pan and add the other ingredients, layering them in the order given above. Pour the con-

densed milk over all. Bake until golden brown. Allow to cool and then cut into small squares. Eat.

SUGAR COOKIES

Save this recipe for a rainy day because these are rolled cookies and they are more time-consuming to make than any of the other cookie recipes. However, they are also the most fun and the results are satisfying both to the eye and to the mouth! Stores sell many shapes of cookie cutters, but you can make your own shapes by cutting out pieces of cardboard.

2   sticks margarine (or one stick margarine, one stick butter)
1½   cups of sifted confectioners' sugar
1   egg
1   teaspoon vanilla
¼   teaspoon salt
1   teaspoon cream of tartar
1   teaspoon baking soda
2½   cups of all-purpose flour

Cream butter and sugar together. Add egg, vanilla, salt, cream of tartar, baking soda and flour. Mix well. Chill dough for one hour in the refrigerator. (You could use this time to try and design your own cookie cutter patterns.)

Roll a small amount of dough at a time on a floured board (or just flour the kitchen table) to ⅛ inch thickness. Keep the remaining dough in the refrigerator until you are ready to use it. Cut out shapes with a cookie cutter that has been dipped in flour. If you are using your own shape of cardboard, cut around the shape with a butter knife.

Preheat oven to 375 degrees. Bake for 8 to 10 minutes or until pale brown. Raisins or nuts may be pressed onto dough to decorate cookies before baking or they may be frosted after they are baked.

Cookie frosting: Blend until smooth ½ stick of butter, 4 cups sifted confectioners' sugar, ¼ cup scalded cream, 1 teaspoon vanilla, a drop or two of any color food dye desired.

New York Cheesecake

BARBARA SEULING

You pour a delicious, creamy filling onto a crust of pressed, buttery crumbs in a special spring-form pan, and come up with one of New York's most delightful desserts. Here's how you do it from scratch:

EQUIPMENT YOU'LL NEED:

a 9″ spring-form pan (it springs open after the cake is baked when you remove the pin that holds the sides together)

a rolling pin, for making crumbs

a medium bowl

a large bowl

small saucepan for melting butter

INGREDIENTS:

For crumb crust

1 box (6 oz.) zwieback crackers or an equivalent amount of graham crackers

¼ cup sugar

½ cup melted butter or margarine

For filling

3 eggs

1 lb. cream cheese

1 cup sugar

½ tsp. salt

2 tsp. vanilla extract

½ tsp. almond extract

3 cups sour cream

Roll the crackers into fine crumbs with the rolling pin (do this between two sheets of waxed paper for the least mess) and mix them in the smaller bowl with the sugar and the melted butter. Put aside ⅓ cup of the crumb mixture. Press the rest into the bottom and sides of the spring-form pan.

Cream the cream cheese and sugar together in the large bowl until the mixture is smooth. Add the eggs and salt and extracts. Blend these very well. Fold in the sour cream. Pour the mixture into the crust-lined pan. Sprinkle the remaining crumbs on top.

Bake at 370° for about 45 minutes or a little longer, until it is set. Take it out of the oven and let it sit and cool for an hour. Do not remove it from the pan. Put it in the refrigerator for 5 to 6 hours, then remove the pin and open the spring-form pan. Be very careful not to smash it.

The Delicatessen-Loving Dog

X. J. KENNEDY

My dog's a deli-loving dog:
He's crazy like a fox.
He sneers if I put bread
Upon his nose and tell him, *Roll!—*
He says, *You call that thing a roll?*
And also, where's the lox?

He'll only speak for liver paste,
He'll sit up straight and beg
For salami,
Hot pastrami,
And a purple pickled egg.

EAST SIDE, WEST SIDE

Brownstone People

TOBI TOBIAS

We live in a brownstone, an old, narrow house with five floors, that we—"we" is my father and mother, two sisters, and I—fixed up ourselves. We bought it cheap, because it was a wreck.

When we moved in, the fixing was only half done. My sisters and I slept on mattresses in what was going to be the living room because there were no bedrooms yet. We camped out there for weeks with our clothes and books and stuff in cardboard cartons. There was no heat, either (that year we ate Thanksgiving dinner in our coats) and not much electricity. Now it's nice—regular rooms and a back yard that all the neighborhood cats have their club meetings in, and a real conglomeration of people living upstairs.

The top three floors in our house we cut up into small apartments—two to a floor—that we rent out so we can afford to live on the bottom two floors. Being the landlord's kid, you really get to know people.

My favorite tenant is Joseph—top floor front. He's not as smart as some people but he's nicer than most. When he stops in the hall and asks, "How are you?" he's listening for your answer, and he's always giving us kids things, like comics from the Sunday newspaper we don't get. He has troubles, my mother says, but he doesn't tell them. Then one night he got drunk and fell down the hall stairs and cut his head; it was bleeding all over and he couldn't get up because of the liquor dizzying him. My father carried him upstairs and put him to bed, bathed his head and put a bandage on it, and made him some coffee. The next morning Joseph rang our bell, stood in the doorway, saying over and over again how sorry he was about what happened. "I don't remember anything happening," my father said to him.

Fifth floor back is Diana, one of those fairy-tale princess types, with the blue eyes and the long, blond hair. She's the one that when the pregnant gray cat came into our yard and tried to adopt us and we couldn't take her because my mom's allergic to cats—Diana's the one who took her in, and kept one of the kittens, too. She says both cats are part ours, that we can visit whenever we want. Which we do. The mother cat is silky, like Diana, but Chaos, the kitten, is black and wild. Must take after his father.

Fourth floor back is Sally, who says, "How you doin', man?" whenever she lays eyes on me. But mostly, as my mother says, she keeps herself to herself.

When Tony moved into the fourth floor front, he painted the walls over four times to get what he called the right shade of terra cotta—looks like plain old clay color to me. He scraped the floors down, sanded them smooth, stained them dark, and waxed them shiny. Then he decorated the whole room so it looks like a museum. "I wish our place looked like that," my sister said. My mother looked up from the card table where she writes her books and said, "*I* don't."

Third floor front is Paul. He has a different, beautiful girl friend every month. He works in TV, invited me to a show; all the women there were crowding around

It's a great place—even for the likes of me.

him. I asked him why that was. He looked back at me and laughed. Said, "Cool dude."

Third floor back is Skye. He's into electronics. Lets me come and take stuff apart and put it together again crazy new ways we figure out. He calls himself and me the last of the great American inventors. He has wild schemes for getting rich. The latest is an idea for making fuel, to heat houses, out of ordinary household garbage. "Make something out of nothing," he says, explaining it to my father. "That's the basic formula for success." My father says, "I already did that. With this house." He says he's come to collect the rent, but it can wait a week.

The rest of the house is us, and I guess the tenants have some of their own opinions about *us,* especially my two crazy sisters. I don't know, you'd have to ask them.

Grand Central Station

PHILIP H. AULT

Grand Central Terminal is the most spectacular railroad station in the world. Tall buildings nearby on Forty-second Street make it look like a dwarf, but just step inside! The domed ceiling of its grand concourse soars high above the marble floor. Light rays slanting down from high windows on thousands of hurrying travelers remind the visitor of European cathedrals.

This station is more than a convenience. It is a symbol of Manhattan grandeur. Travelers emerge from its undergound train shed into the lofty splendor of the concourse and feel a tingle of excitement.

In the days before television, Grand

Grand Central Station during the 1920s.

Central was the imaginary setting for a dramatic network radio show. Each week the announcer opened the program by exclaiming: "As a bullet seeks its target, shining rails in every part of our great nation are aimed at Grand Central Station, heart of the country's greatest city. Drawn by the magnetic force of the fantastic metropolis, day and night great trains rush toward the Hudson River . . . and then . . . *Grand Central Station! . . .* Crossroads of a million private lives."

Few long-distance trains arrive there now, because most people travel by air. Grand Central is still busy, however, as throngs of workers arrive from their suburban homes aboard commuter trains.

The lofty old terminal, built in 1913, has seen many strange sights. The movie cowboy Tom Mix once rode his horse Tony through the station, waving his white ten-gallon hat at the cheering crowd. The marble floor was too slick for Tony, however who slipped and almost spilled his rider.

Another time, thirty-five policemen from Los Angeles who had come to New York for an American Legion convention unloaded their motorcycles from the train and rode in formation through Grand Central. The echoing roar almost sent other travelers running into the street.

When passenger train travel was at its peak, 550 trains a day arrived and left Grand Central. Most luxurious of all was the *Twentieth Century Limited* to Chicago. Scores of Red Cap baggage handlers trotted out to greet its five hundred arriving passengers each morning. Often movie stars and famous political leaders were among the arrivals. A red carpet was laid out for those departing on the *Century* each afternoon.

Grand Central looks a trifle dingy now, compared to its days of glory. Many of its windows sell horse race betting tickets instead of railroad tickets. Real estate developers want to tear it down and build another huge glass-faced office building. But those who love the station fight to save it. New York would never be the same without Grand Central.

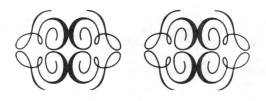

What's Up?

MARGARET F. O'CONNELL

Most people in New York don't take the time to look up. So where do they look when they're walking? With eyes straight ahead, of course.

There's a lot to see up there above the "straight ahead"—lots of unusual sights. You'll find them when you look up to the top of gates, to the decorations over doors, to the sculptures tucked away under the eaves of a building, or around the corner of a building somewhere.

When you look up you might see some Winged Victories, gargoyles, flute players, dragons, and a griffin or two. Then there is the marble sculpture of a man with an eternal toothache. You can spot him, with a kerchief tied around his head and under

The Dakota Building at 72nd Street and Central Park West.

20 East 65th Street.

his chin, standing on a building in Murray Hill. If you want to see him, just look high above the entrance at 285 Madison Avenue.

Can you believe that there are three rats holding up a marquee over the Forty-third Street entrance to Grand Central Station? If you stand across the street you'll catch sight of them as they seem to scurry and gnaw at what look like a ship's hawsers. But these hawsers are really metal cables which hold up the roof cover over the entrance and shield people from the rain.

While you are around Grand Central go to the Grand Concourse. There you'll find a spectacular sight. Painted on the ceiling are the constellations of the night sky—all of them. It's the whole zodiac unfolding before your eyes.

Would you like to see the figures of Br'er Rabbit talking animatedly to an impassive Tar Baby? Then look up at the outside of the Brooklyn Public Library on the Grand Army Plaza in Brooklyn.

If you're north of town in the Bronx you can see a figure that's the spitting image of Mary Poppins, who looks as if she's just come down on a gust of wind with her umbrella still unfurled to rest on the corner of the Parkchester building on East Tremont Avenue.

Why not try this one day? While you're walking on the street, stop dead in your tracks and look up at the sky or a building —really crane your neck. People will stop, look up, and try to figure out what you're looking at. Who knows—it may fire their imaginations, and they may find a little treasure secreted high on some building or around some corner. New York has a million of them.

Park Avenue Rats

Despite constant control methods, there are estimated to be about eight million rats in the various subway and other tunnels under the streets of New York City. One of their favorite gathering places is beneath Park Avenue.

A Ring
of Secret Gardens

PAMELA MORTON

Gardens for reading, for thinking, for smelling, for drawing, for sitting quietly. Gardens for dreaming, for pretending that you are a medieval princess or a poet-scholar or a pilgrim on the way to a holy place.

THE BIBLICAL GARDEN
(AT THE CATHEDRAL OF ST. JOHN THE DIVINE)

In an enchanted walled garden nestled close to the Cathedral are fruit trees, herbs, and flowers mentioned in the Bible, from figs and flax to frankincense. There is even papyrus growing in a pond.

THE HERB GARDEN
(AT THE CLOISTERS, FORT TRYON PARK)

A beautiful thirteenth-century cloister garden high above the Hudson contains the aromatic plants used in medieval households for cooking, dyeing, and making medicines, and for perfuming floors and cupboards.

THE SCENT GARDEN
(AT HIGH ROCK PARK, STATEN ISLAND)

This is a garden of fragrant herbs and flowers for touching and smelling. There are signs in Braille for the blind.

THE JAPANESE GARDEN

(AT THE BROOKLYN BOTANIC GARDEN)

A magic garden designed around a lake with a waterfall. Trees are in the shape of clouds and the hedges are clipped to curve around the lake like dragons. Ducks and turtles and goldfish swim peacefully.

THE TIBETAN GARDEN

(AT THE JACQUES MARCHAIS CENTER OF TIBETAN ART, STATEN ISLAND)

The terraced gardens at the only Tibetan museum in the western hemisphere include a lotus pond and a view of the Lower Bay of New York across the valley.

THE ROSE GARDEN

(AT THE NEW YORK BOTANICAL GARDEN, BRONX)

A garden of dreams is the rose garden with roses of all colors and sizes.

THE SHAKESPEARE GARDEN

(IN CENTRAL PARK)

In this delightful garden, close by the Delacorte Theater where plays by William Shakespeare are presented each summer, you will find many of the plants Shakespeare mentions.

The Explorers Club

NORMAN BAKER

There's an old stone town house on East Seventieth Street near Fifth Avenue where people gather. Most of the men wear business suits, and women are fashionably dressed. Yet these people have been places and done things that you've only dreamed of. The place is the Explorers Club.

Do you see that distinguished-looking man opening the old oak-paneled door? Those feet now treading the carpet have stood upon an Arctic ice cap two miles thick.

Do you see that man with a red beard pointing out the ocean on the three-foot-diameter model of our planet? He's showing the tall thin man the route he sailed across the sea in a papyrus reed boat.

Now the tall man in the business suit has his finger on the globe where he was the first to achieve the summit of a twenty-four-thousand-foot peak in the Himalayas.

That pleasant-looking woman points out the city in Tibet where she was medical advisor to the Republic of the Dalai Lama. She is telling about the six weeks she spent on the Tibetan Plateau, living on yak meat and melted snow.

This afternoon's lecture is open to the public. Young people ask how they can grow up to be explorers. The club secretary explains that when they are older the club may help them organize and finance an expedition of their own, as long as it meets the club's rigid standards of worthiness. In the meantime, she invites them to attend the public lectures given by Explorers Club members on the hardships and dangers, the boredom and excitement of expedition life. Then she sends them up to the third floor, to the Explorers museum, where an Eskimo kayak, an Explorers Club flag that's been on the moon, and a Pygmy's dart gun may inspire them—or you—to venture into lands far and unknown.

Once in a while my sister takes me down to the Brick Church on Beekman Street . . . Mr. Hull is the Sexton, and he puts the coals in the foot-stoves in the pews. Sometimes the heat gives out and the lady gets up in her pew and waves her handkerchief and Mr. Hull comes and gets her stove and fills it again. When church begins he fastens a chain across the street to keep carriages away . . .

FROM *Diary of a Little Girl in Old New York*, 1849–50

SPORTS & GAMES

(typographic illustration of a New York skyline rendered in text characters)

Rubber Ball Games

FROM ANCIENT AMERICA
TO NEW YORK

BARBARA BULLOCK

The streets of New York resound with the smack of rubber balls on cement. Whether it's handball, volley ball, basketball, or a good game of catch, this is a sign that good weather is here and the city streets have come alive.

Games played with a rubber ball have a long history. We can learn a lot about them from a visit to the Museum of the American Indian, Heye Foundation. On the third floor in the hall of Middle American archaeology there is a model of an I-shaped court used in the "rubber ball game" of the ancient Americas. This game,

played for the most part in silence, can be traced back as far as A.D. 200–300. Once a contest between the Lords of the Day and the Lords of the Night, the ball game was an outgrowth of their ancient rites of spring. Mirroring the seasonal transition of light overcoming darkness, the Lords of the Day were expected to triumph. Later local communities cultivated teams and rivalries developed.

The rules of the game varied according to local custom, but use of the hands was never allowed. The use of head, shoulders, knees, thighs, or elbows was acceptable.

The ball had to remain in constant motion. Points were scored by failure to return a play or by casting the ball into the opponent's end zone. Placing the ball through the horizontal hoop on the wall ended the game. The winning captain would be overwhelmed by bounty and the vanquished might lose his shirt, if not his head!

●●●●●●●●●●●●●●●

The First Baseball Game

On June 19, 1846, the first real baseball game was played at the Elysian Fields in Hoboken, New Jersey. The contest featured two New York teams, the Knickerbockers and the New York Nine. The game lasted only four innings, but that was four innings too many as far as the Knickerbockers were concerned—they went down to a sound defeat 23–1. To add insult to injury, a Knickerbocker player named Davis was fined six cents for swearing at the umpire.

DID YOU KNOW?

The longest day baseball game and the longest night baseball game were both played in New York's Shea Stadium. The longest day game lasted 7 hours and 23 minutes and was played between the New York Mets and the San Francisco Giants on May 31, 1964.

The longest night game was played between the Mets and the St. Louis Cardinals on September 11, 1974. This contest lasted nearly as long, 7 hours and 4 minutes.

Oh yes, the Mets lost them both. The Giants won the first game 8–6 in 23 innings and the Cardinals took the 1974 game 4–3.

●●●●●●●

Sports Sites

Over the years New York has been represented by many fine professional baseball teams. In the early years there were the New York Mutuals and the Brooklyn Excelsiors. More recently New Yorkers were rooting for the New York Giants and the Brooklyn Dodgers. Today the city is represented by two teams, the New York Yankees and the New York Mets. The Yankees play at Yankee Stadium in the Bronx. The stadium is nicknamed "The House That Ruth Built" because that great ex-Yankee Babe Ruth had so much to do with bringing championships to New York.

The Mets play their games at Shea Stadium in Flushing Meadow, Queens, site of the 1964 World's Fair.

The New York area boasts two fine professional basketball teams, the New York Knicks, NBA Champs for the 1969–70 and 1972–73 seasons, and the former ABA champions, the New York Nets.

The Knicks play their home games at Madison Square Garden. The Nets play at Rutgers University in Piscataway, New Jersey.

Hockey fans can watch the New York Rangers play at Madison Square Garden or the New York Islanders play at Nassau Coliseum on Long Island.

In the fall and winter professional football is played by the New York Jets at Shea Stadium and by the New York Giants at their new stadium in Hackensack, New Jersey.

Rodeos, boxing, soccer, tennis, track, and many other sports can also be found in New York. Check the sports pages of the New York papers for details.

S.M.

The Umpire Was a Lady

GLORIA PERRY

Being a first in any field is difficult enough, but Bernice Gera found that it was almost impossible to achieve her particular goal. She wanted to be an umpire.

Baseball did not want women on the field in any capacity. Bernice had to fight for years in the courts just to obtain the right to be given the job she wanted so badly. Even after she made it onto the field, the battle wasn't over. She had to endure abusive language from the men and the constant cruelty of being left out of game plans.

Everyone knows that in most sports all players work together as a team. The same applies to umpires and other officials. In her first game with the Minor Leagues, the New York–Pennsylvania League in Geneva, New York, personnel executives and the umpire with whom she was to work held a five-hour-long conference, without her. Afterward, the umpire refused to discuss any work plan with her.

Bernice's life as an umpire was short-lived. Although she did beat baseball in the courts, she could not enforce her acceptance on the field or within the game. She decided, even though it broke her heart, to play the game for the sake of history, and then bow out.

Today, Bernice Gera works as part of the Met organization. Through her job she is able to visit schools, clubs, and other organizations, to speak to young people. Her desire to help kids, together with her love for the game of baseball, enables her to talk to kids on any subject.

After her day's work is done at Shea, Bernice goes over to the West Side Community Center, where she works with kids who are trying to stay off the streets and away from drugs. They play basketball, or baseball, or shoot some pool. Or they just rap with her about the problems they have day in and day out, in school or at home or on the street. Bernice understands the problems. She had a hard life herself, orphaned at the age of two and earning a living any way she could for most of her life.

"It's made me older than I am," she says. "That's why I want to help kids any way I can."

As for her battle to become the First Lady Umpire, Bernice feels that any girl can now become anything she wants to in sports because of her breakthrough. "When I started," she says, "there were no lady jockeys, no lady football players, and there was no women's championship tennis. I'm no women's libber or anything, but you know, what I did paved the way for these things to happen."

Bernice Gera is quite a gal. We're proud that baseball is richer for her struggles, and that she is part of the Mets and New York.

A Talk with the Mets

STEPHEN MOOSER

The New York Kid's Book went out to Shea Stadium and talked to a few of the Mets. Here's what Ed Kranepool, Mets rightfielder, said when we asked him, "If I'm at bat should I try to guess what pitch is about to be thrown (fastball, curve, etc.) or should I just try to see the ball as best I can?"

KRANEPOOL: "My advice to kids is not to be too selective. In Little League and high school ball you're going to see very few breaking pitches thrown anyway. Most everything thrown is a fastball. I think too many kids take pitches and don't swing when they should. If you walk four times in a game, you've wasted a day of batting. Don't be selective, just look at what's coming and swing at it. As far as I'm concerned the name of the game is hitting, that's the fun of it."

Next we asked Mets coach Joe Pignatano if he had any advice to someone who wanted to someday play professional baseball.

PIGNATANO: "If you want to be a professional ballplayer you've got to eat, sleep, and drink baseball, plus, of course, have a little talent and a little luck. Luck is being in the right place at the right time, and it's important in any field. Most important

Thomas

A PROFILE OF A NEW YORK KID

CONOVER

Tom lives in Grant City, Staten Island, and attends Monsignor Farrell High School. Last year he made the Farrell Junior Varsity Basketball Team; 12 were chosen out of 50 and Tom was number 6. His special ambition is to make it again this year. Meanwhile, he also plays on the Queen of Peace, St. Christopher's, and the Intra-Mural teams.

A guard and always the smallest one on the team, Tom gets teased about it but he says he doesn't mind. "I play better than most of them anyway," he adds. Making the school team in the sixth grade was probably the best thing that ever happened to him, says Tom. He really didn't expect to. Now, his confidence has soared, almost to the point where he has to worry about being overconfident.

Naturally, Tom's favorite team is the Knicks, and he is an avid TV-watcher on Saturday and Sunday afternoons, when basketball is on. His most treasured possession is his basketball—he's had six or seven since he got his first one in the seventh grade.

Tom likes to hang out with his friends at the local youth center or at the movies on Friday night. *Rocky* is his favorite movie.

Asked if New York was a good place to live, Tom said, "I like it. Now it's at a bad point, but once it pulls out of the depression, it will be okay again. Too many people are scared of the city."

you've got to have *desire*, you've got to want to be a ballplayer worse than anything. Take me, for instance, when I was eighteen I came up to the Dodgers. The first year I was released, but I came back, and I've been back ever since, because I want to play. I love baseball.

"I think that if a kid has the desire, is able to adjust to different ways of playing, and practices, practices and keeps on practicing, he's going to be a professional ballplayer. It's as simple as that."

The New York Rangers, Larry, and Me

JUDY BLUME

For the first twelve years of his life my son, Larry, lived in New Jersey. But his heart was in New York, in Madison Square Garden, on the ice. I grew up in New Jersey too, but to me, Madison Square Garden meant the Circus. I always thought it would be the same for my children. When Larry was small we made an annual spring pilgrimage to the old Madison Square Garden, on Fiftieth Street and Eighth Avenue, to marvel at the wonders of the circus. Larry's first comment was, "It smells like animals in here!" So much for the circus.

Then hockey struck! Larry became a Rangers fanatic. Even today, living in New Mexico, which is pretty far from Madison Square Garden, Larry remains an ardent Rangers fan. Never mind that this hasn't exactly been a Rangers year. Never mind that right now they are in last place. Larry is quick to remind me that in 1940 the Rangers won eighteen in a row, *and* the Stanley Cup! Not only that, the Rangers were the first team *ever* to win a Stanley Cup. And they've won it three times. In 1928, 1933, and 1940. In 1972 they reached the finals again.

Larry took me to my first hockey game, in the new Madison Square Garden, in Penn Plaza, on Thirty-fourth Street and Seventh Avenue. We saw the Rangers play Boston. I quickly learned that hockey is the fastest, roughest contact sport in the world. It is also very exciting. The players have to be in great shape. I must admit I enjoyed the gracefulness of the skaters, the well-executed team work. I also commented on the goalies' uniforms. "Looks like they're dressed up for Halloween."

"Come on, Mom," Larry said, annoyed, "quit acting dumb and watch the game."

I also found out that fighting is a part of every hockey game. In a fight the idea seems to be to pull the other guy's shirt over his head so that he can't see. Then, *BAM* . . . smack him! The crowd loved the fighting, loved the blood. The grounds crew swept the blood right off the ice. The doctors stitched up the injured players and sent them right back to the game. But I am a peaceful, nonviolent person. Every time one player smashed another against the boards, I cringed. So how did I wind up with a kid like Larry? Me, who loved the marching elephants . . .

The Rangers won that game, 5–2. Larry was ecstatic.

Now Larry plays in a local hockey league. He reminds me that with all his equipment on he's really safe, that I shouldn't worry. His mouth guard is flavored with Hawaiian Punch. I wonder if Phil Esposito's is too . . .

●●●●●●●●●●●●●●●●●●●●●●●

BASKETBALL

Not long after the game of basketball was invented in 1891 by James Naismith, the first professional game was played in Trenton, New Jersey. The Trentons, under the leadership of Captain Fred Cooper, rented the local Masonic Temple and advertised the upcoming contest. To their surprise so many people came that they were able to give each player fifteen dollars. There was an extra dollar left over and the players voted to award a $1 bonus to Cooper in view of his leadership position.

Pro basketball was soon a popular diversion in New York. The greatest of early basketball teams was New York's Original Celtics. The team was founded in 1912 and quickly became one of the top teams in the country's major basketball league, The American league.

The Original Celtics met all comers, and beat most of them. In the 1922–23 season, for instance, they were 204–11. Over the next two years they were 89–10 and 90–12. They played their last game, an exhibition match at Madison Square Garden, on November 11, 1941.

Tennis, Anyone?

There are 535 public tennis courts in the Big Apple, 106 of them located in Manhattan. (If you live in Queens, count yourself lucky—they have the most courts at 173.) In order to use these courts, a tennis permit is required. You should apply at your borough office of the New York City Parks and Recreation Department in March, as the courts generally open in mid-April. In Manhattan, this office is located conveniently smack in the middle of the Central Park Zoo. You must be under eighteen by the end of the tennis season in

November to qualify for a Junior Permit, which costs six dollars. The only requirement for using the courts is that the player wear tennis shoes. Outside of that, you can play in blue jeans or a bathing suit!

There is a free eight-week tennis program in the summer called New York Youth Team Tennis. It begins after July 4, and provides group lessons at all levels, in addition to competition and team finals. Racquets and balls are provided. Tennis permits are not required, but are suggested so that you can practice on the City courts in your free time. Any person under eighteen can join this program. Watch the newspapers and school bulletin boards for sign-up notices. Be sure to enroll quickly as this is a very popular program—over sixteen thousand young people registered for it in 1977.

Jonathan

A PROFILE OF A NEW YORK KID

Jonathan, age ten, is quite an expert at backgammon. He learned the game by watching his uncle and his grandfather play, and then they taught him some more. He is so good at it that it's hard to find people to play with. Does backgammon get in the way of his school work? "Not really," says Jonathan, who lives in Forest Hills, Queens. The truth is, Jonathan doesn't even have a worst subject at school because he likes everything.

Also interesting to Jonathan are piano, reading, movies, and his favorite of all, tennis. If he could be anything he wanted to be, Jonathan would be a tennis pro. How did he get interested in tennis? Another grandparent! His grandmother signed him up for a lesson when he was visiting her in Florida. He learned with a pro, and now plays at the Washington Tennis Academy in Forest Hills every Friday afternoon.

If it's beginning to sound like Jonathan has some really special people for grandparents, it's no wonder. When asked who his hero was, the answer came easily: "Grandpa."

 # Tom Molineaux

FROM SLAVE
TO FIRST AMERICAN BOXING
CHAMP

STEPHEN MOOSER

Tom Molineaux began his life in 1784 as a slave on a Virginia plantation. When he was twenty he was able to purchase his freedom and come to New York. Molineaux's father and grandfather had been boxers, and they passed their knowledge of the sport on to young Tom. They must have trained him well because shortly after his arrival in New York he was boxing, and defeating, all comers, both black and white. When he had beaten every worthwhile fighter around he was declared American champion. He then set out for England to fight the English Champion, Tom Cribb, for the world title.

The contest was held on December 18, 1810, in Sussex, England. Technically, Molineaux won, but he lost out due to a bit of skulduggery by Cribb's seconds. At the end of the twenty-eighth round both men were exhausted, but Cribb more so than Molineaux. When it came time for the twenty-ninth round to begin Cribb was too tired to get up. Technically the fight should have ended then and there and Molineaux should have been declared the world champ. But one of Cribb's seconds began to argue about one thing or another and in so doing gained enough time for Cribb to regain his strength. Cribb then went on to win in the fortieth round.

Molineaux continued his boxing career, winning a great many fights in England and America before his retirement many years later.

On the corner of Fifteenth Street next to Spingler Institute is the Church of the Puritans. Dr. Cheever is the minister, and he and the church people are called a long name, which means that they think slavery is wicked, and they help the black slaves that come from the South, to get to Canada where they will be free . . .

FROM *Diary of a Little Girl in Old New York, 1849–50*

Different Football Shoes

HOWARD LISS

On December 9, 1934, the New York Giants were scheduled to play the Chicago Bears at New York's Polo Grounds for the pro football championship. The Bears were heavily favored to win. They had gone through the regular season undefeated, winning all thirteen games. The Giants had won eight and lost five.

In the morning before the game, Giants coach Steve Owen discussed the game plan with field captain Ray Flaherty. The field, they learned, was like a sheet of ice. It would be difficult to run on the frozen turf.

Flaherty had an idea. "Coach," he said, "why don't we try using different shoes against the Bears?"

"What kind of shoes?" asked Coach Owen.

Flaherty explained. "In 1925, when I was at Gonzaga, we played on a frozen

field against Montana. Somebody suggested using basketball sneakers. It worked. We won the game."

Owen picked up a pair of regular football shoes and examined them. They were made of soft leather and laced around the ankles. Affixed to the bottom of the shoes were cleats.

"Maybe it was just a lucky accident," mused Owen.

"No. Washington University used sneakers once, and they won their game," Flaherty said.

"But I've never heard of sneakers being used in pro football," Owen pointed out. "Still, if we hope to beat the Bears, we've got to try *something*."

Owen called his friend who coached the Manhattan College basketball team. The Manhattan coach promised to deliver the sneakers as soon as possible.

Playing with regular shoes, the Giants managed to score first. Flaherty and tackle Tex Irwin blocked a Chicago punt, and a few plays later backfield ace Ken Strong kicked a field goal. The Giants led, 3–0. But the Bears came back with a touchdown to lead, 7–3. Later, they added a field goal. The discouraged Giants went into the locker room at halftime losing, 10–3.

And then the sneakers arrived. The New York players put them on and went out for the second half.

It took some time for the Giants to get used to the feel of the sneakers on the frozen sod, and the Bears managed another field goal to lead by 13–3. But the Giants were holding their ground now, gaining confidence.

In the fourth quarter, the Giants struck hard. From the Chicago forty-yard line, rookie quarterback Ed Danowski lofted a long pass downfield. Receiver Ike Frankian made a spectacular catch and scored. The extra point made it 13–10, in favor of Chicago.

The Bears took the next kickoff, but were unable to advance the ball against the sure-footed New Yorkers. Trying to kick out of danger, Chicago's Keith Molesworth saw the Giants line come slashing in on him. His hurried punt did not travel very far.

In two plays Ken Strong scored a touchdown. From Chicago's forty-two, he sped through the Chicago line and zigzagged away from the slipping pursuers. Now New York led, 17–13.

The next time the Giants got the ball they ran a series of end sweeps. Again Ken Strong scored.

Chicago was helpless. The Giants scored once more, to make the final score 30–13.

Bronco Nagurski, Chicago's Hall of Fame fullback, said it all when he told reporters, "Ken Strong was just great. The sneakers helped the Giants run. We couldn't get out of our own way."

Today, football players wear all sorts of shoes. They are cut low instead of reaching the ankles, and some types of shoes do not even have cleats. But the first time "different" shoes were used in a pro football championship game, it was done in New York City by the New York Giants.

The New York Marathon

MARTINA D'ALTON

Imagine running around a city block 131 times without stopping, or from New York City to Jones Beach, or up to Stamford, Connecticut. This is about the distance of the Olympic marathon, which is officially 26 miles, 385 yards. Each October a marathon is run through the streets of New York City into every borough. The starting line is on the Verrazano Bridge, and when the gun goes off, the runners follow a long blue line that has been painted on the city streets and the several bridges over the East River to help those in the race stay on course.

The finish line is in Central Park near the Tavern on the Green, but all along the

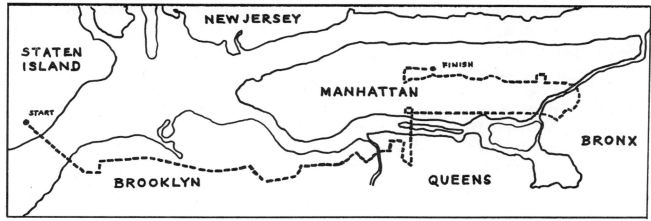

Runners in the New York City Marathon begin in Staten Island and run through all five boroughs before finishing in Central Park.

route crowds of friends, neighbors, well-wishers, and curious onlookers watch and cheer the thousands of runners as they pass. Wherever you live, if it's within the city's borders, you won't have to travel very far to find a good spot to watch the fun.

To enter the race you must train for at least a year. If you're not ready to run in it yet, you can still be a part of the great race by cheering and encouraging the runners. You can do even more by bringing along a jug of water and a stack of paper cups to offer drinks to thirsty runners. In such a long race each runner needs lots of water, and if you can give someone one little cupful you will be doing something important. You might also bring along some oranges for runners who like to chew on an orange slice, or a bucket of ice cubes for the runners who wish to tuck a cube under their hats to keep cool, especially on a hot day.

As a spectator and cheerer, you will see every type of runner. Many travel from England, France, Finland, Italy, Japan, and other foreign lands, as well as from all over the United States, just to run in this race. Often you can guess where they are from by the T-shirts they wear that say things like The Detroit Striders, or The Honolulu Marathon. Whether you watch, cheer, or help with drinks, you'll find a friendly group and a lot of excitement.

For more information, send a self-addressed stamped envelope to The New York Road Runners Club, P.O. Box 881, FDR Station, New York, New York 10022.

The Mini-Marathon

MARTINA D'ALTON

One of the most popular of New York's distance races—and most fun to watch or to run in—is the Mini-Marathon that takes place early in June. It was one of the first big races for female runners only. Beginning and ending near the Tavern on the Green, it has a distance of 10,000 meters (6.2 miles), which is one complete circuit around the park drive in Central Park. Over four thousand women runners and lots of girls five years and older race against each other. Often, new friends are made during the race as the runners work to get to the top of each of the hills and across the finish line. Hundreds of people line the roadway cheering and clapping, and each runner who finishes the race feels like a winner.

Many other short-distance races are open to runners of all ages and take place in Central Park, Prospect Park, and Van Cortlandt Park throughout the year. If you feel ready to test your legs, a complete list and entry blanks for the Mini and other races can be obtained by sending a self-addressed, stamped envelope to The New York Road Runners Club, P.O. Box 881, FDR Station, New York, New York 10022.

The catcher and the pitcher for the New York Baseball team in 1888.

CENTRAL PARK

How to Go Mountain Climbing
in New York City

BEATRICE SCHENCK DE REGNIERS

Go to Central Park
(in daytime
not after dark)
and find a boulder—
a big rock
that sticks straight up
and looks as though
it has been dropped
by plane or copter.

You may find it interesting to know
it *was* picked up quite long ago—
15,000 years or so—

from Bear Mountain
probably
(or in that vicinity)
then dropped here
just where you see it.
All this pick-up-and-delivery
courtesy
of the glacier that was
slowly passing by.

Well, now you've found your rock.
They are scattered through the park.
You will find one easily.

(Near Sheep Meadow
you can see
a big one.)
The boulder that you find may be
six or ten or maybe twelve
feet high.
Or if you're into metrics
make that roughly
two
to three, say almost four,
meters.
(Stay with us now.
We're almost through
with figures.)

Let's say that you
have found a rock
thirteen feet high.
(That's four meters,
give or take . . .)
Now in *inches*
that would be
156.

If all this
arithmetic
makes you sick,
just skip it.

All you need to know
to turn that rock
into a mountain
is that you
must change *your* size.
And this is what you do:

You stand before the rock
Don't close your eyes.
Just stare
and *think* yourself—
shrink yourself—
down down down
and there you are—
two inches high!

Keeping in mind
you will find the rock's
become a mountain.
Now, just standing there,
in your imagination
start to climb.

Take care.
It's really scary.
If you've time,
go to the very top.
That takes a while.
(The climb is difficult
and dangerous
and slow.)

No need to hide.
The passerby
will never know
what's going on.
Perhaps he'll smile
to see the fifty-two-inch
you
standing in a kind of trance
before the rock.
And all the while
your two-inch self
is halfway up
the mountain!

With a maximum of truth
and a minimum of rhyming
I have told you all I know
about
how to go mountain climbing
in New York City.

SOME OF THE
BIRDS BEES
AND
FLOWERS
BY
RICHARD ROSENBLUM

TREE MOVING MACHINE

TREES IN CENTRAL PARK

ROBERT M. MAKLA

There are several million trees and shrubs in Central Park. Some of the trees, such as the American elm, the Osage orange, and the tulip tree are native American trees. The American elm is a glorious tree which has a silhouette against the sky resembling a giant bouquet of flowers. The Osage orange has orange-colored bark which was used by the American Indians as a dye. The tulip tree has bright yellow flowers in the spring and a very tall straight trunk, which the colonists used as masts for ships.

New Yorkers get together to make their neighborhood a nicer place to live.

The Windmill

SAM REAVIN

The person who told me this story said it happened to her when she was a little girl. She didn't say how little.

One sunny day in June, she said, she walked into Central Park at Fifth Avenue and Fifty-ninth Street. Not far from the entrance she saw a strange-looking object on the ground. It was half-hidden by a big gray rock under a weeping willow tree. The rock is still there, a little older than it was then, but still in pretty good shape.

The strange object was about the size of a pitcher of ice-cold lemonade, and it was covered by something that looked like a red bath towel. When the girl (her name was Penny) knelt down and removed the red cloth she saw a toy windmill with four arms joined together the way hands are joined on a clock.

Most windmills are built to pump water, and that's what this toy did. As soon as the sunlight touched the arms of this little machine they began to spin, and out spurted a stream of water.

It didn't pump up a big stream, such as you'd expect from a fire engine. But it was a strong jet of water, even larger than the kind that shoots out of a drinking fountain. And when Penny covered the windmill with the red cloth the toy stopped working immediately.

Penny soon learned that it didn't matter where the little windmill was set—on the walk, on a park bench, on the gray rock—the water would flow from it in a high arching stream.

Penny wanted to take it right home. She wasn't sure though, that her parents would like having their apartment sprayed with water—water on the floor, water in the beds, water in her father's empty shoes. Maybe it would be wise to think about it first.

So Penny sat down on a park bench to plan what she would do. She put the covered windmill beside her and considered all the fun she and her friends could have with it.

As she sat there a tough-looking kid came by. He wore a new pair of jeans with colored patches sewn on the seat of his pants, and he swaggered as he walked.

He stopped when he saw Penny. He sat down beside her. Then he began crowding her toward the end of the bench. You could see he thought it would be a great joke if she fell off. Then he saw the windmill.

"Watcha got under that red rag?" he demanded.

She put the covered toy in her lap and hugged it tightly.

"Leave me alone," she said.

"Lemme see watcha got there!"

The boy jerked the windmill out of Penny's arms, and pulled off the red cloth.

The arms of the windmill began to spin and a stream of water shot out. It struck the boy right between the eyes. The water ran down his nose, down his chin, under his shirt, and wet the front of his jeans.

At that moment two small boys rode by on bicycles. One of them saw the wet jeans and began to laugh. "You waited too long!" he shouted.

This made the tough kid angry. He wanted to take off after the boys but the bicycles were too fast. Besides, the crazy thing he held in his hands kept shooting water at him. He dashed the windmill to the ground and jumped on it with both feet. Then he ran off as fast as his soaked clothes would let him.

Penny was shocked. She looked around for the pieces of the toy, hoping she could put it together again.

She could not find even one tiny piece.

But she still has the red towel. I saw it with my own eyes. The label on it says, "Made in Japan."

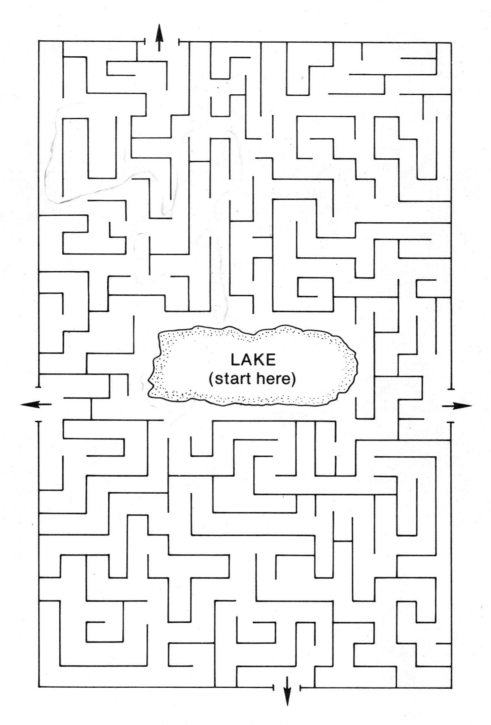

LAKE
(start here)

Lost in the Park

You just went rowing in Central Park and lost your flash map in the lake. Now you have to find your way out of the park on your own. Can you do it? (SOLUTION, PG. 370.)

A LITTLE BIRD
IN CENTRAL PARK

IDA CHITTUM

A little bird sat
In Central Park twitting.
She took out her needles
And soon began knitting.

Along came a breeze.
The yarn came unwound.
Wrapping the little bird
Around and around.

Sang out the little bird.
I shall be wise quitting
This knitting, while sitting
In Central Park twitting.

Sheep Meadow

JUDY DONNELLY

Sheep Meadow in Central Park got its name for a good reason. A flock of sheep grazed there until 1934. Every morning the city shepherd herded the sheep across the Park Drive for a day of munching. Every evening he herded them back to the Sheepfold which had been especially constructed for them. In 1934 the sheep were sent to Prospect Park, and the Sheepfold became a restaurant—Tavern on the Green.

Storytelling

BARBARA ROLLOCK

Perhaps the most traditional and best way of introducing books and literature is through storytelling. Children's librarians may be heard telling stories in neighborhood branch libraries from fall to midspring or in Central Park in the summer. Some storytellers tell at museums or even in local department stores. One storyteller in a community with many young listeners once arranged for parents to bring children in their pajamas for special bedtime stories.

Children are always welcome even without a borrower's card to attend programs, take part in workshops, and sometimes meet in person the authors and artists who created their books. It's all free, and the borrower's card accents the lifelong "magic" of discovering, learning, and enjoying life through books and other media.

Lizzie and Jessica

A PROFILE OF TWO NEW YORK KIDS

Lizzie, nine, and Jessica, eleven, are sisters. They live near Kip's Bay in Manhattan.

Lizzie loves to play handball and tag, to skateboard in the plaza, and to bike around a nearby complex overlooking the East River. Her favorite place, however, is Central Park, where, if she had anywhere in the world to choose, she would take her best friend. She loves to walk there and climb the rocks and rest. Reading is her favorite pastime. "We have more than a thousand books in the library, and you pick a book and do a project on it. So far I've read twenty-three books since October. I get carried away. We're supposed to read for twenty minutes and I end up reading for two hours!" At the moment she is reading, among others, *Little Women* and *The Secret Garden*.

She loves the Baronet card shop on Twenty-third Street, where she can buy her school supplies and comics. "I love comics. I have about two hundred now. I like *Wonder Woman* the best, though *Captain Marvel* was the first I ever bought."

Jessica's favorite place is also Central Park. "I love the merry-go-round. I would take my best friend to climb the statues—Alice in Wonderland and Hans Christian Andersen. I love the monkey house at the zoo there. Once the ape kept roaring and grunting . . ."

Jessica collects post cards. "More than

two hundred of them—I've started on my second box. They come from all over— Hong Kong, Japan, Europe . . . I have some beautiful ones of animals, like a fox and a bluejay and a deer. It tells all about them on the back."

Lizzie has already named her favorite restaurant—Denos (the Greek part of it, upstairs), on Twenty-sixth Street. Jessica adds, "I like Trattoria Siciliana; and I like Shu Yu up on Third Avenue"—she spells it —"and the pizzeria on First Avenue."

Jessica loves to dance, and takes ballet lessons every Saturday. Lizzie is learning to play the recorder. She just started in October.

They like the city, though it could be a little cleaner, they say, and the people a little nicer. "They litter so much," says Lizzie. "The subways are too noisy," says Jessica. San Francisco, which they visited last summer, is very clean and the subways are very quiet. This summer they're going to visit Washington, D.C., and go to day camp in Vermont.

A few days later they ran up to me, both talking at once. "Don't forget," they said breathlessly, "to put in Pot au Feu— it's on Forty-ninth Street between Sixth and Seventh. It's another favorite restaurant. We just came back from there, and we love it!"

EARLY SPRING

CHARLOTTE ZOLOTOW

There is a softness in the air
and the birds sing differently.
Small green shoots
are showing
through last fall's dead leaves.
Soon
spring will turn to summer
with lilacs and lilies
and clover
(that sweetsmelling purple weed)
and along with it
comes
bumblebees
and time to read
　　　　　　and read
　　　　　　　　and read!

POTPOURRI

Monologue

A. D. GOLDSTEIN

Everybody always says it's great to be a kid. But I don't think they know what they're talking about.

First of all, you're too small to do a lot of things, like going on the bus or subways alone. Anyway, only real little kids are too small for that. But it's also hard even to get a drink of water from a fountain. You have to get someone to give you a boost, sometimes.

And when you go to the bathroom to wash, you have to reach up to get to the sink. Then after you finish washing, your mother scolds you, sometimes, because you made a mess in the sink. Parents don't stop and think it's hard enough just reaching the sink and turning the water on, and all. How do they expect you to keep it clean when you can't even see the bottom of it?

The hardest part of being a kid is you have to listen to everybody. You have to do what your teachers say, and what your parents tell you, and if you go to camp in the summer, you have to listen to the counselors. And if you play Little League you have to listen to the manager. Everybody's always telling you what to do.

One time some of us were playing stickball in the street. Everybody yells at you then, anyway, and says you shouldn't be in the street because you'll get killed. But one time a big kid came over and told us we weren't playing with the right rules. We always played the game that way, but he was a big kid, so we had to listen to him. Even when you're having fun everybody tells you it's the wrong way to do it.

That's why we try to grow up. So we can do things and everybody won't tell us what to do. My father comes home and complains about his boss telling him what to do. But at home nobody tells him anything, except my mother when she says he should take out the garbage. And my father sometimes tells her what to do, and he can tell me what to do whenever he wants. But I can't tell anyone.

With other kids you can't tell them, unless you're the captain of the team, and then they don't always listen. If you have a little brother or sister you can tell them what to do, but not always, because they might cry, and then your mother will get mad at you. The only person you can tell what to do is your dog if you have one. We don't have a dog, because my mother says it's too expensive to feed it, and who's going to take care of it and take it out for a walk? I tell her I'll do it, but she says I'm too small.

For Itchy Fingers

By just dialing a number you can find out your horoscope for the day, get the results of the latest sports events and hear interviews with the players, listen to a Christmas or Chanukah story, or break out into giggles over a funny line. Try one of these for fun.

WEATHER	936-1212
TIME	936-1616
DIAL-A-JOKE	999-3838
SPORTS PHONE	999-1313

HOROSCOPE: YOUR	
ARIES	936-5050
TAURUS	936-5151
GEMINI	936-5252
CANCER	936-5353
LEO	936-5454
VIRGO	936-5656
LIBRA	936-5757
SCORPIO	936-5858
SAGITTARIUS	936-5959
CAPRICORN	936-6060
AQUARIUS	936-6161
PISCES	936-6262

NEW YORK REPORT gives information on current happenings in the Big Apple 999-1234

During the winter holidays, there are also these additions:

DIAL SANTA (a different Christmas story each day during the period between Thanksgiving and Christmas) 999-2929

DIAL-A-CHANUKAH STORY (one for each of the eight days of Chanukah) 999-1313

My Super and Me

BEBE WILLOUGHBY

I can't wait until my parents come home—this day has been too much for me. They went off to visit my grandmother. They said I could come along but I said I wanted to stay home. "You won't get into any trouble, Debra?" they asked.

"No trouble, I promise."

I didn't get into trouble, but trouble just seemed to find me. Keeping an old apartment in order is hard, my mother says, and now I see what she means.

Just after my parents left I turned on the faucet and the shower head fell off. I couldn't turn the water off, and our bathtub drain doesn't work too well so I knew I needed help fast. I grabbed the keys and went in search of the super. He has an apartment in the basement, but he's a hard person to find. I knocked on the door and his wife told me he was out.

"But we've got an emergency," I said. "There is water everywhere and the faucet won't turn off."

"Well," she said. "He'll be back. You could try apartment 10A. He might be there. They're having a problem with water too."

Sam was there, all right, mopping up water.

He smiled at me pleasantly. "What's the matter, Debra?"

"Water," I said. "Water everywhere."

"Well, it can't be that bad. I'll look at it this afternoon."

"No," I said. "It can't wait. Our apartment is being flooded." My mother says you have to be stern with supers, but this was the first time I'd tried.

"I'm busy right now," he said.

"Sam, you've got to come."

He sighed, put down his mop, and followed me.

After he stopped the water, he mopped up the floor. I gave him a dollar the way I've seen my mother do.

"May have to put in an entire new system here. Pipes are old," Sam said.

"This afternoon?" I asked.

"No, sometime in the future," he said on his way out.

Then I was in a hurry, and when I got my jacket the rod in the hall closet fell down. I had to go back to see Sam and ask him to come up to our apartment and fix the coat rack. In no time at all he had it back up. I gave him another dollar.

That's something about living in an apartment in New York—you must always tip. My mother says she gets tired of it, that nobody will do anything for free.

But our super is really nice. Sometimes I just go down to the basement to talk to him. He tells me things that are going on in the building. He told me that the Carrisons are probably going to get a divorce because they fight so much. And Mrs. Jackson is expecting. And he always tells me about new people moving in. I know just about everyone in the building and it's a large building.

"Being a super teaches you a lot about human nature," Sam told me.

After the closet was fixed, I grabbed my baseball and bat and set off for the park. That was one of the important things I'd planned to do all day. I pulled the apartment door closed and it locked automat-

ically. Then I realized I had locked myself out. I felt like crying. It was frustrating. But I found Sam for the third time and he let me back in. I offered him another dollar, but he shook his head, and said I'd paid enough that day. That was the last dollar I had, anyway.

Out of the City

EVE MERRIAM

"Eugene,"
 said Claire,
"let's drive somewhere
 and picnic in the open air."
"Keen,"
 said Eugene,
"the air will be clean,
 and the grass will be green."
So they drove
and they drove
and they drove and they drove
and they drove and they drove
and they drove
        and they drove
until they found
some open ground
and they hurried and ate
because it was late
and they turned the car around
and they drove
and they drove
and they drove
and they drove
and they drove
and they drove
and they drove
and they drove
back from the clean green scene.

Distances in Miles from New York City

Philadelphia, Pennsylvania	100 by land
Boston, Massachusetts	200 by land
Montreal, Quebec	330 by air
Raleigh, North Carolina	490 by land
Columbus, Ohio	540 by land
Detroit, Michigan	640 by land
Louisville, Kentucky	750 by land
Chicago, Illinois	800 by land
Atlanta, Georgia	840 by land
Nashville, Tennessee	900 by land
St. Louis, Missouri	950 by land
Springfield, Missouri	1,160 by land
Topeka, Kansas	1,260 by land
Miami, Florida	1,300 by land
San Juan, Puerto Rico	1,400 by sea
Pierre, South Dakota	1,565 by land
Houston, Texas	1,600 by land
Denver, Colorado	1,770 by land
Mexico City, Mexico	2,100 by land
Phoenix, Arizona	2,400 by land
Las Vegas, Nevada	2,550 by land
Los Angeles, California	2,800 by land
Seattle, Washington	2,815 by land
San Francisco, California	2,930 by land
London, England	3,469 by air
Moscow, U.S.S.R.	4,680 by air
Rio de Janeiro, Brazil	4,800 by air
Honolulu, Hawaii	5,000 by air
Cairo, Egypt	5,600 by air
Tokyo, Japan	6,750 by air
Cape Town, South Africa	6,800 by sea
New Delhi, India	7,300 by air
Bangkok, Thailand	8,670 by air
Singapore	9,500 by air
Melbourne, Australia	10,350 by air

Spring in New York

One Fourth of July, my father got a carriage from Hathorn's sta-
ble and took my mother and my sister and my brother and me out
to see the High Bridge. It is built with beautiful arches, and brings
the Croton water to New York . . .

FROM *Diary of a Little Girl in Old New York, 1849–50*

Tube Time

EVE MERRIAM

I turned on the TV
and what did I see?

I saw a can of cat food talking,
a tube of toothpaste walking.

> Peanuts, popcorn,
> cotton flannel,
> jump up, jump up,
> switch the channel.

I turned to station B
and what did I see?

I saw a shampoo bottle crying,
a pile of laundry flying.

> Peanuts, popcorn,
> cotton flannel,
> jump up, jump up,
> switch the channel.

I turned to station D
and what did I see?

I saw two spray cans warring,
a cup of coffee snoring.

> Peanuts, popcorn,
> cotton flannel,
> jump up, jump up,
> switch the channel.

I turned to station E
and what did I see?

I saw dancing fingers dialing,
an upset stomach smiling.

> Peanuts, popcorn,
> cotton flannelette,
> jump up, jump up,
> turn off the set.

A Funny Crossword from England

ROALD DAHL
(SOLUTION, PG. 371.)

ACROSS

1. A hit
2. A drink
3. A tool
4. Judy's friend
5. An English magazine

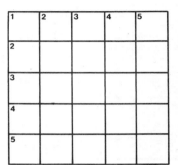

DOWN

1. Vegetables
2. Sheep
3. Chickens
4. Oceans
5. They are often dropped

Still More Far-out Figures

There are 200 chestnut vendors in New York City, 300,000 pigeons, 600 statues and monuments, and (since 1931) 100 suicides by people jumping from the George Washington Bridge.

Crossing

Q. What goes across the Hudson River but cannot swim or float?

A.   The George Washington Bridge.

ALL AROUND THE TOWN

CATHEDRAL
TREASURE HUNT

PAMELA MORTON

If you're game for a treasure hunt, this one at the Cathedral of St. John the Divine involves plenty of leg-work. Two football fields could be placed end to end inside the building, the largest cathedral in the world.

The first stop is at the steps outside the Cathedral at the west end. Before you are the great bronze doors (each weighing three tons) which were cast in the same foundry in France that cast the Statue of Liberty.

Find—two imaginary animals.

Inside the Cathedral your clues for finding treasures will come from the Pilgrim's Pavement under your feet. Standing on the medallion marked Nazareth, take two steps forward and turn a half circle, then look up.

Find a rose—with a diameter of forty feet and made of ten thousand pieces of glass.

Standing on Gloucester, find eight sportsmen.

Standing on Jamestown, find the Signing of the Declaration of Independence.

Standing on St. David's, find a skeleton and a toad.

Standing on York, find a news broadcast.

Standing on Durham, find two heroic charred beams.

Standing upon five loaves and two fish find a space tall enough to enclose the Statue of Liberty.

Turn one-quarter circle and walk north until you find the future completed cathedral.

Proceeding eastward toward the seven chapels of the different language groups of New York around the altar find a donkey

a pair of treasure chests from the King of Siam

a guardian angel behind gates

two vases from the Emperor of Japan

four lamps of alabaster

a Magna Carta stone.

The last treasure, as you leave the Cathedral by a side door, can be seen blowing a trumpet on the roof!

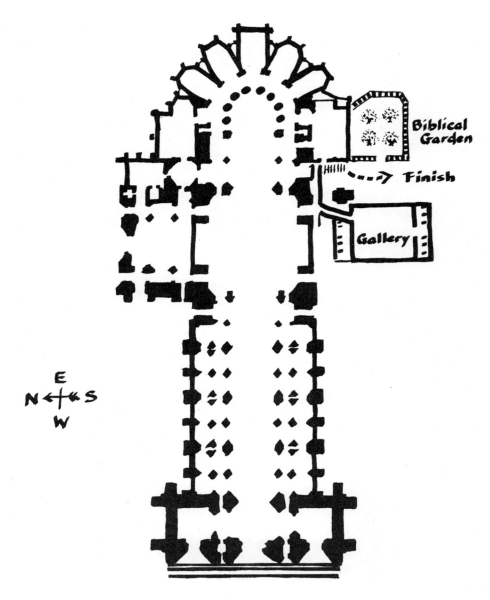

Blue-green and Free!

SUE ALEXANDER

As you walk along Amsterdam Avenue toward 110th Street, you find yourself in front of the Cathedral of St. John the Divine. Suddenly you hear a loud, raucous, most un-churchlike SCREE-EE-ECH! What can it be? Enter the Cathe-dral grounds through the Amsterdam Avenue gate and there, amid the dogwood, magnolia, and cherry trees, you see one of New York City's most intriguing sights:

PEACOCKS! ROAMING FREE!

While you are watching, one of the pea-

cocks spreads his shimmering fan, a mass of blue-green feathers dotted with what look like darker blue-green "eyes," and parades back and forth. It's almost as if he were saying, "Look at me! Am I not beautiful?" He's quite used to people admiring him. He and his two companions have lived on the Cathedral grounds since 1973, a gift from the Philadelphia Zoo. Because peacocks originally come from the high Himalaya mountains of Asia, they are quite accustomed to cold weather. New York winters are just what they like!

Perhaps, if you are there at the right time, you will see the peacocks (actually two peacocks and one peahen) asleep in the trees—they never sleep anyplace else! Spread along the branch of a tree in full bloom the peacock's tail hangs down and you may have trouble finding where the tree ends and the peacock begins!

"Here, Matthew! Come, Luke! Time to eat, Martha!" That's what you may hear if you decide to visit the peacocks in the very early morning. It's feeding time then and the birds stroll happily toward their meal of grain.

The people who live in the neighborhood of the Cathedral visit the peacocks almost daily, as do the children who attend the day school at St. John the Divine. Everyone enjoys watching the peacocks roam over their domain—occasionally flying over a hedge or an azalea bush—or seeing their brilliant fans highlighted against the gray stone of the Cathedral walls. Though the peacocks could fly far away if they wanted to, they are content to remain at the Cathedral, and everyone who sees them is glad they are there.

St. John the Divine, the largest Gothic cathedral in the world, is a fitting home for these majestic birds, who are like the ones brought to King Solomon as tribute from Tarshish (I Kings 10:22).

We use the book "Watt's & Select" in our church, and I know lots of [hymns] . . .

Sometimes when the sermon is very long, Ellen and I count the bonnets, to keep ourselves awake. She chooses the pink ones and I take the blue, and she generally gets the most . . .

From *Diary of a Little Girl in Old New York,* 1849–50

Big Game Hunting in the City

GEORGESS McHARGUE

When I walk through New York, I am usually doing what I call Big Game Hunting. The thing I am looking for, however, is not live tigers or rhinos or reticulated pythons, but the sculptured stone or metal creatures that perch on or prowl in front of New York's buildings.

I can't possibly introduce you to all of my favorite New York beasts, partly because I sometimes forget exactly where they are and then rediscover them. (Can anyone find the white marble centaur I once saw on a private house in the East Twenties?) However, here are a few beasts to look for as you go around Manhattan.

You could start at the Museum of Natural History, which has wonderful, lifelike friezes of African animals all across its main front. Then there's Teddy Roosevelt's horse, part of the statue at the foot of the Museum's steps. If you like horses, don't miss the two fiery Spanish chargers that carry South American liberators José de San Martín and Simón Bolívar beside the traffic entrance on the south end of Central Park. I think they are the best horses in

the city, except for my favorite horse on the merry-go-round—the black stallion with the lion skin for a saddle. The whole of Central Park is full of sculptured beasts, from the rather lumpy eagles by the sea lion pool at the zoo to the crouching puma on the rocks near East Sixty-fifth Street and the bronze dog Balto who is always shiny on his back and nose where people have patted him. (He can be too hot to touch in summer though.)

Of course, everyone knows the two noble lions that guard the entrance to the New York Public Library at Forty-second Street, but have you seen the equally beautiful pair of lionesses just a few blocks away, in front of the Morgan Library? I have always wondered whether they play together on moonless nights, and if so, whether they are hiding a family of stone lion cubs somewhere.

You are probably also familiar with the bronze statue of the giant Atlas in front of Rockefeller Center, but have you stopped to look at the delightful little turtles, crabs, and fish that adorn the reflecting pools leading down to the skating rink? In fact, Rockefeller Center is one of the best places in town for my kind of hunting. Check inside the lobbies of the various buildings, as well as the outsides.

Some of the best beasts are not big public statues like the ones I've just mentioned, but part of perfectly ordinary buildings. I used to live at 36 East Seventy-second Street, so I'm well acquainted with the two stone griffins that are carved in low relief over its front door. When I was about ten, I named them High and Mighty.

Somewhere between Third and Park on the north side of Sixty-seventh Street, there is an apartment building that has squirrels, birds, and (for some reason) hound dogs carved over its doors and windows. Maybe the sculptor was homesick for the Deep South.

On the east side of Lexington Avenue, somewhere between Fifty-fourth and Forty-eighth streets, there is a hotel that has elephants' heads supporting its marquee. The elephants are facing forward with their ears flat against the wall and their trunks wrapped in spirals around the poles that hold up the marquee. Probably not one out of every ten thousand people who stay there notices them.

If you really get into Big Game Hunting in New York, you will find that some places are much better hunting grounds than others. In general, the older the neighborhood is, the more likely it is to have surprises for the beast collector. Streets of brownstone houses are very good, and so are churches and synagogues, which often have wonderful gargoyles or biblical monsters along with the saints, prophets, and patriarchs. (Don't bother with St. Patrick's Cathedral, though. For some reason there is hardly a beast in the place.) Older public buildings such as theaters, courthouses, and armories are good too.

If you are like me, the more you find the more you will want to look, and eventually the whole city will be part of your mental map of beast hunting locations. It's true that the place is all made of stone and metal, but that just means that everything in it is linked together into the biggest piece of sculpture in the world—a sculpture that sprouts unexpectedly into owls or dragons or leopards.

Any woodsman will tell you that if you want to see animals in the forest you have to know where to look and what to look for. It seems to me that New York is just the same.

TINTINNABULATION

WINNETTE GLASGOW

If you don't know what that word means, here's how to find out.

For a penny a floor, ride the elevator to the top of Riverside Church. From there, take a staircase up to the bell tower past the carillon room—perhaps you will be able to peek in and see the massive instrument with a "keyboard" that must be hammered upon with gloved fists. Keep climbing until you come to the little door that takes you outdoors to the bells. Step outside and look up. There are bells as far as you can see. Some are five feet tall. There's a narrow winding staircase that takes you in and out and all around the bells.

When the carillon plays you may want to run—or cover your ears—but stay if you can. It's great to see (and hear) them all in motion. *That's* tintinnabulation. Edgar Allan Poe made up the word to use in his poem "The Bells."

While you're up there, look out over Manhattan and the Hudson River. You may be able to spot the building you live in. You can be sure the Hudson River will never look quite so beautiful as it does from here.

On your way out, stop at the mini-museum on the twenty-fifth floor. There are fascinating instruments in the collection, including some extremely old bells.

All Around the Town

ACROSS

3. Traffic sign (var.)
6. Ocean or Avenue
7. Beginning of the alphabet
8. _____board
9. "_____, it's off to work we go!"
11. Unit of energy
13. But___ or oct___ (ending for lighter fluid or gasoline)
14. Do _____ others
15. Bowling _____
17. New York's public transportation system (abbr.)
18. Famous navigator; Circle or Avenue
20. Stocks _____ bonds

DOWN

1. George or Square
2. Central or Avenue
3. _____ Island
4. Bell or Street
5. Occupation: abbr.
8. ___Ho (New York neighborhood)
9. Half a laugh
10. Tribune or Square
12. Stop and ___ traffic
14. New York's international meeting place (abbr.)
16. Graceful shade trees
17. W_____, New York radio station
19. Jr.'s dad

(SOLUTION, PG. 371.)

THE FLAG ON THE GEORGE WASHINGTON BRIDGE

CATHARINE EDMONDS

Early in the morning, when holiday traffic is sparse, the largest free-flying flag in the world appears on the George Washington Bridge. The flag, big as a basketball court, unfurls sixty feet across and ninety feet down. The flag weighs almost a quarter of a ton. Its stars are four feet in diameter and its stripes are five feet wide. It is an impressive sight, fit for the noblest of Hudson River bridges.

It used to take twelve to fourteen men to get it flying. The waiting traffic would watch the men lay it folded on a covering, its full width spanning the roadway, and hook it to the huge, swaying boom. Then they would hoist it with winches on either side, and gradually fold by fold it would grow to its massive height and ascend until it hung gracefully between the towers.

A new apparatus was tried for the first time on Memorial Day 1976. There were two men to push a few buttons, and the flag was swinging and curling in the breeze in fifteen minutes. The plan was to fly the flag every weekend as well as holidays for the Bicentennial. Once however, on June 10, a strange thing happened. The mechanism failed and a cable snapped. Luckily there was only one vehicle—a truck—on the roadway when the flag came down, boom and all. All the truck driver could see was blue. The falling flag cracked the windshield and bent the exhaust stack, but the driver wasn't hurt. Policemen struggled to remove the irreparably damaged boom lying across the roadway. Sad to say, the great flag was ripped to shreds from cars driving over it. Now there is a safety mechanism to prevent such sudden calamities.

Now that the Bicentennial is over, the flag is displayed on holidays and other special occasions, if it is not too windy or stormy out. When the flag is flying, there is something exciting about crossing the bridge; it lends a special majesty to the grand Palisades, the river and the skyline ahead.

Unicorns Uptown

If you're not too old to look for unicorns (and some of us never are), then look in the Cloisters, the museum of Medieval art up in Fort Tryon Park, overlooking the Hudson. There hang the famous Unicorn Tapestries, woven in the fifteenth and sixteenth centuries to commemorate the wedding of Louis XII and Anne of Brittany in 1499. They tell, in pictures, the story of the Hunt of the Unicorn. These tapestries are among the most valuable in the world.

Unicorns Downtown

There is a magical shop on a sunny street corner in Greenwich Village filled with unicorns. It is a place for kids of all ages, featuring dolls, ornaments, jewelry, books, even clothing. Proprietor Marty Proctor even had a friend in California design a unicorn kite for high-flying spirits. The most popular item is a unicorn pattern that can be made into a doll or pillow. The unicorns reside at Unicorn City, 55 Greenwich Avenue.

THE OBSCURE OWL

Alma Mater, the "soul mother" of the students at Columbia University, sits with her back to Low Library, facing Butler Library across the campus. Tradition has it that a student may not graduate from the university until he or she has found Alma Mater's companion, an owl hiding somewhere on the statue. The next time you're on Morningside Heights, see if you can find this symbol of wisdom.

CLOCKS AND WATCHES

The most comprehensive collection of clocks and watches in the Western Hemisphere—the James Arthur Collection—can be seen at the uptown campus of New York University, 181st Street and University Avenue. It consists of more than two thousand timepieces.

THINGS THAT GO BUMP IN THE NIGHT

A *True Ghost Story*

BEBE WILLOUGHBY

A ghost lingers in SoHo around Spring and Greene streets. Her name is Giuliana Elmore Sands. The well in which she was found years ago is located on the premises of 129 Spring Street. It still stands today.

Giuliana Elmore Sands left her house one night in 1799. The snow was falling and it was shortly before Christmas. She never returned home. Her body was retrieved from a well on January 2, 1800. She had either fallen or been pushed.

Her fiancé, a man named Levi Weeks, was charged with the murder. At the trial Alexander Hamilton and Aaron Burr pleaded his defense and he was acquitted.

But that is not the end of this story, for an angry relative of Giuliana's is said to have pronounced a curse on Hamilton, Burr, and the presiding judge. Whether or not you believe in curses and hexes, the facts are that all met with tragedy after Weeks's acquittal. Hamilton's life ended in a duel with Burr, which also ended Burr's political career. And Burr died in poverty in New York. The presiding judge went for a walk one day and never returned.

There are people living in SoHo who will testify that Giuliana does indeed live there. They say they have seen her or felt her presence.

In the 1950s a sanitation man looked up in the early morning light and said he saw a shadowy woman's figure rising like mist in the alley.

An artist in 1974 did not "see" but rather felt her presence and painted a pic-ture that captured what the artist had felt. The picture contains a face not quite human, but not quite ghostly. It is a painting of a woman suspended in the air wearing a long dress; the figure is tense, fearful, and moving in a hurry to some unknown desti-nation.

During the same year that the artist painted the picture a man in SoHo said that he was having visitations. A female figure seemed to rise from his bed during the early morning.

The Game of Ghost on Fifth Avenue

(A HALLOWEEN STORY)

IDA CHITTUM

There was a game the Wokeskies and their cousins played along Fifth Avenue out-of-doors on warm fall nights. It was called the game of Ghost.

Clara Wokeskie would fetch two large strips of canvas and lay them side by side. All the Wokeskies and their cousins would gather on the canvas and one of the older children would be the ghost. A frightful, fearful figure clad in flowing, flapping sheets, the ghost would come running, howling, around the canvas, eager and anxious to haul off anyone daring enough to stick an arm or a leg out over the edge. Every so often someone would take a chance and get caught by the ghost. They would then be hauled off screaming into the darkness and have to help the ghost catch the others.

The game of Ghost was noisy and scary.

The game of Ghost was the greatest fun to play *until—the Wokeskies and their cousins played it on a Halloween night.*

This night, all the Wokeskies and their cousins were crowded shouting on the canvas tempting the ghost, throwing their arms out and drawing them back before the ghost could drag them off. The ghost was Clara, one of the older cousins. Suddenly in the middle of the game Clara said, "I'll be right back. I have to go upstairs and get a drink."

The strange thing was, it seemed Clara returned in two seconds. She had grown taller, thinner, and danced more wildly, her sheets aflapping in the wind. She began calling out in an eerie voice, deep and blood-chilling. A voice that had never come from the throat of a young Wokeskie.

"That doesn't sound like Clara," whimpered one small cousin. No one paid any attention to him. Then little Carl Wokeskie put out his foot. The ghost was on him in a flash; she snatched him up, and bounded away. That second Clara returned. Every one of the Wokeskies and their cousins started to scream and point. They leaped as one from the canvas and set off in pursuit of poor little Carl. Down the avenue they raced whooping; in and out of streets and doorways the mass of children sped through the night. In an uneven line they ran to the rescue, stumbling, falling and rising again, shouting. Led by Clara, following Carl's cries, they kept after the ghost. At last after a breathless chase the ghost dropped poor little Carl and zoomed off hooting into the night.

The game of Ghost was sometimes played again on Fifth Avenue by the Wokeskies and their cousins, but never, never on a Halloween night.

The Halloween Witch

BEBE WILLOUGHBY

Stella was cruising over Central Park West looking for trouble. She was looking for someone to pull a good trick on, someone she could really upset. "I could tie a little girl to a tree for the night," she said to herself. "Or I could sneak up from behind on a little boy and scare him till his hair stood on end." Stella wanted everyone to know that she was a powerful witch and could scare people.

Stella could see children dressed up as gypsies, pirates, and astronauts strolling along the sidewalk. One little girl pointed up and shouted, "Look at that old woman. She looks funny."

Stella pulled on the handle of the broomstick and headed down toward the girl. "I'm going to give her a good scare," Stella whispered to herself. "I'm going to show her who's powerful on Halloween. She won't forget me so quickly." The girl was dressed like a skeleton in a shiny black jumpsuit with bones painted all over it. Under her arm was a large bag of goodies she'd collected. As soon as she saw the bag, Stella knew exactly what she would do.

Stella became so excited at the trick she planned to play that just before landing she got the gears mixed up and crashed into the sidewalk. Jumping up, she checked her broom. It was unharmed. And her hat was still on her head.

"I'm a witch with magical power," Stella said as she brushed her skirt off. "I'm going to play a trick on you." Her lips parted into a mischievous smile.

"You're not a real witch. I don't believe in witches," the girl said. "I'm not scared."

"What!" said Stella. "I'll show you." She reached forward and grabbed the girl's trick-or-treat bag.

The girl yelled for help. Stella hopped on the broomstick and flew off down the street. High above the trees in Central Park, she laughed at her cleverness. "That'll teach that girl," she said.

Stella parked in the top of a tree and opened the bag. Candy corn was on the top, and she stuffed a handful into her mouth. As she chewed she felt very pleased with herself. When the corn was gone, she ate chocolate kisses until her stomach started to ache. "Oh, what a bore," she said to herself. "There must be something better to do than eat. What shall I do now?" she asked.

Stella put the bag on the end of the broomstick and took off. She headed out of the park, down Fifth Avenue, and finally over the Empire State Building. She felt good because the night was young and there was so much she could still do in the way of troublemaking. "I could turn out all the lights on Madison Avenue or break the windows in the World Trade Center or tear up the streets so that cars couldn't move," she thought.

Stella was flying over Greenwich Village thinking of all those horribly wonderful things when she saw a boy crying. "He'll be easy to scare," she mumbled. When she landed, the boy looked up at her but continued crying. She walked toward him, frowning and pursing her lips. Then she blew and out of her mouth came a strong wind that lifted the boy up and then set

him down. Still he continued crying and didn't seem to notice what Stella had done. "What's the matter?" she asked sharply. The boy didn't answer so Stella asked again, "What's the matter?"

"It's Halloween," the boy said, "and some kids stole my costume."

"What a rotten thing. It's Halloween and you don't have a costume." After a moment she said, "I can help you. I have magic powers. I'm a witch."

The boy stopped crying and looked scared.

"Don't worry. I do good tricks," Stella said. "Sometimes, anyway."

She pulled out a white sheet from the straws in her broom and dropped it over the boy's head. It had two holes for his eyes. "Now you're a ghost," she said proudly. "You can help me scare people!"

"Gee, thanks," said the boy. "You're wonderful!"

Stella thought for a moment. She could picture the girl in the skeleton costume without her trick-or-treat bag. Stella hopped on her broomstick. "Happy Halloween," she shouted. Suddenly Stella knew what she had to do. She pushed the broomstick into high and zoomed back to Central Park West. She was going to find that girl again.

On Ninety-fourth Street she saw the

skeleton outfit and made a landing. The girl started to run away, but Stella stopped her.

"I brought your bag back," Stella said. "That wasn't a nice trick to pull. I'm sorry."

The girl took her bag and looked inside.

"I ate some," Stella said. "But I've brought you a wonderful present." Stella reached into the air and suddenly produced a giant pumpkin. It was orange and glowed brightly in the darkness.

"Oh thank you, thank you," the girl shouted.

"Hop on my broomstick and I'll take you for a ride." The girl climbed on and the two of them set off. As they started across the park Stella smiled to herself. On Halloween she had discovered it was more fun making people happy than sad with her tricks.

Later Stella parked in front of the girl's apartment building and the girl got off.

"Thanks," the girl said.

"Happy Halloween," Stella shouted as she set off. Silhouetted against the moon, she waved and the girl waved back.

The World of Darkness

BARBARA BEASLEY MURPHY

Sunset, not sunrise, is the wake-up signal for many creatures who live on this planet. On forest floors, in burrows, caves, and caverns, on limbs of trees and in pools of water . . . everywhere, hosts of creatures arise and start their day. At night.

In the World of Darkness the New York Zoological Society has reversed the order of day and night, making it possible for you and other visitors to see some of these nocturnal inhabitants. When you enter the black granite building you'll be plunged into a dark and rather spooky place. It is faintly lit by a red light that is indiscernible to the night creatures but which enables you to see them. You can peer into naturalistic exhibits and observe bats and owls, kit foxes, flying squirrels, banded ar-

madillos, porcupines and slow lorises, the brush-tailed phalanger and the little leopard cat, the hog-nosed skunk, tiny mice and slithery snakes in their native habitats. It's exciting. Bring a friend; you might feel scared. And if the visitors that day are quiet, you'll hear some fascinating sounds.

The World of Darkness. It's one of New York's most mysterious and surprising places. And after you and the other visitors have gone, the lights inside come on as bright as day. Then the animals in this kingdom of night rest and go to sleep.

The Ghost Bus

JULIA CUNNINGHAM

My name is James. I'm nine and yesterday I stopped pretending. Before yesterday I used to do a lot of it. I mean my apartment just isn't ten rooms with windows on the park and a maid to take our five wolfhounds out walking. It's three rooms of gloom and too small for my mother and father and me. Adding a dog would make a crowd. The two of them are not so big but they're very nervous. It would be better if they sat down more and talked and laughed with me. More space. More peace. More fun. I used to pretend about those rooms and about them when they weren't there and have out loud conversations with me taking all the parts. It was okay, this business of a secret life. Until yesterday.

Yesterday I got fed up with being alone all the hours between school and late dinner. Or, more exactly, I had a fit, a fit of loneliness. And when the phone call came that they couldn't make supper and I'd find enough to eat in the frozen food compartment and would I mind, I gave my usual answer, "Have a good time," but I fell as low as a hole to China. Somehow it was kind of the end and I couldn't pull myself up. I looked through one of the squinchy windows and saw that the dark sky was almost ready to snow or rain. That sky matched me and I decided to join it. I grabbed a handful of change, pushed my arms into a jacket, and ran down the four flights and out into the evening.

When I got to the sidewalk there wasn't anybody around and that's very strange for New York. My insides pinched up into hard knots too tight for tears. It was as if the city had been wiped clean of real people, as if it was waiting to pounce, all of it, the buildings, the trees in the park, even the stones that walled those trees in. I was so alone I felt like yelling but I knew there wouldn't be anybody to hear me.

At that moment a bus drew up where there wasn't a bus stop, right in front of me. It was too dusky to see the driver but I knew somehow that the bus was empty of passengers. I scooped the fare from my pocket and got on. There was nobody to take my money. This bus was old. It had two decks, the top one open, with a curved staircase leading upstairs. I scrambled upward and took one of the seats in the front. Silently, with no grinding of gears, it lurched forward and the ride began. Faster

and faster it careened down the avenue at such a speed that all the buildings blurred into a gray smear. The wind tore at my hair and iced my hands.

I knew, suddenly, that I had to get off or I'd be trapped forever in the terror that was deadlier than the cold in my bones. I fought my way back to the stairs. I fell. I couldn't feel my feet anymore. I got to my knees and went down backward. But when I came to the platform I couldn't make myself dive into the rushing river of pavement that passed like rapids under the bus.

Then I knew there was only one way out and off. I had to forget. I had to forget the loneliness and the pretending. I had to fight.

In a voice that sounded like a squeak I forced the words from my mouth. I shouted, "My name is James, James, James!"

The bus stopped. The bus vanished. I was standing on the sidewalk in front of my apartment and the sidewalk was full of people. An old woman bumped into me and I laughed when she grunted at me. I wanted to hug her. I raced up to the three rooms and I stood, safe at last, in the center of myself.

New York Nightworkers

CATHARINE EDMONDS

A whole other life begins at night in New York City. Thousands of people rise in the evening, go to work at night, and come home to sleep in the morning.

There are cab drivers, nurses, police officers, bartenders, elevator operators, pharmacists, disc jockeys, news reporters, toll collectors, truck drivers, subway conductors, telephone operators, printing press operators, office cleaning squads, grave diggers, factory workers, firemen, bus drivers, fishermen, waitresses, airport tower control operators, cooks and night club singers to name but a few. New York City never sleeps.

Most of the these jobs are divided into three shifts: 8 A.M. to 4 P.M., 4 P.M. to midnight, and midnight to 8 A.M.

Lots of people love a steady night job. They can sleep when it's noisy and frantic outside, and enjoy working when the bustle is over. They can shop at leisure after work, in the morning, when the stores aren't crowded. It's hard, too, though, missing friends, the city nightlife, and places open in the daytime when they're asleep.

"There are good parts and bad parts," says a former toll supervisor on the George Washington Bridge. "It was depressing leaving the family there in the house to go off to work, especially in the winter. Sometimes it's very boring in the dark there. All you see are occasional headlights and the bridge lights overhead—though sometimes some pretty weird people come through, or there is an accident. When the Palisades Amusement Park was still open, sometimes we'd find lost children wandering across the bridge at all hours . . . It's a whole different feeling working at night. You get a sense of the movement of the earth—one minute the moon is over here, and you look up a couple of hours later and it has moved over there. You make closer friendships working at night. People really make a point of remembering each other's birthdays and things.

"The last two hours, before the sun comes up, you really want to sleep; then when it starts getting light, you wake up again. I've seen the most beautiful sunrises —really magnificent. The sun's coming up and you're going home."

THE MOVIES

Making a Movie in New York City

DENNIS SEULING

New York City is a great place to make a film. All you need is a Super-8 movie camera, a few rolls of film, and a good imagination. The city itself will provide you with hundreds of great locations and backgrounds.

The first thing you'll need is a script. A script is a breakdown of the scenes you want to show into shots, or individual pieces of the movie. A shot is to a completed film what a word is to a full sentence: a single, component part.

The easiest kind of script to write lists shots in numerical order. A script will save you money on buying film because it will serve as your blueprint or guide, reminding you exactly what to shoot.

Your cast can be made up from friends on the block or at school and, of course, your family. As director, you will have to tell each actor exactly what to do. If you're not working with sound film, don't worry. A story can be told with pictures, and you can always play a record or tape with the movie when it's finished. A good time to work on your film is during the weekends or in the summer. This way you'll have a longer time to find locations, rehearse and shoot.

Possibilities for location filming are end-

150

less. Central Park offers—at no cost—large grassy areas, small hills, secluded pathways, a zoo, trees galore, and a lake, all picturesque backgrounds. The Brooklyn Heights promenade offers a superb view of the Manhattan skyline. The Wall Street business district early on a Sunday morning is a virtual ghost town and you can do leisurely filming on real city streets against some famous historical landmarks with no crowds of people or traffic to bother you. This elaborate set's cost? Nothing.

Chinatown has many narrow, winding streets dotted with neon signs in Chinese, and many possibilities for highly atmospheric shots. Rockefeller Center is a treat year round. In winter, an ice skating rink is set up beneath the huge gold sculpture of Prometheus. In summer, the rink gives way to several outdoor cafe tables and chairs with large colorful umbrellas. Above this are flags from scores of nations, which would be terrific for adding splashes of color to your movie.

Hollywood has often taken advantage of the scenic riches of New York City by filming important sequences—or entire films—right here. The following map gives just a few examples of the places used in the films listed.

Key to Movie Map

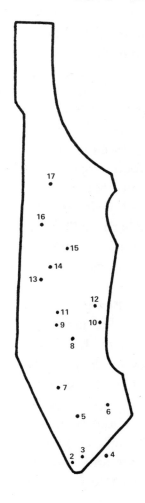

1. Statue of Liberty: *Up the Sandbox*
2. The Battery: *Funny Girl*
3. Wall Street: *Sweet Charity*
4. Brooklyn Bridge: *Marathon Man*
5. Little Italy: *The Godfather*
6. Lower East Side: *The Mad Adventures of Rabbi Jacob*
7. Greenwich Village: *My Sister Eileen*
8. Empire State Building: *King Kong*
9. Times Square: *Midnight Cowboy*
10. United Nations: *North by Northwest*
11. Rockefeller Center: *On the Town*
12. 2nd Avenue: *The Prisoner of Second Avenue*
13. Lincoln Center: *West Side Story*
14. Central Park West and Seventy-second Street: *Rosemary's Baby*
15. Central Park: *The Out-of-Towners, Godspell*
16. Upper West Side: *Harry and Tonto*
17. Morningside Park: *Death Wish*

151

The Movies
in New York

ED EDELSON

When we think about the movies today, we usually start with Hollywood. Yet a lot of motion picture history has been made in New York City and the area around it. Did you know that the very first Western movie, *The Great Train Robbery*, was made in New Jersey in 1903? By 1905, Thomas A. Edison, the great inventor and movie pioneer, built an $11,000 studio in the Bronx. Samuel Goldwyn, another movie great, had an early studio across the Hudson in Fort Lee, New Jersey. The early studios were strictly indoors. Their windows were painted over and they used electric lights for illumination.

New York lost out to California because the Hollywood area had weather better suited for outdoor movie-making. Almost every day, all year round, there was sunlight in Southern California. But even after Hollywood had become the nation's film capital, many films were still made in New York.

Paramount Pictures had a studio in Astoria, Queens, for many years. It used its location to have Broadway stars literally make movies in their spare time. The stars could come over to Astoria for a few hours of film-making in the morning, and then go back across the river to appear on stage at night. The first two Marx Brothers films, *The Cocoanuts* and *Animal Crackers,* were made in the Astoria studio, in 1929 and

1930. If you should see either one of these films, on television or in a theater, you'll see pretty much what the Broadway audiences of those days saw. Instead of trying to adapt the shows for film, Paramount simply set up a camera and filmed the Broadway production. In *The Cocoanuts,* you can even see some of the supposed Florida palm trees, actually painted on canvas, flapping loosely.

Some of the other stars who made either full-length films or shorts for Paramount at the Astoria studio include Rudy Vallee, Ethel Merman, Eddie Cantor, Jack Benny, Burns and Allen, George Jessel, and Victor Moore. Meanwhile, on Avenue M in Brooklyn, Warner Brothers had a studio that was making films. The productions were done by the Vitaphone Corporation, a subsidiary of Warner Brothers, that is most famous for first using sound in the movies. Vitaphone's Brooklyn studio mostly made short musicals, which were shot in just three days—half of the time for planning, the rest for actual filming. You could have seen such budding stars as June Allyson, Betty Hutton, and Phil Silvers in those Brooklyn-made musicals.

Eventually, New York lost those studios, as the Hollywood monopoly grew. But times have changed. Instead of making films in studios, producers and directors are going to the places where the action occurs to do their shooting there. In recent years, the streets of New York have been alive with production units. Such films as *Naked City, The French Connection, The Godfather, Hospital, Cops and Robbers,* and more have been shot on location in New York. And the Astoria studio, which was unused for many years, is now back in action. The film version of the Broadway musical *The Wiz,* the latest version of *The Wizard of Oz,* was filmed in the studio, and also on location throughout the city. New York is still making movie history.

Free Movies for Kids

RICHARD MERAN BARSAM

Kids love to sit in the dark at the movies, and fortunately there are movies for kids all over New York City, usually on Saturdays, and almost always free of admission charges.

The best sources for film programs are the Central Children's Room at the Donnell Library Center, 20 West 53 Street, New York 10019 (phone: 790-6359) and the Children's Film Theater, 400 East 74 Street, New York 10021 (phone: 288-0363). The Children's Film Theater, a project of the Media Center for Children, is an ambitious undertaking, offering films made for children, films made by children, and workshops on film-making. Most important, though, is the opportunity they provide for young people to discuss film and its relationship to the other arts. Children are encouraged to make films, and experts are invited to share their ideas and to help create a perspective for viewing the work of young film-makers. They also offer workshops for adults who are interested in the rich world of children's films.

Other places offering movies for kids include the American Museum of Natural History, the Brooklyn Museum, the Metropolitan Museum of Art, the South Street Seaport Museum, and various branches of the New York Public Library. The Museum of Modern Art film programs are not offered specifically for children, but many of their films are of interest to young people, and there is no better place in town to get a comprehensive film education than at MOMA; there is an admission charge, but student memberships are available at a minimum fee and represent a wonderful bargain, especially when one considers the cost of admission to regular theaters.

In addition, many other churches, schools, museums, cultural centers, and foreign missions and embassies make films available to kids. Some of these institutions require reservations for their showings, and some will supply films for your own showings. A phone call in advance will inform you of their services, film titles, screening times, and costs, if any.

Finally, a word should be said about the film books available at the Library & Museum of the Performing Arts at Lincoln Center. Here, young people can learn more about the films and film-makers that interest them. The Educational Film Library Association, 17 West 60 Street, New York 10023 (phone: 246-4533) provides comprehensive information, including reviews and ratings, of many educational films.

The Biggest Movie Theater in the World

BARBARA SEULING

A few days after Christmas in 1932, Radio City Music Hall opened. With six thousand seats, it was the largest indoor theater in the world. On its giant stage, such stars as Martha Graham, Ray Bolger, the Flying Wallendas, and the Rockettes performed. It was a spectacular vaudeville show, but a failure. Vaudeville was on its way out. Then someone had a bright idea, and ten days later, a movie, *The Bitter Tea of General Yen,* was added to the show, with phenomenal success; a great tradition was born.

Ever since, Radio City Music Hall has been the greatest showplace of them all. Threatened constantly with extinction, it remains the only movie palace that still brings the audience live entertainment plus a movie.

The interior of the theater looks like a sunburst. The ceiling arches up over you, never giving away the fact that it is hiding the lights which are used for stage effects. The curtain in front of the stage, two thousand yards of it, shimmers in gold. It is so heavy that it had to be carried to the

Music Hall in five separate pieces and sewed together on the stage by a corps of seamstresses.

The show begins with music from the mighty Wurlitzer, a huge organ that pops into sight on the left wall. Especially built for the Music Hall, the organ has so many pipes that they have to be housed in eight separate rooms behind the scenes. The largest one is thirty-two feet tall and the smallest is no bigger than half a pencil.

Next, as the stage show begins, the orchestra rises on a huge elevator, musicians playing. Whatever the theme of the show, you can be sure the latest in modern stage equipment is being used to produce it, from rain curtains to a forty-three-foot revolving turntable built into the stage. With their famous high kicks and precision dancing, the Rockettes conclude the stage show.

Then comes the movie. The screen on which the movie is projected is seventy feet wide by thirty-five feet high, and has millions of pinholes in it to allow the sound from behind to come through. A fresh screen is installed about every six months.

After the show you can explore the elegant lounges and various works of art around the lobbies. The Music Hall is one of the best examples of the Art Deco architecture and interior design which was very popular in the 1920s and is again in fashion today.

When the last show is over and the audience has left, a crew of one hundred sweeps the popcorn from under the seats, empties ashtrays, vacuums the carpets, and polishes the mirrors. Tomorrow, at ten o'clock in the morning, everything has to be spanking clean when the "Showplace of the Nation" opens its doors once again.

Before going to Radio City, be sure to call their Program Information number, 757-3100, to find out what's playing.

ROCKEFELLER CENTER

DOREEN

A PROFILE OF A NEW YORK KID

Doreen lives in Newspringville, Staten Island, and goes to St. Patrick's School. It is a neighborhood with big yards to play in and lots of kids.

Doreen wants to be a Rockette at Radio City Music Hall. She has studied dancing for seven years and she is only eleven years old. Her favorite kind of dancing is jazz.

A second love of Doreen's is the piano. She has been studying for four years and loves to play. Her favorite pianist is her teacher.

Once, on the way to Radio City, Doreen fell asleep from fumes in the car and had to be rushed to the hospital. It was scary —but it was also the most interesting thing that ever happened to her.

When she grows up, Doreen wouldn't mind being a piano teacher or a dancing teacher—after her career at Radio City Music Hall is over, that is.

Kicking,
Kicking,
Kicking

BARBARA SEULING

The road to Radio City Music Hall is a long hard one if you're an aspiring Rockette.

All her life, June Taylor had been teased about her name, the same as a famous dancer. In high school, she was chosen for a dancing part in a school program, even though she had no dance training. "With a name like June Taylor, you've got to be good," they told her. In frustration, June was determined to live up to her name.

At the advanced age of sixteen, she joined a dance class in her home town in Baltimore County, Maryland, where most of her classmates had been dancing since they were three years old. Sometimes she danced with children barely up to her shoulders, but she was dancing, she loved it, and she never wanted to stop.

To make up for all those years without training, June did nothing else in her spare time for a whole year except practice. Her teacher saw how important it was to her, and helped her quite a bit. Then, on a field trip to New York City with her high school class, June found herself sitting in the front row of Radio City Music Hall for the first time, memorizing the steps of the Rockettes' routine. One week later, she was auditioning to become one of them.

June's dance teacher had requested auditions for her students in writing, according to the rigid rules of the Rockettes. The Rockettes' director sent a list of the physical requirements—height, weight, experience in ballet, tap, jazz, very limber kicks, etc.—and requested a photograph of each applicant. Two girls from her class were called to come to the audition in New York. June was one of them, but she was a newcomer to dancing. All bets were on the other girl to pass.

At the audition, the girls were asked to do some of each kind of dancing, plus some kicks from different angles, to be sure that they weren't leaning over from the shoulder to make the kick higher. The director, Violet Holmes, asked them to improvise a tap dance to piano music. She also gave them a small combination to memorize to test their ability to pick up a routine fast.

To everyone's surprise, June passed the audition and was put on a waiting list. While she waited back home, she worked at temporary jobs to pay the fare from Baltimore to New York for the audition, and turned in an application for a job training program to become an engineer with the telephone company, in case the dancing didn't work out.

June waited from March to December. Then, the day before the opening of the big Christmas show, she got a long distance call from New York. There had been an accident during rehearsal—one of the few in the Music Hall's history. Many of the Rockettes were out with minor breaks and bruises and had to be replaced. June was to open immediately in the Toy Soldiers number, probably the most complicated number ever performed by the Rockettes. She sat in the front row of the theater, as she had done on her field trip to New York, memorizing the steps.

From that day, five years ago, June Taylor has been a regular member of the Rockettes. Her routine is not easy. There are thirty-nine dancers in the group, nine of whom are out each week on vacation. Each Rockette works three weeks and gets a fourth week off. In addition to shows at the Music Hall, the women perform in benefits, in the annual Macy's Thanksgiving Day Parade, and on tour around the country when their schedule permits. There are rehearsals every Wednesday after a new show is introduced, so that the dancers who have been out on vacation can keep up to date on the routines.

Despite the rigorous program, no Rockette seems to regret her choice for a moment. June has become a devoted New Yorker since joining the Rockettes. She loves the theater; her favorite show is *Chorus Line,* a show about dancers. June walks wherever she wants to go, and loves the independence of not having to depend on a car to get around. "There's so much choice in New York," she says. "If you want to go dancing, you can go, anytime . . . there's always some place open in New York for the things you like to do. And so many movies to choose from!"

June's family comes up from Baltimore often to see her perform. Little sister Joan Marie is most awed by it all. She's 11, has been taking dancing lessons for years, and wants to follow in the steps of her big sister. Although the Music Hall may close one of these days (it's too expensive to run, says the management), Joan Marie remains hopeful: she wants to become a Rockette.

Crash on 47th Street

X. J. KENNEDY

Truck stopped.
Taxi didn't.
Bumper bopped.
Windshield splintered.

Jerk! says truck,
Why didn't you stop?—
I did, says hack.

Fists whack.

AMERICA'S
FIRST WORLD'S FAIR

America's first World's Fair was held in the Crystal Palace at Sixth Avenue and Forty-second Street in 1853.

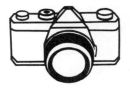

Where Is Sixth Avenue?

JOAN GROSS

Many visitors to New York wish to find Sixth Avenue and wonder where it is. They have heard that Radio City Music Hall is on Sixth Avenue. They know many famous office buildings are on Sixth Avenue. They can see some parts of Rockefeller Center are on Sixth Avenue. So people naturally try to find it. But everybody says the same thing—there is no Sixth Avenue. There is a Fifth Avenue of course. And there is a Seventh Avenue. And Sixth Avenue should be right in between. But instead there is this street with a long name.

There is no Sixth Avenue because in 1945 Mayor Fiorello LaGuardia dedicated the street to the unity of all the American republics. He signed a controversial bill changing the name of Sixth Avenue to the Avenue of the Americas. Two statues of Latin American heros, Simón Bolívar and José de San Martin, were placed at the very end of the Avenue in Central Park at Fifty-ninth Street. Later, emblems of all the Latin American nations were hung at street corners.

Nobody really wanted the name of the street to be changed, and in fact a bill to put the name back to Sixth Avenue was introduced only three hours after its new title had become effective. Even the Mayor regretted it. "I sort of wish I had never named it Avenue of the Americas," he said. And today New Yorkers still call it Sixth Avenue.

Where is Sixth Avenue? Right where it should be. You really can't miss it.

PRIVATE PROPERTY

The street which crosses Rockefeller Plaza from north to south is a private street owned by Columbia University. It must be closed for one day each year so that it does not become public property.

Peepholes

New Yorkers can thank the Rockefellers for many things, including Rockefeller Center, but few people realize that they were also responsible for one of New York's favorite pastimes—peepholing. It seems that John D. Rockefeller, Jr., stopped to watch the work on his own Rockefeller Center one day and was curtly asked to move on. From that time on, the peephole has been added to every construction site, for the benefit of curious observers.

Gods—Alive and Well in Manhattan

JANE YOLEN

A few of the Gods of Greece—Atlas, Prometheus, and the fishtailed sons of the great sea god Poseidon—still live in the middle of Manhattan. They have marked out several blocks as their own. New Yorkers call their territory Rockefeller Center, but the gods know it is theirs, a piece of Mount Olympus in New York.

Between Fiftieth and Fifty-first streets, mighty Atlas looms twenty-four feet over the mortals who struggle along Fifth Avenue. Atlas, one of the Titans, the giants who ruled Greece before the gods, and his brother Titans once lost a terrible war with Zeus. As punishment, Atlas was condemned to stand forever with the world on his back. Through the thousands upon thousands of years, he bore this terrible burden. Only once was he allowed to put it down, when the hero Hercules carried it for him. Atlas tried to leave Hercules with the task and sneak away, but the crafty hero tricked him back.

"Just one moment, mighty Atlas," said Hercules. "Take the world from me while I place a pad on my shoulders to ease the pressure."

And Atlas, who was strong but none too bright, took the globe back from Hercules.

If you look up to the bronze feet of the Titan on Fifth Avenue, up beyond his powerful thighs and bulging biceps, you will see it there still—a twenty-one-foot sphere, ringed with the zodiac and stars—the world that he has been carrying at this particular spot since 1937.

His brother Prometheus, lying carefully on his side, is eighteen feet high and overlooks the skating rink in the center of Rockefeller Plaza. Bearer of fire and knowledge, Prometheus was the Titan who was punished for helping humankind. Because he stole the fire from the sacred torches of the gods, Prometheus was chained to a rock on Mount Caucasus. Every day a vulture came and tore out his liver. But because Prometheus was immortal, his liver grew back again each night. The Prometheus who reigns over the skaters is not the suffering chained god but the light bearer who carries in his outstretched palm a fiery coal. Behind him is a fountain of colored water jets that rise and fall in rhythm.

On the east entrance to the plaza, guarding pools of polished granite, are six bronze tritons, fishtailed godlings of the sea. Under the sea in Greece, they would blow on conch shells to announce the entrance of the great sea god Poseidon, but in Manhattan they are landlocked, gamboling with sea nymphs called nereids and riding on dolphins above the concrete walks.

In Rockefeller Plaza there are other gods' images: Pegasus, the winged horse, sails over Sixth Avenue, and Mercury, with his winged shoes and helmet of invisibility, sails on the Rockefeller Center's British Building.

It does not matter if you believe in their power, the old gods' glory is still there for anyone to see. And from their places, high up on buildings or along the cement walkways, the Greek gods watch over—and perhaps they guard—the people on the streets of New York.

SHOW BIZ

ONE TIMES SQUARE

PHIL SEULING

Maybe it's true and maybe it isn't that if you sit at the intersection of Forty-second Street and Broadway (Times Square) you will sooner or later see everyone you ever knew. But if you sit at home on New Year's Eve watching the bright electric light globe descend as the crowd counts down the seconds, you can be fairly sure that every one you ever knew is probably watching that Times Square tradition along with you. Watching the New Year light up on the Times Building has been a New York tradition since 1905 and is now a genuine national ritual which begins each year for us.

Times Square got its name from the building standing at New York's most famous crossroads, which was owned by the New York *Times*, one of the world's greatest newspapers. The news appears in lights which seem to travel around the building, a service to the public begun by the New York *Times* in 1928, and still going on. The five-foot-tall letters are made up of more than fourteen thousand light bulbs (count them!).

In the past, One Times Square, also known as the Allied Chemical Building, has housed a newspaper, a giant industrial corporation, and the main offices of many companies. Today it features the Walt Disney licensee for New York City; the official fan club of the Six Million Dollar Man; the Songwriter's Hall of Fame; an excellent restaurant called Act One; and plans are being made for a Superman Hall of Fame.

And all of these features are year-round, not just on New Year's Eve!

Florence Mills:
From Dixie to Broadway

STEPHEN MOOSER

Florence Mills's funeral was like nothing ever seen in New York. Over 100,000 people jammed the streets in early November of 1927 to see the funeral procession for one of Harlem's, and the world's, brightest stars.

Florence Mills was born in Washington, D.C., on January 25, 1895. She was on the stage practically from the time she could walk. When she was six years old she appeared a number of times as the singer and dancer "Baby Florence." She performed in the Washington theater for a while, then toured in vaudeville with her two sisters, Olivia and Maude, as the Mills Sisters. She never earned more than forty dollars a week until she came to Broadway in 1921 to star in a musical, *Shuffle Along*. For many years black theater companies had been entertaining New Yorkers with musicals and plays, mostly performed in Harlem theaters and clubs. Many actors and musicians, such as Paul Robeson, Ethel Waters, Duke Ellington, and Jelly Roll Morton made names for themselves in the Harlem theaters and clubs of the twenties and thirties. But no one excited the city more than young Florence Mills. It was said that as a dancer, comedienne, and singer she had no superior. Her voice was described as bubbling, bell-like, and magical.

Her New York success earned her a trip to London with the show *From Dover to Dixie*. An Englishman said her performance was "something unequalled by any American playing here in the last decade. She is by far the most artistic person London has had the good fortune to see."

She returned to New York to star in *Dixie to Broadway* and then, in the spring of 1926, in *Blackbirds* at Harlem's Alhambra Theater.

With *Blackbirds* she toured London and Paris again to excited audiences. She returned to New York on October 12, 1927, and checked into a hospital for an operation for appendicitis. She died in the hospital on November 1.

The theatrical world was stunned. At first no one believed the news. The newspapers carried serialized accounts of her life, and tributes poured in from around the world.

On the day of her funeral five thousand people packed the Mother Zion Church in Harlem. A hundred thousand more jammed the streets. As the procession moved slowly through the streets an airplane circled low and released a flock of blackbirds. They fluttered briefly above the crowd, then, with a gentle beat of their wings, lifted into the sky above Harlem and were gone.

* * *

NEW YORK: INSIDE OUT

If all the chewing gum ground into the sidewalk at Times Square were softened, pried up, and laid end to end on Fifth Avenue, it would be a very sticky street.

Bright Lights

Place the definitions of the words below on the numbered blanks. Then print each letter in the right puzzle square, and you will have the name of a famous popular song. (SOLUTION, PG. 372.)

A. hair piece   __ __ __
                     21   2   9

B. father's nickname   __ __ __
                     20   10   12

C. cast a ballot   __ __ __ __
                     3   18   14   8

D. limb   __ __ __
                     22   11   5

E. kind of bread   __ __ __
                     17   23   4

F. old torn clothes   __ __ __ __
                     7   19   1   13

G. male child   __ __ __
                     16   15   6

1	2	3	4	■	5	6	■	7	8	9	10	11	12	13
■	■	■	■	■	■	■	■	■	■	■	■	■	■	■
■	14	15	■	16	17	18	19	20	21	22	23	■	■	■

THE NAMING OF BROADWAY

Manhattan has many famous streets, such as Wall Street, Park Avenue, and Fifth Avenue. But the most famous of all is Broadway. It is eighteen miles long and the only street to run the entire length of the island.

Broadway began as an Indian pathway which followed the high ground between the swampy meadows of lower Manhattan.

The Dutch built the first houses along the pathway, down near what later became Wall Street, and called it the Broad Wagon Way.

THE TIMES SQUARE THEATER BOOTH

If you're willing to take a chance, there's a great opportunity in New York to see Broadway shows at half price. The Times Square Theater Booth, in Father Duffy Square at Broadway and Forty-seventh Street, sells half-price tickets for theater, dance, and opera. The Booth is open seven days a week, 3–8 P.M. On matinee days it is open from 12 to 2 P.M. They never know what tickets they will receive, but you're sure to find something among the many attractions they handle. Telephone: 354-5800.

THE FIRST PLAY

The first theater in New York was opened in 1732 with the play *The Recruiting Officer*.

Dance Theatre of Harlem

JOAN GROSS

The Dance Theatre of Harlem is the brain child of dancer Arthur Mitchell. A soloist with the New York City Ballet, and for years its only black dancer, Mitchell felt a great desire to help other dancers. Blacks had been told that their bodies were unsuitable for classical dancing, but Mitchell knew this was untrue. All that black dancers needed was proper training. He determined to start both a school and a company for them—a school to train dancers, and a company in which they could perform.

In 1969 the Dance Theatre of Harlem started in a garage with thirty young students and a fledgling company of four dancers. There are now twelve hundred students, and the school is a true "community of the world." It accepts pupils of all races; dancers have come from as far away as Australia (the first Aborigine to be awarded a scholarship by the Australian Government chose to study at the school), and students from Mexico, Holland, and Italy are in residence at present. Although classical ballet is the mainstay of the curriculum, the school offers a varied program of ethnic dance, modern and tap dancing.

In addition to dancing, students may study voice, percussion, or join a chorus. There is even a sewing department. When young sewing students become proficient, they are hired to make the company costumes.

The company now travels all over the world and numbers twenty-six dancers. Most of the members started as students at the school, and have had their entire dance training there. It has been invited twice to London to perform for the Royal Family and is now regarded as one of America's leading ballet companies. Its repertoire runs the gamut from abstract classical ballets to energetic jazz and ethnic dances. The company and its founder, Arthur Mitchell, give many lecture-demonstrations and are in constant demand by schools everywhere.

For a young black child, the dream of dancing in a ballet company is no longer unattainable. At last he has a home of his own.

We are a musical family, all except my father; but he went with my sister to hear Jenny Lind in Castle Garden, and when she sang, "I Know That My Redeemer Liveth," the tears ran down his face . . .

FROM *Diary of a Little Girl in Old New York,* 1849–50

Alicia

A PROFILE OF A NEW YORK KID

Alicia is an outspoken twelve-year-old who admires another outspoken person: Muhammad Ali. She attends the New York Tutorial School on East Fiftieth Street in Manhattan and lives a block and a half from Broadway, where all the movies are. (Alicia thinks that's a really neat thing about living in New York.)

Alicia is in a show business family, and has done a good bit of traveling, to places as far away as Australia. She fell in love once with a theater, the State Theater in Cleveland, where her mother was singing. An old building with beautiful ceilings, nice dressing rooms, and lots of "cozy places," "It was like two old mansions put together," says Alicia.

Blond and blue-eyed, Alicia wouldn't mind being in show business herself some day. Actually, she's quite a natural comedienne, with a lively, affectionate personality.

All of her special interests seem to involve animals, which makes her happy: She collects Snoopy clothes; her most treasured possession is a picture of a lion that a friend made for her; she has two pets, a cat named Sammy and a South American tortoise named Jujube; and her dearest possession is her little lamb, Lamb Chop. "I lent him to a friend when she went to the hospital," says Alicia, "and she got better. I got him when I was born."

Alicia likes New York City but doesn't especially like living here. There is too much noise and too many fires. "I lived in Connecticut," she says, "and it was quiet. I liked it."

Lincoln Center

JUDIE WOLKOFF

Where might you go in New York City to see a giant Christmas tree rise from a stage or to walk beneath a five-ton, one-hundred-and-ninety-foot-long sculpture that is suspended in space by thin steel wires? The answer is: Lincoln Center.

Long ago this fourteen-acre area on Manhattan's Upper West Side was farmland. Today it is the home of some of our country's greatest performing arts companies, including that one favored by all young audiences, the New York City Ballet. A ticket to any of the company's productions is a treat, but it is undoubtedly the magic of *The Nutcracker* with its unforgettable journey to the land of the Sugar Plum Fairy that thrills children most.

Much can be seen and heard at Lincoln Center that doesn't require a ticket, however. There are a hundred free concerts scheduled annually in the Center's parks and plazas, and free daily programs of music, dance, experimental drama, and opera are given in the Library and Museum's auditorium just inside the Amsterdam Avenue entrance.

In addition to these, there are dramatiza-

tions by children's theater groups, magic acts, folk singing, and mini-operas performed with dolls at Heckscher Oval in the Children's Library. While you're in the library you'll probably also want to read books, listen to records, or look at the display of dolls, costumes, and letters that once belonged to Elsie Leslie, a child opera star of the late nineteenth century.

If you find yourself in the mood for more browsing, there are wonderful works of art to be seen in all of the Center's buildings. Alexander Calder's sculpture of the ticket-seller's window and Marc Chagall's two thirty-by-thirty-five-foot murals are at the Metropolitan Opera. Richard Lippold's enormous space sculpture can be found in the promenade of Avery Fisher Hall. And there are many others.

By all means, don't forget to visit the fountain. Sixteen thousand gallons of water are circulated through it each minute and you might just be there on a day when somebody has added a bottle of bubble bath to the water. This isn't one of the Center's scheduled events, but it's certainly a spectacular sight.

COMICS!

Comic Books

PHIL SEULING

The *Daily Planet* may be in Metropolis. Yancy Street may be part of an unnamed city. The Batcave may be under Gotham. But most comic book readers can spot the truth—all of those magical places are aliases for New York City.

The streets and buildings and neighborhoods of New York can be seen in Spider-Man's adventures, or recognized during a Green Lantern–Green Arrow campaign. And why not? The comic book use of our city seems reasonable when you know that every great comic book publisher has its headquarters in Manhattan. *Marvel Comics* and *Mad Magazine* and the *National Lampoon* are all on Madison Avenue, while *DC Comics* is in Rockefeller Plaza.

The art and the stories are sent to these main offices from South America or Europe or the Philippines as well as from all over the United States. Later the books are printed in Illinois. But without New York, there would be no comic books at all. Here is where they are devised, edited, assembled, colored, and given their final check before printing. Although other businesses may come and go, the comics have always been in New York. This is where they were "invented" in the 1930s and where they have been ever since.

In the 1940s a young boy named Billy Batson was gifted with wonderful super-powers and became Captain Marvel. This incredible event took place in an old subway tunnel.

Now in what city do you think we could find one?

DC Comics	75 Rockefeller Plaza
Marvel Comics	575 Madison Avenue
Mad Magazine	485 Madison Avenue
Warren Magazines	145 E. 32 Street
Archie Comics	1114 First Avenue
Charlton Comics	529 Fifth Avenue
Harvey Comics	15 Columbus Circle

DC Comics has a good way to keep in touch with what's happening in their comics. You can reach their "hot-line" at 757-9517 or (800) 223-7760.

COMIC BOOK STORES AND GALLERIES

PHIL SEULING

New York City used to have "candy stores" on every other street corner. These stores had all the necessities and luxuries of daily city neighborhood life. There are still a few, but in today's faster, more specialized world, each item is usually sold in its own specialty store —a stationery store for stationery, for one example, or an ice cream store for ice cream, for another.

Which all means that there are now *comic book* stores! They have new comic books, and older ones, and some very old and rare ones. They also have posters, some comic character toys and games, and "fanzines," which are magazines *about* comics, put together by fans. For the comic book reader these stores are very much like Shangri-La. Outside in the "real" world it may be any bleak season. But inside you are young and it's always summer.

MANHATTAN
Bat Cave
120 West 3 Street
New York, New York 10012

Back Issues
960 Eighth Avenue
New York, New York 10019

Black Star
2nd Avenue & 2nd Street
New York, New York

Cee See Books
128 West 23 Street
New York, New York 10011

Charles of Bleecker Street
195 Bleecker Street
New York, New York 10012

General Lee Fun
424 East 82 Street
New York, New York 10028

Gotham Book Mart
41 West 47 Street
New York, New York 10036

J & B
776 Eighth Avenue
New York, New York

New York Comic Arts Gallery
132 East 58 Street
New York, New York 10022

Old Friends
202 East 31 Street
New York, New York 10016

Thoughts and Things
371 West 34 Street
New York, New York 10001

BROOKLYN
City Wide Books
735 Wythe Avenue
Brooklyn, New York 11211

Comics and Fun
382 Avenue P
Brooklyn, New York 11204

Discount Books
1908 86 Street
Brooklyn, New York 11214

Sheepshead Bay Discount Books
3735 Nostrand Avenue
Brooklyn, New York 11229

QUEENS
Bell Boulevard Books
39–34 Bell Boulevard
Bayside, New York 11361

Discount Books
184–01 Horace Harding Exp.
Fresh Meadows, New York 11365

Forest Hills Bookstore
63–56 108 Street
Forest Hills, New York 11375

Jackson Heights Books
77–15 37 Avenue
Jackson Heights, New York 11372

Little Nemo Shop
108–30 Ascan Avenue
Forest Hills, New York 11375

Joseph

A PROFILE OF A NEW YORK KID

Joseph is a seventh grader at Shallow Junior High School in Bensonhurst, Brooklyn. He lives on a very colorful corner at a busy intersection in an Italian neighborhood, where the smell of fresh-baked bread drifts out from the bakery, stands are packed with fresh fruit and vegetables, and stores specialize in Italian delights: pizza, pasta, espresso, pastry, pork, cheeses.

Joey is very good at fixing bikes and working with tools, and thinks he would like to be a carpenter. He earns extra money as a newspaper delivery boy, getting up each morning at 6:30 A.M. Right now, he is happy collecting things, like matchbox cars, stock car racing sets, and comic books—especially comic books. He goes to comic book stores the way other kids go to the ball park or the movies or the pizza parlor. His special super-hero is Hulk, and his most treasured possession is his collection of comic books.

The large number of stores in New York

is a special treat for Joseph, who likes to spend money (when he has it). Although he hasn't lived in any other city, he thinks New York is pretty good. "There's something for everybody," he says.

BUSTING THE CODE

DANIEL MANUS PINKWATER

I don't care what anybody tells you about comics, there has to be something good about them. I think it is this: You get to buy your *own* comics, and they belong to *you*. No one hands them to you and tells you that reading them will make you a better person. I learned to read from comic books. In fact, I can remember the exact moment when I learned to "code-bust," that is, to figure out words I'd never seen before. I had spent a dime (that's what they used to cost!) on a *Batman* in 1947—I was six years old—and I was going to read *my comic*—every word. And I did it. I've been reading things ever since—all by myself. I wish I still had that *Batman*.

Comic Book
Fan Conventions

PHIL SEULING

Comic book readers love to talk about comic books, but there's not always someone to talk to who shares that love. They want to know what's behind the stories, who does the artwork, what's coming up in their favorite hero's life, what old comic books look like, and how much their collections are worth lately. For this reason comic book conventions are very popular.

At a typical comics collector's convention, you'd find guest artists and writers, exhibits of artists' original drawings, hundreds of thousands of comic books for sale, panel discussions, question-and-answer sessions, slide shows, films, and auctions.

These events are now held in all the large cities in the United States and even Europe. New York, in 1964, was the first city to host a comic book convention and it continues to have the biggest and best-attended ones.

It would be the perfect place to meet and talk to other comic book readers.

CREATION CONVENTION (usually held in November)

INFORMATION: Adam Malin, 16 East 2 Street, Freeport, New York 11520

COMIC ART CONVENTION (usually held in July)

INFORMATION: Box 177, Coney Island Station, Brooklyn, New York 11224

COMIC BOOK MARKETPLACE (one Sunday each month)

INFORMATION: Box 177, Coney Island Station, Brooklyn, New York 11224

LAW AND ORDER

Captain William Kidd

PIRATE OR SCAPECOAT?

STEPHEN MOOSER

New York has, over the years, given birth to many infamous people. Among its citizens New York has had more than its share of cutthroats, thieves, and swindlers. Many of these people justly deserved their evil reputations. But for Captain William Kidd, whom history has labeled a bloodthirsty pirate, the reputation seems decidedly undeserved.

In the 1690s William Kidd was one of New York City's most respected citizens. As a sea captain, trader, and businessman Kidd had made a great deal of money. He owned property on Pine, Pearl, and Water

streets as well as a fine brick home on Wall Street, which he shared with his wife, Sarah, and his children.

The last half of the seventeenth century was a time of treachery on the high seas. It was a time of pirates, and of privateers too. Pirates were cutthroats who attacked and plundered any ship they could lay their hands on. Privateers were just slightly more respectable. They were legal pirates commissioned by a government to prey upon enemy ships. The spoils from privateer attacks were usually split between the crew and the government.

In 1695 Kidd was asked by the new Governor of New York, the Earl of Belle-mont, to captain a ship that would not only prey on ships belonging to France, England's enemy at the time, but on other pirate vessels as well. A secret agreement was drawn up between Kidd, the Earl, and a syndicate of high-ranking English lords to sail to the Indian Ocean and attack and plunder pirate ships. The agreement was made in secret because the English lords, as members of the government, were using inside information about pirate activity to turn a quick doubloon. The lords were to receive 60 percent of the spoils. This was all very unethical, and illegal.

In 1696 Kidd set sail on the ship *Adventure Galley* and headed for the pirate-infested waters off Africa. His crew was working on a strict percentage of the take. If they took no booty they would receive no pay. This arrangement caused Kidd a great deal of trouble because for almost a year he captured no pirate ships and only one small French fishing vessel. Kidd was primarily after pirates, but he was also interested in French ships. Since France and England were at war it was considered privateering, not piracy for an English ship to take a French vessel.

But not even rich French ships could be found and the crew became mutinous. During a wild argument with the first mate Kidd bounced a bucket off the poor man's skull, killing him.

By and by Kidd did take a number of French ships, looted them of treasure, and set sail for New York, and home. Mean-while, however, rumors of Kidd's exploits were reaching London. It was said he was a murderer for killing the first mate. Worse yet, he was accused of boarding and loot-ing English ships. Kidd was no longer playing the role of privateer; if the rumors were true, he had become a pirate.

When Kidd landed he went right to the Earl of Bellemont and showed him docu-ments that proved he had only attacked French ships. The Earl, and his friends the English lords, however, were not interested in Kidd's innocence, but in saving their own necks. They didn't want their illegal syndicate exposed; they wanted Kidd si-lenced. So the Earl had him sent to Lon-don to stand trial for piracy.

The documents that could have saved Kidd were never turned over by Bellemont and Kidd was condemned to death. In late May of 1701, before a large crowd on the banks of the Thames River in London, Captain William Kidd was hanged. In 1910 an American historian came across the missing documents, which could have cleared that unfortunate New Yorker, but it was two centuries too late for Captain William Kidd.

PIRATES

Where the George Washington Bridge now stands there once stood a gallows. In Colonial times pirates were hanged by the banks of the Hudson as a warning to other would-be pirates.

A PIRATE
AND AN EXPLORER

STEPHEN MOOSER

What explorer was the first European to discover New York Bay? Here's a clue; one of New York's most famous bridges is named after this man. If you guessed George Washington, or even George Brooklyn, I'd have to mark you wrong. The correct answer is Giovanni da Verrazano, whose name adorns the Verrazano Narrows Bridge, one of the world's longest suspension bridges.

Verrazano, who, history tells us, spent his early days as a pirate, was commissioned in 1523 by Francis I, King of France, to find a northwest passage to the fabled spice islands of the Orient. Of course we now know such a passage does not exist, but in January of 1524 Verrazano set out in his ship, *The Dauphine*, to cross the Atlantic and begin his search. Two months later Verrazano sighted the New World, at Rockaway Beach, Long Island. He spent the next few months exploring up and down the coast for the elusive gateway, which, of course, was never found. On April 17, 1524, however, he made a historic discovery—New York Bay. According to Verrazano's diaries, *The Dauphine* anchored off Staten Island and the crew explored the bay in smaller boats. Verrazano did not stay long, but in his report to the King upon his return he said that the area was fertile, populated by friendly Indians, and worthy of French colonization. The French King was bogged down in a war at the time of Verrazano's return and paid little attention to his report. Had he colonized as Verrazano recommended we might not be New Yorkers today—we'd be Angoulêmese. For the name that Verrazano gave to the area was Angoulême, after the family of the French King.

The New York City Police

CATHARINE EDMONDS

What is it like being a New York City police officer? It's sort of like a baseball game. A couple of strikes (the mugger got away), a few balls (false alarms, empty complaints), maybe whole empty innings. Then all of a sudden—*crack*—bat meets ball and everyone jolts into action. Sometimes it's a shutout, which is tough on the nerves, considering that you've been trained to handle a thousand risky situations, any one of which you *may* have to tackle. Sometimes it's a wild game, energies high, wits at a peak, and coordination split-second—an armed man with a hostage, a heart attack, a bomb somewhere in a building. In New York, a hundred different ball games are going on at once.

The New York police officer is a special breed—World Series caliber, you might say. The city comprises many extremes, the very rich and the very poor, almost every race, creed, and religion in existence, the fusion and fission of vast cultural differences. People from every part of the world don't just visit here, they live here. Such extremes make the city exciting and special, but they also mean conflicts, and New York City cops have to know a lot in order to do their jobs. They study psychology, languages, and law besides the usual defense and emergency training.

The most recent annual statistics include some extraordinary facts: New Yorkers called the police every five seconds; that is, about seven million calls a year were followed up. These involved settling family disputes, car accidents, rescuing people trapped in revolving doors or a cat from a ledge, collapsed buildings, gas leaks, homicide, "aided cases" (such as taking sick people to the hospital or delivering babies), and much more. City patrol police cars drove fifty-two million miles (not to mention scooters and horses), harbor police boats traveled the equivalent of five times around the world, and police helicopters could have gone to the moon and back. Every incident or emergency was as different as the people involved.

Of course there are different kinds of police officers: crime-prevention officers to advise you on protecting your home, your car, your business; detectives to investigate crimes; anti-crime squads who dress up in disguise to surprise the "bad guys" in the act. There are also five thousand uniformed volunteers in the Auxiliary Police and twenty-five thousand civilian patrol volunteers. And behind the scenes, the City police have the most modern laboratory in the world, where last year thirty-five thousand tests took place—from handwriting and fingerprint analysis to studying evidence under a microscope.

Being a New York City police officer means living in a particularly complex world—much more unpredictable than a baseball game—and much more human. It's not a game.

HORSES CAN BE COPS TOO

BARBARA BURN AND EMIL P. DOLENSEK

Everyone has seen mounted policemen in New York City—in Coney Island, around the United Nations when a demonstration is going on, in the theater district near Broadway, or in Pelham Bay Park in the Bronx. Although automobiles have replaced horses in police work just as they have in other parts of city life, New York's mounted troops are still effective in many ways—in controlling crowds, particularly. A policeman on foot or in a car can't see much better than anyone else, but on horseback the officer can add an extra five feet to his height. Also, people can see the policeman from quite a distance.

Police horses were once used in parade work, which is why they look alike. Each horse must be a bay gelding about fifteen hands high at the shoulder (since each hand is four inches, that means sixty inches tall). There are several police-horse stables in New York City, each one devoted to a troop of horses and riders: Troop A in lower Manhattan, Troop B in Brooklyn, Troop D in the Bronx, and Troop F in Queens.

Some police horses have worked with the department (and even with the same riders) for many years. Unlike the life led by racehorses, the police horse's life is relatively calm; they do much more walking and standing than running. But they do have their share of excitement and must become accustomed to lots of traffic, noise, and people. Many horses are easily frightened by such things and will bolt at the drop of a hat, but a police horse is trained to accept all the commotion and trust his rider even when the going gets rough. Each horse has his own officer, who looks after his feeding and grooming and the cleaning of his tack (saddle and bridle).

The police department originally established the mounted division about a hundred years ago because it needed some way to control and arrest those who raced their carriages through the city streets, risking the lives of pedestrians. But times haven't changed all that much. Not long ago, a horse-drawn carriage in Manhattan was seen racing up Broadway at full speed, quite out of the driver's control. Two mounted policemen raced off after the carriage and were able to catch the runaway and apprehend the driver, who was then charged with disobeying a hundred-year-old law that prohibits "overspeeding on a city thoroughfare."

Scuba Cops

JOAN GROSS

Everything that happens above New York happens below New York," says Sergeant Joseph Mottle, supervisor of the Underwater Recovery Team—a unit of the New York Police Department. The Scuba Cops, as they are sometimes called, have as their domain everything "under" New York. They patrol six hundred miles of shoreline in addition to rivers, streams, reservoirs, and lakes. Their beat ends above Spuyten Duyvil near the George Washington Bridge and includes all the five boroughs of New York as well as a good part of the New Jersey shoreline.

How did this unusual unit start? It was founded in 1967 by two policemen, both trained scuba divers, who volunteered for the exacting job of policing the underwater world of New York City. There are now six hand-picked men in the team who must take four difficult qualifying examinations before joining. In fact, the minimum standards for this job are more stringent than those for Navy divers. All men have had years of experience in both sport and commercial diving; Officer William Reddam is even a Scuba instructor, who takes his twelve-year-old daughter with him on weekend dives—for fun only!

"Your life depends on your partner, and his life upon yours," says Officer Charles O'Donnell, a veteran diver. The unit never uses fewer than three men on any job—two divers in water and one man standing by on the launch. Sometimes, in very dangerous conditions such as extra swift currents, two men will go down and two will stay up. They maintain voice and line communications at all times. "It's like walking into a closet and closing the door behind you," continues Officer O'Donnell. One of the main problems is the amount of raw sewage in the Manhattan waters. That, plus debris and the dust created by soft mud on the river's floor, make their work difficult and exhausting. Underwater flashlights, with 100,000 candlepower, aid them. The visibility isn't always so bad, however, and both Mottle and O'Donnelly feel the waters around New York are definitely cleaner than before.

What do they find in the water? Anything and everything, including guns, cars, and bodies. The recovery rate is an astounding 93 percent. Ten years ago, when a gun disappeared in the water, it was gone forever. Now it can be recovered, and the Ballistics Lab, after scraping off the barnacles, can trace its ownership. By checking the license plate, they can determine if a car has been stolen and they always check the car trunk too, for contraband. The sad task of recovering bodies is made easier by the knowledge that they are giving comfort to distraught relatives.

Occasionally they make an exciting find. Once, while searching for a helicopter under the East River, they came across two fixed-wing airplanes. One was a seaplane and the other a fighter. They are probably still sitting on the bottom of the East River today! In 1976 they discovered a two-hundred-year-old anchor weighing over a thousand pounds. They presented it to the South Street Seaport Museum on July 2, just in time for the Bicentennial Celebration.

Policemen first, scuba divers second, they have occasionally made arrests wearing their black and orange wet suits, and

once even wore them into court with a burglary suspect.

Despite all the discomfort, danger, and fatigue, would they change jobs? "We love our work and we're proud of it," says Sergeant Mottle. "We dive in places where other city agencies won't go, but it's our city and our responsibility," he explains.

The Great New York Fire

STEPHEN MOOSER

December of 1835 was alternately one of New York's hottest and coldest months on record. The cold was caused by a terrible storm which plunged temperatures well below zero, and the heat was brought out by a rash of fires that sprang up in various parts of the city. New York's fire department had failed to keep pace with the rapidly growing city. Fifteen hundred firemen were charged with protecting the homes and lives of New York's nearly 250,000 people. In the early days of December 1835 the overworked fire department fought and brought under control a number of stubborn blazes, but on December 16 a fire broke out that not even the combined New York, Brooklyn, Newark, Jersey City, and Philadelphia fire departments could contain.

The blaze began in a warehouse at 25 Merchant Street at the height of a freezing gale. By the time the first firemen arrived on the scene the blaze had already jumped across Exchange Place and was racing away toward Hanover Square. To their horror the firemen discovered that there was no water available to fight the fire. All the wells were frozen solid!

The fire chief ordered a dozen engine companies to proceed to the East River to get water. It was quickly discovered that the river was also frozen, so holes were hurriedly chopped in the ice. A string of hoses was set up to carry the water back toward the fire, but before the water could reach the gale-blown flames it too froze.

The temperature was −17°. A little water was finally coaxed from the hoses, but the wind blew it back into the firemen's faces, where it promptly froze. Some of the firemen poured brandy into their boots to keep their feet from freezing.

All the efforts to control the fire failed in the high winds.

The next morning, with the fire still raging, a local merchant climbed to the roof of a building, and wrote down this account:

"From Maiden Lane to Coenties Slip, and from William St. to the East River, the whole immense area, embracing some 13 acres all in a raging, uncontrollable blaze!!! . . . An ocean of fire with roaring, rolling, burning waves, surging onward and upward and spreading certain universal destruction; tottering walls and falling chimneys with black smoke, hissing, clashing sounds rising up on all sides . . ."

Finally, on December 18, the Navy came in and dynamited a number of buildings in the fire's path. The downed buildings created a firebreak which at last stopped the flames, but not before 674 buildings had been destroyed in the worst fire ever to strike New York City.

When [my stepbrother] was twenty-one years old he joined a fire company, and it was called The Silk Stocking Hose Company . . . But they didn't wear their silk stockings when they ran with the engine, for I remember seeing my brother one night when he came home from a fire and he had on a red flannel shirt and a black hat that looked like pictures of helmets the soldiers wear. He took cold and had pain in his leg, and Dr. Washington came and he asked my mother for a paper of pins and he tore off a row and scratched my brother's leg with the pins and then painted it with some dark stuff to make it smart, and it cured him . . .

FROM *Diary of a Little Girl in Old New York, 1849–50*

THE FIRST OF THE FINEST

In 1658, Peter Stuyvesant established the first police force, of eight men.

A GRIM BUSINESS

Each day fifty-six tons of choice items such as old iron, tin cans, bottles, tires, dead animals, and packing materials are removed from New York Harbor.

A street cleaner in Times Square, 1900.

A DAY AT THE MUSEUM

Calder's Circus

ELIZABETH LEVINE

 lexander Calder, one of America's greatest artists, created an entire miniature circus for fun.

The idea came to him fifty years ago, while he was covering a story on the Ringling Bros. Barnum & Bailey Circus for the *National Police Gazette*. He worked on his own circus for six years, using ordinary found materials: cloth, paper, wire, string, corks, buttons, bottle caps, sequins, wood, etc.

When it was finished, Calder packed his circus into five suitcases and gave "performances" at different friends' houses. When he arrived, one of the first things they had to do was to push all the furniture against the walls. Then Calder put on basketball knee pads, because he had to be on his knees for the whole show. While he made the figures perform, he would roar for the lion, bark for the seal, and make all the other necessary sound effects. His wife played music on a Victrola. Most of the time Calder gave these performances free, but once a man on Long Island paid him one hundred dollars.

These 55 figures and animals, tent, trapeze, ring, cages, etc. are now at the Whitney Museum, where Calder himself arranged the circus in a beautiful display.

Barnum's American Museum

by JAY WILLIAMS

Back in the middle of the nineteeth century, there was one sight in New York nobody wanted to miss—a five-story building with a curved front, its roof lined with the flags of all nations, standing on the corner of Broadway and Ann Street near City Hall Park in what was then the heart of the city. In letters taller than a man the sign across the front read BARNUM'S AMERICAN MUSEUM. And inside there were wonders.

There were stuffed animals and birds from every corner of the earth crammed into glass cases. There were sea creatures in tanks, including live whales from Labrador. There were astonishing animals such as a troop of performing bears, a hippopotamus, and a giraffe—a cartoon of the period showed a farmer looking at one and saying, "I still say there's no sich animule." There was entertainment of all sorts—a company of Industrious Fleas, a Wild West show with Indians, and Moral Plays in the great Lecture Hall. There were strange people: a genuine bearded lady, a three-legged man, a pair of twins from Siam joined together at the waist, and the amazing General Tom Thumb, a man only thirty inches high, who had appeared before the kings and queens of Europe and was the most famous midget in the world. And the cost of all this was only twenty-five cents.

One of the most popular sights was the Fejee Mermaid, the dried-up body of a strange little creature with a monkey-like face and hands and the body of a fish. No one was ever able to prove whether it was a fake or a freak, but in the first four weeks it was shown the museum made $3,341 in admissions.

P. T. Barnum, the great showman, had bought the building in 1842. It was then called Scudder's Museum, and was well known as an exhibition of curiosities. But under Barnum's direction it became the most exciting attraction in town. Huge colored pictures hung outside, portraying the marvels within. At night, powerful lamps on the roof lighted up Broadway all the way down to the Battery. A band played on one of the balconies. And Barnum used every trick he could think of to bring in the public.

He claimed to have a Glorious Aerial Garden—it was actually two cedar plants, a dozen flower pots, and some tables on the roof where ice cream was served. He had a poster showing a famous violinist hung outside, but he had it hung upside down and people flocked in thinking the man was going to play standing on his head. He advertised *The Great Model of*

Niagara Falls with Real Water. It drew crowds, but when they got inside they found that the model was only eighteen inches high. However, nobody was ever too disappointed because there was so much else to see.

Once, Barnum used one of his tricks to get people out of the museum instead of into it. On St. Patrick's Day, in 1843, the place was so crowded that no more tickets could be sold. Barnum had a workman paint a sign pointing down a back stair: TO THE EGRESS. People hurried down the stair and out the door at the bottom, and found when they were in the street that "egress" means the same as "exit."

The American Museum flourished until one day in 1865 when the engine which pumped water to the aquarium overheated and started a fire. The building burned to the ground. A new museum was built, but only three years later it too was destroyed by a fire. Even then, it provided a real Barnum spectacle which everyone came to see, because the day was bitterly cold and the water from the fire hoses froze to make an icy vision one newspaper called, "a picture no artist could have painted."

The Tall and the Short of It

BARBARA SEULING

Probably the most fascinating wedding ever to take place in New York City occurred at Grace Church, an elegant Episcopalian landmark on lower Broadway. Quite a crowd gathered on February 10, 1862, when Mercy Lavinia Warren Bump, thirty-two inches tall, was married to thirty-five-inch-tall Charles Sherwood Stratton. The bride, from Massachusetts and a descendant of the *Mayflower* Pilgrims, looked beautiful in a white satin gown worn over a corset, especially made for her and adorned by tiny jewels. Her hairpins were also made to order in miniature, and she carried a bouquet of roses and camellias. The groom, originally from Bridgeport, Connecticut, was familiar to the public as "General Tom Thumb," the featured attraction of P. T. Barnum's circus. The bridesmaid was Minnie, Miss Bump's thirty-one-inch sister.

For their honeymoon, the pair visited the nation's capital, Washington, D.C., where they were guests of the President, who, incidentally, was the tallest man ever to live in the White House—Abraham Lincoln.

The Museum
of Modern Art

ELIZABETH LEVINE

The Museum of Modern Art on West Fifty-third Street shows the paintings and sculptures of the greatest masters of modern art. Some of the works you will see here have influenced the shape of art around the world.

If you look closely at Picasso's sculpture "The Baboon and Young," made in 1951, you'll notice that Picasso used his son Claude's toy car to form the head. The windshield becomes the eyes, and the bumper becomes the mouth!

Mondrian's famous picture, "Broadway Boogie Woogie," painted in 1942 after he came to New York, really expresses the excitement and fever pitch he felt about New York City.

The large water lily paintings by Monet occupy an entire room in the museum. When you enter, you will notice the quiet and still mood that Monet has caused you to feel. Some people begin to whisper.

Vincent Van Gogh's "Starry Night," painted in 1889, and reproduced in posters, postcards, books, and magazines all over the world, is here. It still looks alive with its swirling sky, stars, and glowing moon. Van Gogh's enthusiasm and emotion in this painting makes the nighttime seem more appealing for us than the day.

Modern art is often experimental, and people are sometimes shocked by what they see in the museum. But you'll proba-

bly have fun seeing George Segal's sculpture "The Bus Driver." The reason the driver is life-size is that Segal wrapped a live man for the sculpture. He used Nivea Cream to protect the man's skin, and then covered the whole body, clothes and all, with wet plaster-of-Paris bandages (the same kind doctors use for a broken leg). After about 15 minutes, it was dry enough for Segal to gently cut the plaster sections away from the body. The model's clothes were ruined, of course, and his hair was full of plaster! But he was probably glad to have helped in the creation of a new art form. Segal then put the dried sections together to complete the sculpture. The coin box, which is so important to this sculpture, is a real one direct from an old city bus.

Don't forget to go out to the museum's beautiful sculpture garden. It is filled with pools, fountains, trees, and sculpture. You may want to see your reflection in a pool, or toss in a penny and make a wish. Near the garden, on the first floor, is a restaurant.

The museum bookshop has games, toys, stationery, cards, posters, jewelry, and other well-designed gifts. Upstairs, there are galleries for photography, drawings, architecture, and design. Charlie Chaplin, Buster Keaton, and other silent and "talkie" films are shown every day downstairs in the auditorium. Check at the museum desk in the lobby for schedule and tickets.

The Solomon R. Guggenheim Museum.

Who's at the Guggenheim?

1. The Stewardess ate pizza for lunch.

2. The person who went to Macy's rode the bus.

3. The Model stopped for a hot dog on her way to the Bronx Zoo.

4. One of the women parked her motorcycle and went in for a frozen yogurt.

5. The Actress spent the day in Central Park.

6. The Writer ate a bagel.

7. One person took the subway.

8. The Stewardess rides a bicycle.

WHO'S AT THE GUGGENHEIM?

(SEE ANSWER PG. 372.)

Have You Ever Been to an Art Gallery?

MARGO FEIDEN

Have you ever been to an art gallery? They aren't like museums, you know. Less stuffy. Now, as an adult, I do love to wander through museums. But when I was a child there was a lot I didn't like about them. I was intimidated by giant, cold rooms with uniformed guards who looked like they stood for "No touching, no talking, no laughing. No smiling?"

People, and especially young people, seem more relaxed in galleries. They seem to smile more. I think this is because galleries are built to human proportions. When you look at pictures hanging in a gallery it's somehow easier to believe that they were created by real people. New York is the art gallery capital of America. There are more galleries here than anywhere else, and of much greater variety.

You'll find five distinct areas in our city where art galleries cluster and thrive.

1. SoHo. (Located between Chinatown and Greenwich Village.) The word SoHo is a "portmanteau"; this means that it is a word made by combining parts of other words. SoHo was named for its location, SOuth of HOuston Street. Its popularity as an art center began in 1971 when New York City's government rezoned SoHo to make it a special neighborhood for artists. For years before that the streets were lined with deserted, vacant warehouses and old factories. Although these spaces weren't being used commercially, they did not meet the legal requirements for residential occupancy. Rents in these buildings were very low, but people were not allowed to live in them. Our City Planning Commission changed these laws, for artists only, because even great artists usually are broke until they become successful. Landlords in the area were given permission to rent living space to people who could prove that they made their money by producing art. Artists then converted the factory lofts into homes and studios. When space like this is rented, the artist must hang a shingle outside with his or her name, followed by "A.I.R.," which means "Artist in Residence." Where there are artists, art galleries will follow. This is why SoHo has become a major center for art. And, of course, its popularity has pushed property values up, and rents are higher now.

What you'll find: The new and the different. Lots of work by as yet undis-

covered artists and newly famous ones. You'll see work which is totally abstract, that is, not representing a recognizable object. For example, you may find a painting whose entire surface is covered with one color only and nothing else. Or it might have a thin strip or two of some other color running through it. And you'll also find the "apparent" opposite of abstract art —Super Realism. This concept in art was born in SoHo. Super Realism is also called Photo Realism because the artist uses a slide projector to produce a photographic image on the canvas he or she is about to paint. The image is then painted over exactly as it appears.

2. TriBeCa. (An irregularly shaped triangle, closer to a trapezoid, which zigzags its way roughly from Canal Street to the World Trade Center.) The name TriBeCa is also a portmanteau, again derived from its location "TRIangle BElow CAnal." This is New York's newest center for the arts. As rents in SoHo become higher and space harder to find, artists have been converting TriBeCa's lofts into living and working space. This area had once been a center for wholesale fruits and food importers. With the closing of the Washington Market wholesalers have left the area leaving empty space behind them. The Planning Commission rezoned TriBeCa in 1976 for artists and nonartists as well. This is an exciting neighborhood to visit now because you can actually watch the changes as they happen.

What you'll find: The very new and very different.

3. Greenwich Village. (Houston to Fourteenth Street, between Third Avenue and the Hudson River.) In the first half of this century there were two places to be if

you were an artist: Greenwich Village and Paris.

What you'll find: In the 1950s New York's most popular street for art galleries was Tenth Street. It still has fine galleries. This is the street that my gallery, the Margo Feiden Galleries, is on. We are a gallery devoted to art which arises from the artist's love of New York City, its theater, or its people. For example, we have all the work of the late Don Freeman, whose illustrations appear in this book. Before Freeman wrote and illustrated children's books, he was an illustrator of New York and everything about it. We have his original paintings, drawings, and lithographs for you to see. You may also know another of our artists, Al Hirschfeld, whose drawings heralding the opening of Broadway shows have appeared in the New York *Times* for more than fifty years, and in other newspapers and magazines throughout the world. Greenwich Village is also a good place to buy posters of all kinds. A poster can be simply a three-dollar reproduction which is printed on a machine. But there are also "original posters" which are printed by the artist and signed by hand. These can be very good investments which even young people may be able to afford. Because original posters are not mass-produced on machinery, relatively few are made. When many people want the same poster, the price keeps going up. Sometimes a $15 poster becomes worth $150 in a year. Sometimes. But I never advise people to buy art for an investment. I always say, "Buy what you like."

4. Fifty-seventh Street. (Between Park and Sixth avenues.)

What you'll find: Expensive. In general I would not recommend this for young browsers. One gallery in this area that you should know about is Cityana at 16 East 53 Street. This gallery is privately owned and is devoted to exhibitions which show off New York.

5. Madison Avenue. (From the lower Sixties to the upper Eighties and on the side streets between Fifth and Lexington avenues.)

What you'll find: Everything. There are galleries that carry only old, old things and those that carry only the newest things. There are galleries that carry only European art, or Asian art, or African art, or American art. There are galleries that carry museum quality masterpieces and others that carry strictly commercial art—anything salable. The good work is usually very expensive and the bad work is usually overpriced. Madison Avenue does offer you the most galleries to choose from and also the largest variety of art. Madison Avenue art dealers tend to dislike children who are not in the company of at least one mink coat.

When you visit any of these galleries it is important to remember that just because something is hanging doesn't make it art. Question everything you see. Your opinion is as valid as anyone else's. After all, professional critics themselves violently disagree with each other.

Ideas:

1. Have your name put on gallery mailing lists and you will receive announcements of exhibitions.

2. Keep a scrapbook. When you visit a gallery you can ask for an announcement or brochure of the exhibition you've just seen. Usually at least one work will be reproduced. You might write down your feelings about the artist. Then you can

watch your own taste changing and you can watch what happens to the artist's career over the years.

3. Write a letter to the artist (in care of the gallery). Honesty may be appreciated more than flattery, but either will probably get you a letter in reply.

4. If you find a gallery you think your classmates would like to visit, ask your school to arrange for a guided tour. Most galleries are not crowded during school hours, and they may welcome enthusiastic company.

Revan

A PROFILE OF A NEW YORK KID

A colorful papier-mâché dragon lies as guard outside Revan's Upper West Side apartment in Manhattan. "I made him in a pottery class at the YMHA on Ninety-second Street," Revan explains.

Revan is twelve years old and goes to the Spence School. She hasn't always gone to school in New York though. In grades two and three she attended Kodi Kanal in the mountains of southern India. Maybe that explains why her favorite subject is languages.

When asked what her career plans are, she says she might like to become a doctor. Or maybe a lawyer. "My main ambition, though, is to help people," she adds.

What about food? She's "addicted" to pizza but can't stand lima beans. Naturally she loves curry—but not too hot.

In addition to pottery-making and pizza-eating, Revan reads . . . and reads . . . and reads. Her favorite poets at the moment are E. E. Cummings and Ogden Nash. She's just finished reading *Black Boy*, the autobiography of Richard Wright, and thinks it's wonderful. Revan loves the works of Mary Norton. "I feel a children's book just has to have great illustrations," she says, "and Mary Norton's books certainly do." Putting her beliefs into practice, Revan is collaborating with a classmate on a book for children.

What else does she do? She likes visiting the New-York Historical Society in particular, and museums in general. "New York must be the museum capital of the world," she says. And she really enjoys getting "lost" in one of the city's biggest bookstores—Barnes and Noble.

Revan sums up New York: "You can never be bored here."

DO YOU SEE A FAMOUS VASE FROM THE METROPOLITAN MUSEUM OF ART, OR TWO NEW YORK TAXI DRIVERS DISCUSSING A FENDER-BENDER ON SIXTH AVENUE IN RUSH HOUR?

The Mystery of the Stolen Painting

JOAN M. LEXAU

Find the names of seventy-five Manhattan streets in the mystery. Some are hidden (Fulton is in "aw*ful to nearly*"). After one search, consult the list on pg. 373 and try again.

"Only the painting is missing," said Charles Montgomery, rector of St. Dominick's in Manhattan. "It was here in the vestry an hour ago at nine thirty."

Clare Montgomery, his wife, said, "Allen Smith and Howard Jones were here when Adrian York brought it last night to be auctioned at the Spring Fair. They know we work for an hour in the office downstairs each morning from nine thirty to now with the front door open."

"The painting is worth a lot. York is a member of the Academy of Fine Painters. He would be better known if he didn't hate to sell his paintings," the rector said. "But can Howard be a thief? Can Al? I'll call them and see if they can account for

their time this morning." Side by side, he and his wife returned to the office.

"I've often thought," his wife said, "that we should keep that door locked when we're downstairs. We must be extra careful from now on."

The rector phoned Howard Jones. Jones had been patching the vestry walls the night before. The rector hired him whenever he could talk him into doing some work, but Howard never accepted much pay.

"Hello, Rector," Howard said. "Would you believe I was washing tons of clothes at the laundromat from eight thirty on? My wife Hester says she works hard enough at the Post Office without doing laundry. Just got back seconds ago and I'm downing a cherry soda when who pops by? My mother-in-law."

"That's great, Jones," said the rector, ready to hang up.

Howard went on talking. "Right away she's at me about getting a job so we can move to one of those nice brownstones a block uptown. She's always saying, 'If Howard and Hester moved north a block, wouldn't it be grand!'"

They exchanged a few more words and the rector hung up without having to explain why he called.

He got Allen Smith on the phone. "What's up?" said Smith. "Got some more legal work for me to do on the side? You know I'll help." The attorney did all the church's legal work free.

The rector explained about the missing painting.

"I have an alibi if that's why you called," Smith said. "Left at seven thirty for an appointment in New Jersey, smashed into a van on Ninth Avenue. The van damage was slight but the driver was surprised when I admitted it was my fault. I told him I only finagle legally, that's my motto. Got back half an hour ago after stopping off at Judge Jackson's chambers and the bank. Just gave my staff instructions for tomorrow. I'm driving tonight to Albany on business."

"Thanks, Smith," the rector said. "I shall see Adrian York now and tell him his painting is lost so he cannot hear it elsewhere first."

"He'd feel awful to nearly lose a nickel. That guy is tight with a buck," Smith said before hanging up.

The rector's church was in the east For-ties and York lived in the east Fifties. The rector, a good walker, went up Third Avenue. He missed the old El even though it had made the street below bleak.

In York's small but pleasant studio, the artist greeted him with, "I'm bushed. I went to Fiftieth Street to St. Patrick's Cathedral early to sketch the exterior and at nine thirty went downtown to John Jay Park at Seventy-seventh Street."

The rector told York about the stolen painting.

"That's terrible," the artist said. "That was one of my best."

"I'd planned on buying some wide pews with the money," said the rector. He rose to look at the bookshelves. York was a reader. On the top shelf were *Oliver Twist*, *Life of Lincoln*, *Shakespeare's Plays*, then *Shaw's Plays*, a travel guide by Henry Kissinger, and a row of income tax guides.

"But I think I know who took the painting," the rector stated suddenly.

WHO WAS IT?

"Smith wouldn't risk his career by stealing and Jones isn't interested in money," the rector said. "You were in a hurry to give me an alibi that couldn't be proved but you said you went downtown from the Cathedral to the park when you should have said uptown. You did go downtown to take the painting which you had donated to give yourself a tax deduction."

The artist hung his head. "I did mean to give up the painting but I found I couldn't part with it and was too embarrassed to ask for it back."

Art Tells a Story

PENELOPE PRODDOW

Have you ever longed for a good story about a mythological hero or heroine, the rise of a country or civilization, or simply life as it was a hundred years ago in the country or a distant city? Next time this happens, go to the Metropolitan Museum, where you can find a story in every work of art.

How do you get to the museum? If you are under twelve, you must take your parents or an older friend. If you are over twelve, go on your own. Just pick up an admission button in the Junior Museum. Then you are ready to explore the galleries.

No sooner do you walk up the Grand Staircase than you see Perseus, the famous Greek hero, holding out the head of Medusa. Walking through the painting galleries, you will see another statue which tells another part of the same story. The princess Andromeda is crying out to Perseus to save her from a sea monster—which he does.

You will find other art works with stories to tell in the Islamic Section, the Egyptian Galleries, among the Greek vases and in Medieval tapestries. If, at some point, you need to refresh your memory on their details, return to the Junior Museum. There the weekend program "Art Tells a Story" not only gives the story, but enables you and other visitors to share your thoughts on works of art from all over the museum.

Charge!

PAMELA MORTON

With a clatter of horse's hooves a jouster, wearing a helmet of ox horns, thunders out to meet you as you enter the armor galleries at the Metropolitan Museum of Art. Close behind him are more mounted knights in armor. All around the great hall there are bright shields and standards of houses at war with one another. You have just stepped backward in time right into the Middle Ages!

Among the standing suits of armor you will find a beautiful blue and gold suit made for George Clifford, a Knight of the Garter, when he was appointed Champion of Queen Elizabeth I in 1590. There are many family and royal symbols to look for

on his elegantly worked armor, which weighs sixty pounds! Such an adventurer was he that he sailed often on the high seas. Could he have worn this suit of armor when he captured the Castle of El Morro in San Juan, Puerto Rico?

In rooms off the great hall there are other treasures and trappings of the man at arms. Many have marks of battle upon them, a grim reminder of the dangers of the soldier's life. History whispers most strongly, however, when you come upon a simple helmet, pierced with holes made by crossbow bolts. It is believed to be the helmet worn by Joan of Arc when she rode into the Battle of Orléans.

A Visit to the World of the Egyptian Dead

GISELA MORIARTY

A tomb doesn't sound like a homey place, but to the Egyptians that's what it was expected to be. Since they believed that life went on after death, they furnished their tombs with all the things that were important to them. Sometimes these were real objects, sometimes models, sometimes paintings. It was believed that paintings and statues had life in them.

At the Egyptian Galleries of the Metropolitan Museum of Art you can visit ancient mummies and tombs. You can walk right into Pernebi's tomb, which dates from about 2415–2375 B.C., with its chapel, where priests and relatives could leave food or drinks for him. Its statue chamber helped guarantee that his spirit would live on and have a resting place. Another section of the tomb includes a display of a human skull and some bones found along with Pernebi's possessions.

We are lucky that the Egyptians furnished their tombs so well, for it has made it possible for us to get a very clear idea of ancient Egyptian life. Because of the dry climate in Egypt, objects have been well preserved through the centuries. (You'll notice that the museum galleries are climate-controlled.)

Among the best-preserved objects ever found in Egypt are the enchanting models made for Chancellor Mekutra's tomb. Beautiful small boats displayed include traveling boats with singers, a kitchen tender boat to come alongside and prepare food, and a sporting boat. Other models include a stable where cattle are being fattened (one is already too fat to stand up), a slaughterhouse where oxen are having their throats cut (the blood is being caught in bowls to be made into pudding), and a granary with the old grain still in place.

In the Study of Dynasty 11 (XI), a sort of alcove, you will find a model of women working in a combination weaving shop and granary. The original thread, thousands of years old, is in the small jars. Don't miss the photos on the wall of the unwrapping of mummies Wah and Mayet, right down to skin and bones.

In the outer room of Dynasty 11 is Wah himself. His coffin has painted eyes so that his mummy can see out. In front of the coffin is a model of Wah's mummy with its ancient golden mask. That long bony thing with a hoof is a real beef joint from the tomb, and those sandals may look like yours, but are actually from Wah. Some things just don't change.

If you're tired, there's a wonderful resting place to come. Brilliant copies of wall paintings, done by the Museum Expedition in the early twentieth century, have been mounted all around a large room. There are chairs to sit in, or you can collapse on the carpet in a glass house which is really a facsimile painting of the tomb chapel of Nakht, around 1420 B.C. Even if you're not tired, you might enjoy sitting down for a while to look around at all the activities pictured. You probably do many of the very things the Egyptians did.

The Ptolemaic Period, 305–30 B.C., isn't nearly so ancient, but the coffins and mummies shown from it are more colorfully decorated. There are little mummiform figures that look like fairy-tale animals with human bodies. One looks just like Red Ridinghood's wolf. That cat statue in a case is not a statue at all, but a cat coffin. Egyptians thought their gods could come to earth as animals. When a sacred cat died, it was mummified, just like a person, and put into its own cat coffin. There were even sacred animal cemeteries.

The mummies and masks displayed from the Roman Period (A.D. 50–100) often have classical Roman faces and hairstyles but Egyptian designs, such as serpents and falcons, around the faces.

As you leave the world of the dead, you pass the chapel of Prince Ravemkal, back in 2415–2375 B.C. Behind its false doors he waited for the living to bring his food.

The Door to Eternity

DEMETRE BOVE

Where is there a door that doesn't look like a door, a door that is made of solid stone that doesn't open, a door that leads nowhere?

The Egyptians believed that after a person died and was buried in a tomb, his ghost could go through a false door in the outer part of the tomb and eat the food that was left there for him. If you look carefully at the pictures around an "undoor" of such a tomb, you will see people carrying goats, sheep, ducks, bowls of food, bread, and grain toward the door.

This is to keep the ghost inside the tomb, to keep it from wandering around outside in the villages in search of food.

A picture of the person who died is also on the walls near the false door. The ghost was thought to live in this picture when it came through the door. In this way it had a body and could look at the pictures in the room, see the visitors, eat the meat and drink that were brought in, and smell the incense that was left burning.

A story is told by the people who study these tombs of a husband who went to complain to his dead wife of all the troubles and problems that had happened to him since her death. He stood before the door and talked of his merits and of how generous he was to her when she was alive. He said that these difficulties she had caused him since her death could not go on! How could she do this to him? It was unfair! Just in case his wife didn't hear him, the husband wrote all of this down in hieroglyphics on papyrus and left the papyrus near the door so that her ghost could read it when it came through the false door.

One of these magic "undoors," from the tomb of Pernebi, is in the Metropolitan Museum.

WHAT DOES THE CURATOR SAY?

Q. What does the curator of the Egyptian Galleries of the Metropolitan Museum of Art say when he's lost?

A. "I want my mummy!"

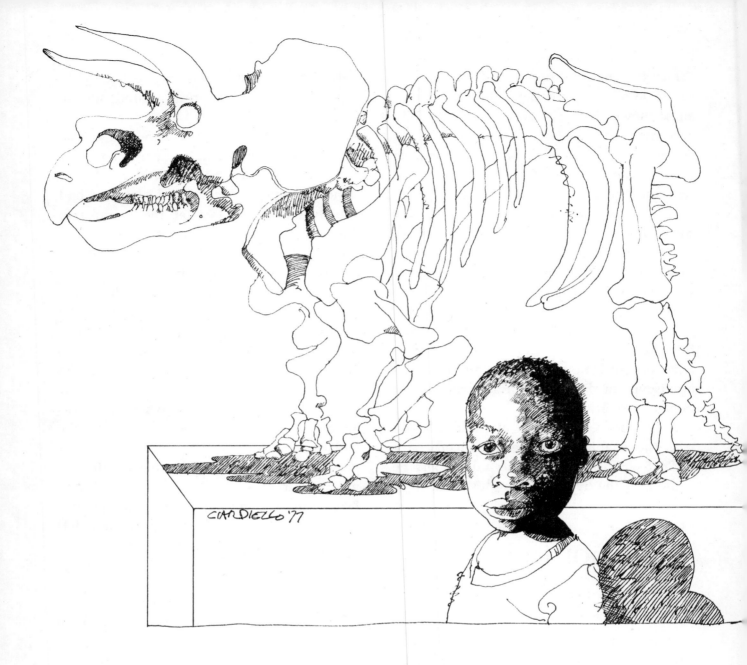

The Last Visit

OLGA LITOWINSKY

Clump. Thump. Sigh.
Clump. Thump. Sigh.
The boy and his friend slowly made their way up the marble staircase to the fourth floor of the American Museum of Natural History.

"Buck up, Boris. We're almost there," the boy said encouragingly.

"I don't think I can go much farther," his friend said. "Let's rest for a minute."

"No, no. Impossible. Someone might see you and call the guard. Come on, Boris. It was your idea."

Clump. Thump. Sigh. "Maybe it wasn't such a good one."

"Don't talk any more. Save your breath. Just three more steps."

Clump. Thump. "Ahhhh. We made it."

"Okay. Now be quiet. Just follow me." The boy led his friend across the highly polished floor. "It's in here." They went into the next room.

"There. What about it?" the boy asked.

"I don't know. What does the sign say?"

"Brontosaurus . . ."

"Is it spelled right?"

"Sure, sure. Brontosaurus. This specimen probably weighed thirty-five tons when alive," the boy went on.

"That sounds about right," his friend said, nodding his head. "You did say this is the largest museum of its kind in the world, didn't you? You don't suppose they could make a mistake about all this."

"It's not likely. There's more." The boy went on reading. "About one hundred and fifty million years ago, during the Jurassic period, there were more dinosaurs than any other kind of animal. But then—"

"So it's true. The good old days are gone," his friend said. Suddenly he began to cry. Great tears fell from his eyes, splashing the boy. Pools began to form on the floor.

"Stop it. You're flooding the place!" the boy cried.

"I can't help it. It's just as you told me. Plenty of bones but no more dinosaurs. No more diplodocus hanging around with stegosaurus under the old pine trees, munching on ginkgo leaves, splashing in the swamps. It's all over. Over! Great sobs nearly tore Boris apart. The brontosaurus bones on display began to wobble—and then fell with a crash.

"Hey, what's going on here?" A guard rushed in. "Don't you know animals aren't allowed. Get out. *Out!*" The guard was furious.

Boris looked at the guard, tears still welling in his eyes. "Don't worry. I'm going. It's all over anyway. I'm extinct."

Splashing through his own tears, the last brontosaurus in the world turned and lumbered toward the stairs.

[We] have finished "Common Things" which tells us about science—why the steam comes out of the kettle, and what makes the clouds, and the rainbow, etc., and now we are going into a harder book called "Familiar Science" . . .

Professor Hume teaches us natural science . . . and one day he brought the eye of an ox and took it all apart and showed us how it was like our own eyes. And another time he brought an electric battery and we joined our hands, ever so many of us, and the end girl took hold of the handle of the battery, and we all felt the shock, and it tingled and pricked . . .

From *Diary of a Little Girl in Old New York,* 1849–50

DINOSAURS IN THE RAIN

What better way is there to spend a rainy Saturday than among the dinosaurs of New York City? There are thirty of them—or their skeletons, to be exact—on the fourth floor of the American Museum of Natural History, part of the largest dinosaur collection in the world. There is enough for the most serious paleontologist. Dinosaur eggs, found in Mongolia, belonging to the horned dinosaur, protoceratops, are on display. Skeletons of ancient flying and swimming reptiles can be seen.

The star of the show is the huge but peaceable brontosaurus, and hot on his trail is a carnivorous dinosaur, smaller but much less agreeable. The scene represents the way it could have been millions of years ago, as flesh-eating dinosaurs pursued the vegetarian ones. When you get up close to the brontosaurus, look behind at his tracks. They are actual brontosaurus footprints found in Texas.

Monsters in the City

**BARBARA BURN
AND EMIL P. DOLENSEK**

Although King Kong never really made it to the top of the Empire State Building or the World Trade Center, there are plenty of other scary animals in New York City if you know where to look. Luckily, they are mostly behind bars or in cages and aren't likely to cause you damage, though they might give you some interesting dreams. Look at the sharks at the New York Aquarium in Coney Island (telephone

266-8500 for information), or at the rattlesnakes in the Staten Island Zoo (442-3100), or at the crocodiles and alligators at the Bronx Zoo (220-5100). If you're into insects, take a peek at the tarantula at the Children's Zoo in the Bronx or gaze upon the gorillas in Central Park or in the Bronx. Keep in mind, though, that gorillas aren't nearly as fierce as they look (they are naturally very gentle with each other in the wild and only become hostile when threatened) and that tarantulas aren't as deadly as most people think. (Don't touch them or try to tease them, though, because they *can* do a lot of harm!) If you want to see a truly huge monster, one that lived on the earth several thousands of years ago, the Museum of Natural History has a terrific display of dinosaur skeletons that have been restored to show what these beasts originally looked like (call 873-1300).

COULD ANY DINOSAUR HAVE LIVED IN THE NEW YORK CITY AREA?

The answer is *yes!* Experts at the Museum of Natural History say that the first dinosaur fossils found in America, of the duck-billed dinosaur, were found in southern New Jersey, near Philadelphia, and dinosaur tracks have been uncovered in the Connecticut River Valley, two areas just outside of New York City. There is no evidence so far that dinosaurs ever stalked the New York City area, but then . . . there is no evidence that they did *not*, either!

The Museum of Broadcasting

JOAN GROSS

Are you interested in watching the historic Kennedy-Nixon presidential debates, or listening to a twelve-year-old unknown named Judy Garland make her radio debut? Perhaps you'd rather watch Mary Martin fly through the air in the television production of *Peter Pan,* or hear some of the campaign speeches of President Franklin D. Roosevelt.

The Museum of Broadcasting (phone: 752-4690), 1 East 53 Street, has more than two thousand television and radio programs on tape, with new additions catalogued daily. This unique museum is dedicated to the preservation of radio and television broadcasting, and is the first one of its kind in the United States.

An eighteen-minute tape, narrated by Alistair Cooke of *Upstairs, Downstairs* fame, introduces the museum, and explains how to use the card catalogue and viewing consoles. There is also a small but excellent reference library as well as books and periodicals about broadcasting. Leisurely browsing is encouraged.

Each of the eight viewing consoles has seats for three, so by all means bring a friend. You are limited to one hour viewing time when the museum is crowded, and a small contribution is requested. There is no charge for using the library.

The Museum of Broadcasting is open between 12 noon and 5 P.M., Tuesdays through Saturdays. Visitors are encouraged to use the facilities on weekdays. As you might expect, this small museum has become one of the most popular places in New York.

A SPECIAL STAR

FRANKLYN M. BRANLEY AND HELMUT WIMMER

In our galaxy there are at least one hundred billion stars. Some are a thousand times larger than the sun, and a million times brighter. Others are a thousand times smaller, and dimmer. Most of the stars are made of hydrogen and helium; but some contain trace amounts of other atoms.

In the past few years stars have been discovered that are made only of neutrons. These are the massive parts of atoms. The neutrons are packed tightly together. One of these neutron stars was found in Taurus in the Crab Nebula—a huge formation of dust and gases left over from the explosion of a gigantic star that occurred about two thousand years ago.

Astronomers think that the star contains about as much material as the sun contains. But the neutron star is only about ten kilometers across—the sun is over a million kilometers across. The picture shows how large this neutron star is compared with New York City. The star is called NP 0532. N means it was discovered by the National Radio Astronomy Observatory, P means it is a pulsar—a star that gives off a pulsating radio wave, and the numbers are clues to its location in the sky.

If this star ever got this close to earth, earth would long ago have disappeared. It would be pulled apart by the gravitation of NP 0532—the parts of the atoms thrown into space and only the neutrons remaining.

EDITOR'S NOTE: To find out more about the stars and the heavens, visit the Hayden Planetarium at the American Museum of Natural History, Central Park West and Eighty-first Street.

SOME SPECIAL PROGRAMS FOR SOME SPECIAL KIDS

STEPHEN MOOSER

FOR THOSE WITH PHYSICAL DISABILITIES

The Association of Community Mayors regularly sponsors an afternoon at the circus, and another at Shea Stadium for children with physical disabilities.

For information contact: The Community Mayors of New York, 16 Court Street, Brooklyn (phone: 624-1100).

The United Cerebral Palsy Association can provide transportation for those with physical disabilities. The Manhattan office of the Association is at 122 East 23 Street (phone: 677-7400).

Information on other ongoing and special programs for children can be obtained from The Mayors Office of the Handicapped, 250 Broadway (phone: 566-0972), or from their Center at 51 Chambers Street (phone: 349-5205).

FOR THOSE WITH VISUAL DISABILITIES

The Botanical Gardens on Empire Boulevard in Brooklyn offers a special nature walk for those with visual disabilities. There are lots of things to smell and touch and all the information plaques along the trail are in Braille.

Information on other ongoing and special programs can be obtained from the:

New York Association for the Blind, The Lighthouse, 111 East 59 Street (phone: EL5-2200);

Jewish Guild for the Blind, 75 Stratton, Yonkers (NYC phone: 549-7523);

Industrial Home for the Blind, 57 Willoughby, Brooklyn (phone: 522-2122).

FOR THOSE WITH HEARING DISABILITIES

The New York Society for the Deaf sponsors a program for teenagers. The group meets every Saturday morning at the Society's building on Fourteenth Street between First and Second avenues. The Society also sponsors a Boy Scout Troop especially for children with a hearing disability.

Information on other ongoing and special programs can be obtained from:

The New York Society for the Deaf, 344 East 14 Street (phone: 673-6500).

GREEN NEW YORK

```
                                                                    ogoodo
                                                                  ogoodyearodo
                                                                 ogoodyearogoodo
                                                                ogoodyeargoodyear
                                                                goodyearroodyear
                                                                goodyeargoodo
                                                                 ogoodyearo
                                                                  theblimp
                                                                  theblimp
                                                                   floats
```

```
                                        talltalltalltalltalltall          busybusybusy
                                        talltalltalltalltalltall          busybusybusybusy
                                                                          busybusybusybusy
      t                  7777777777      talltalltalltalltalltall         busybusybusybusy
   t   r   t  r  t       9999999999      talltalltalltalltallta           busymacysmacysbusy
  tree  e  r e  r       11111111111      talltalltalltalltall             busymacysmacysbusy
  ree    eee   e        22222222222      talltalltalltalltall             macysmacysmacys
  ree     eee           33333333333      talltalltalltall                 macysmacysmacys
  tree      us          44444444444      talltalltall                     macysmacysmacys
  r       bush          55555555555      talltall                         macysmacysmacys
         shrubs                          tall
         bushes
          bush
  grassandsomeleaves,green
  grassgreengrassgreengra
  tinthemiddlecentralpark
  andshellandsummermusics
  aliceinwonderlandstatues
  adafountainandhippiess
  omeadowandemonstrators
  speareinthesummernight
  nahmemorialschaeffertoo
  aroselcalinopemerrygoub
  enplayingchessncheckers
  arensaiterdarkarethere
  akewithboatsandducksess
  akefrozenandskateduponn
  neegreenwalksandtalking
  odtearswhoselllyouaworld         madisonsquare ircus rowsnoflowers
  tinthemiddlecentralpark          madisons  cuscircuscirc  noflowers
  tinthemiddlecentralpark            uscircuscircuscir
                                   mad  circuscircuscircuscir    wers
  zooZooZooZooZooZooZoZoo          r circuscircuscircuscircuscircusc s
  zsnzarz zzruznt  z Z             ma  big   big   big   big     ors
  zsnzarz zzruznt  z Z             mo                           ors
  ZooZooZooZooZooZooZoZoo          ma  p                         rs
```

Life in a Corner Yard

ALVIN AND VIRGINIA SILVERSTEIN

It's amazing how much "wildlife" can flourish in the midst of the city. Our Brooklyn house stood on an odd-shaped corner lot, with two triangular patches of yard. The owner before us had planted neat lawns of green grass, but we had grander ideas: we were determined to have our own mini-farm. The backyard patch we planted mostly in beans, and the side yard with rows of corn. Half a dozen sunflowers along the edge seemed to feel they had to try harder to compete with the corn for a place in the sun. They grew and grew until they nearly reached our second-floor windows. (A friend who came to our house one night saw their huge, shadowy forms outlined by the street lamp and asked us nervously, "What are those *things* out there?")

As our crops grew, animal life appeared. A field mouse was surprised in the bean patch. Butterflies fluttered in the summer breezes and delighted us until we discovered that the eggs they laid hatched into hungry green caterpillars that grew fat chopping down our bean sprouts. We took to prowling through the garden at two in the morning with a flashlight to catch them at their munching. (The neighbors thought we were awfully odd.) We watched a tall green praying mantis suddenly reach out from a corn stalk and snatch a butterfly out of the air. Grasshoppers and leaf hoppers flitted among the plants. Ladybugs perched for a moment on an outstretched finger.

And then there were the aphids. We knew that these tiny plump insects have very special food needs. A corn aphid will not grow on bean plants, a bean aphid cannot live on corn. Each kind of aphid must suck the juices from just one kind of plant, or perhaps a very few closely related kinds of plants, like peas and beans. Each kind of plant in our garden seemed to have its own aphids. There were fat green aphids on the beans (so many that we sometimes found stray aphids inside the house, clinging to the windowpanes), and red aphids and black aphids on the weeds. When we looked closely, we noticed a few ants, busily patrolling the plants, pausing now and then to stroke an aphid and catch a drop of sweet liquid that squirted out from it. When we pulled up some of the old cornstalks, after we had picked the ears, we even found aphids on the corn roots. What a scurrying there was. Frantic ants ran to and fro, picking up aphids from the uprooted plants and carrying them to safety.

And we wondered . . . Where did they all come from? Some aphids can fly. But where was there another cornfield in Brooklyn? How did they find our yard, and how many blocks of sidewalks and streets did they have to fly over to reach it? And how did ants that knew exactly how to take care of aphids happen to be living in our yard, too?

Shallow Roots

Park Avenue is only a few inches thick. The grass island running down the center of the avenue is too shallow to support the roots of shade trees. Buildings on the avenue have no basements; foundations are only half an inch below sidewalk level. The Waldorf-Astoria Hotel, for example, has its wine cellar on the fifth floor.

WATCH OUT

for a thousand vegetable farms which will appear on rubble-filled lots in New York City! The Federal Department of Agriculture has funded the Cornell University Cooperative to work with community groups clearing the garbage from vacant lots, improving the soil, and growing vegetables.

Perhaps we'll even need some new street signs:

Ginkgo Biloba: A Relic

OLGA LITOWINSKY

Undaunted by pollution, steel, or concrete, the hardy ginkgo tree flourishes in New York City parks and on city streets. In a sense, the spiky ginkgo's presence is as incongruous as a brachiosaurus bathing in the pools in front of the Seagram building, for it is as old as the great reptiles of the Age of Dinosaurs.

Like the willow and the wisteria, the ginkgo came to America from the Orient during the days of the China Trade. Ginkgo fruit is still featured on the menus of some Chinese restaurants in New York; it is especially good with chicken. It looks like a beige olive, but there is no pit, and its firm texture is reminiscent of a hard-boiled egg, slightly bitter in taste.

As befits its great age, the ginkgo tree is in no hurry, the female bearing fruit only after the tree is thirty years old. Nor does the ginkgo wait for the wind, insects, or birds to do the work of pollination. Its pretty little fanlike leaves—green in summer and yellow in fall—are really fern leaves (another name for the ginkgo is maidenhair tree). And like fern sperm, the pollen wriggles through rain or dew, as it did two hundred million years ago.

There is no other tree like it, a relic from the Jurassic jungles, alive and well in New York.

FOREST IN THE CITY

PAMELA MORTON

Did you know that there is a natural forest in New York City? Forest Park in Queens covers about three hundred acres and if you go to visit it you can imagine how Long Island looked to those first settlers in 1626.

There are over fifty species of birds living in the dense forest, from hawks to mourning doves. Animals have not fared as well, for where bears, foxes, and wolves used to live there are now only rabbits, moles, and mice. Humans fare best of all, for there are many trails for walking where we can see a natural forest community undisturbed and self-sustaining.

How to Decorate a Wall and Learn Botany at the Same Time

CHARLENE JOY TALBOT

Collecting leaves and wildflowers used to be pretty discouraging. They began to crumble as soon as they were pressed and dried. Now, thanks to adhesive plastic, you can pin each specimen on your wall, neatly labeled and impervious to decay.

All you need to create a leafy wall is a roll of clear plastic contact paper, some stickpins for hanging, and, of course, leaves.

There are as many kinds of collections as there are collectors. You might want to demonstrate how many kinds of plants and trees are growing in the nearest vacant lot. Or, with the help of a book, you might collect and identify only the leaves of unfamiliar trees or wildflowers. Needless to say, you will not collect growing things from city parks or from other people's yards unless you have their permission.

If possible, pick a twig with several leaves on it, to show how they grow. Some grow opposite each other, some grow alternately. Next, dry the specimens by placing them between layers of newspapers and covering them with something heavy—a stack of bricks or books. Change the papers every day or so as they absorb the moisture. By the end of a week the plants should be ready to mount.

While the leaves are drying you'll have time to study the unknown ones and try to discover their names. When you have identified them to your satisfaction, write out the names on slips of paper, ready to seal up with the specimens.

Plastic contact paper comes attached to a backing marked off in one-inch squares. A good size for displaying most leaves is 8½×11 inches. Cut two pieces (8½×11) for the leaf you are ready to mount. Peel the backing paper from one piece and lay the plastic flat on the table, sticky side up. Place the leaf on it, right side up, and place its name label beside it. Now peel the backing off the second sheet and place it, sticky side down, as closely aligned with the bottom sheet as you can. Press. If a pocket of air gets trapped between the sheets, simply pull them apart and smooth them back together. If the edges don't quite coincide, trim them a little. There! You have your first mounted leaf.

Some of the compound leaves, such as ailanthus and sumac, need bigger sheets of plastic. Keep them the same width—8½ inches—but cut the sheets longer, to whatever measurement the leaf needs.

Whether you hang them on the wall or keep them in a folder, you'll soon find yourself with a fascinating and personal collection of leaves or flowers that can be shown at school or on other occasions without its coming to harm.

WATCH OUT

for a new green world growing at the New York Botanical Garden in the Bronx. The "Greenworld for Children" is a new exhibition and workshop space designed to help children in New York discover all about plants and their importance in our lives. In the Greenmuse Grocery Store you can see how the food we buy in stores is grown and cultivated as you walk through a wheat field or a rice paddy, or sit in the shade of a banana tree. And this is just the first of the adventures which are planned in the "Greenworld."

Ailanthus altissima: a Tribute

OLGA LITOWINSKY

Some call it the weed tree, as if to scorn the ailanthus for growing, it seems, anywhere. It's found on vacant lots, in backyards, and between cracks in the sidewalk. It even sprouts high above the ground, from between the bricks on apartment buildings. The wood is pithy and of no commercial value, which is another reason for calling it a weed tree.

Since it is so prolific, and seems to flourish on city rubbish, it is easy to imagine the ailanthus "escaping" from cultivation a century ago when it was first brought to New York from the Orient. Its seeds are like twisted airplane propellers, and a breeze will send them spinning into the air and perhaps into a waiting plot of earth; it doesn't need much.

Medium tall, with branches like swaying tropical ferns, the ailanthus is also known as the tree of heaven. But, when the leaves are crushed, a rank odor is given off, and this has earned the ailanthus another name: the stink tree.

Whatever you call it—weed tree, tree of heaven, or stink tree—think of how it turns New York green, usually where it is needed most, and survives under conditions that would daunt any other tree. Without a doubt, the ailanthus is a true New Yorker.

THE WRITTEN WORD

Two Lions, Five Million Books

JEAN FRITZ

At New York's Fifth Avenue and Forty-first Street there are two lions and five million books. The friendly looking lions were carved out of pink Tennessee marble, and the books take up eighty miles of shelf space in the New York Public Library. That doesn't count the special books which are kept in separate rooms behind locked doors and iron bars. You have to have written permission to go inside those rooms and then you better be careful. You are not allowed to use a pen for fear you might get ink on the books, and you have to turn pages gently, for the books are old and rare. Sometimes there are only a few other copies in the world; sometimes there are no other copies anywhere.

One of the world's first printed Bibles is in a special room, as is a copy of the first book printed in North America. There is the original version of *The Secret Garden* in the author's own handwriting and one of the few surviving copies of the first edition of *Alice in Wonderland*. (The author didn't like this edition so he threw it out.) The smallest book in the world is here too. It is called *Book* and on each page the word "book" appears in a different language. The print is tiny, for the book itself is only two millimeters square. (One millimeter is .003937 of an inch.)

There are other treasures as well: a letter from Columbus, a copy of the Declaration of Independence in Thomas Jefferson's handwriting, and part of George Washington's personal library. What else? You can go to the New York Public Library and read about the Battle of Lexington in a newspaper of that very time. You can look up the telephone number of anyone in the world, as long as that person lives in a major city. And you can find books in every language, including three hundred dialects used by American Indians.

But if you had come to this corner of New York in the middle of the last century, you would have seen no books at all. Instead, behind a high stone embankment you would have found the city's water supply. If it were a Sunday afternoon, you would have seen people promenading on top of the embankment—ladies with parasols, gentlemen with canes.

When the library opened in 1911, people were happy with the building and the books. But not everyone was happy with the lions, which at that time were facing each other. Some people even said they did not look fierce enough. Later the lions were turned to look out on Fifth Avenue, and today New Yorkers think of them as old friends. They even have names. Mayor La Guardia called them Patience and Fortitude but there are others who call them Astor and Lenox in honor of two of the people who started the library.

You may call the lions whatever you want. When they wear wreaths around their necks, you can wish them a Merry Christmas on your way into the library. If you

are not yet eighteen, you won't be able to use the books there, but you can see some of the library's treasures on exhibit. You can browse through the library store. You can take a drink from a lion-headed fountain. You will be one of twenty-five hundred people who visit the library every day.

Sincerely Yours, Piece of Ham

M. E. KERR

"Richard," Birch says to me, "you have no flair, no game in you, no guts." All this with his arm around me as we walk to the Jefferson Branch of the New York Public

Library. (Deets, Derby, and Lonnigan are with us. We are a gang, with me the runt of the litter. Deets, Derby, and Lonnigan are jokers like Birch. I never joke.) "What do you want from me, Birch?" I groan. But I know. Birch wants to be featured, to sound off endlessly on whatever comes to his nutty mind. With me for a friend, how can he miss?

I go to the library a lot after school. It's my hangout. Our apartment on Greenwich Avenue is too small for my sisters and me. I'm not unhappy at home, just crowded. I spend about fifteen hours a week at the library. I read like fat kids eat candy bars.

No one's ever called me Dick or Richie. I'm not that type. When I'm not reading, I daydream. When I was little, I dreamed of being a king, then a spy, then the kind of man Kissinger was, bags always packed, ready to take off on another mission only he could control. I dream of power. Birch would howl; so would Deets, Derby, and Lonnigan.

At the library, Birch suddenly decides to steal a book. He's not a thief; it's a stupid whim. Deets, Derby, and Lonnigan giggle

at the note he leaves on the library shelf. *Help! I've been Abducted! Sincerely, "A Classical Dictionary."*

I can't forget Birch took that book. Next day in Earth Science, I print a message on a piece of notebook paper. Then in cafeteria while Birch is up getting a Coke, I secretly remove the piece of ham from his sandwich. When Birch returns, he bites down on two slices of bread, a piece of lettuce and my note. "What the—?" Birch reads my note. It says, *"I am missing. Sincerely, Piece of Ham."* Birch socks Lonnigan, trips Derby, spits Coke in Deets's face, trying to get the culprit to confess.

I keep this up all week: his pen, his sweater, his cap. First Birch laughs, then gets steamed, then relents and takes the book back. I sneak a package with his things in it outside his locker.

A week later we walk to the library, just the two of us. "Do you know why I returned the book?" "Because it was stolen property?" I say, with a blank look. "No, dummy, because Lonnigan or Deets or Derby reached me. The moral here is that you make a better world by dramatizing your points! It takes flair, and a game, and guts! You never get anywhere unless you roar, Richard!" Then he leans down and shouts in my ear, "Learn how to ROARRRRRRRRR, RICHARD!"

Inside the library I am deaf from the assault. But the king is in his counting room, the spy is removing his disguise, and Kissinger has returned from another mysterious mission. It isn't a daydream. I go back to the reference room and stare powerfully at "A Classical Dictionary," there in its proper place.

My Friend Stanley Reads New York Like a Book

LOUISE ARMSTRONG

My friend Stanley is a very serious thinker. Only his serious thinking takes place in a very funny way.

Like when he says why he likes New York:

"New York is a year 'round serious place," Stanley says. "Because all year 'round it's good to read."

"Aw, c'mon, Stanley," I say. "What do you mean good to *read?*"

"Well, look," Stanley says. "On sunny days you walk around and—boom—you find the Waterproof Hat Store. It's important to know there's a good place to keep your hat dry when it rains.

"'Course you've always got Do Not Enter, Enter, Step Up, No Standing . . . But even in a big building you'll find something educational. Even in an elevator. That's where I learned to always carry a hammer."

"Where?"

"In an elevator. There was a box in the elevator with a glass front and a telephone locked inside. The sign said, 'In Case of Emergency, Break Glass with Hammer.'"

"And there *was* no hammer?"

"Precisely," said Stanley.

"Some things you read can be confusing, though," Stanley went on. "Like the sign that said, 'Throw Pillows $1.79.'"

"That seems pretty clear to me," I said.

"*Clear?*" Stanley said. "*Clear?* Why should I have to pay $1.79 to throw a pillow when I can do it at my house for free?"

"Swell, Stanley. So much for sunny days. What about when it rains?"

"Even better!" Stanley exclaimed. "Then I go look up the fur farm maybe or . . ."

"The *fur farm?* That's ridiculous."

"Why?"

"Nobody can raise furs without raising the animal that comes inside."

"Someone says they can," Stanley says.

"Someone *where?*"

"In the Yellow Pages. There's one listing

under 'Fur Farm.' You know, if you own all five directories you get 501,200 listings —5,160 glorious pages to fill a rainy day. If you're hungry you can look under 'Appetizers, Snacks, etc.' . . . Or there are four and a half pages of Bakers—including Table Talk Pies, for people who like to chat with their food while they eat.

"When I feel insecure I go to 'Gates.' Did you know you can get Stronghold roll-up doors and grilles equipped with exclusive super-lock which are virtually burglar resistant?"

"Burglar *resistant*?"

"Virtually."

"For how long?"

"Until the burglars coax them enough, I guess. No question—the Yellow Pages present a real challenge for a serious thinker." Stanley squinted at me. "What do you think of a place that offers to locate husbands, wives, friends . . . and anyone missing?"

"I don't know, Stanley. What do you think?"

"I think it's definitely fishy."

"How come?"

"Well now, why would you want to pay someone to locate a husband, wife, et cetera—who *wasn't* missing?"

Mary Poppins in New York

P. L. TRAVERS

I would like to say, first of all, that this short note for the *Kid's Book* is not written for kids. It is written for children or, rather, for human beings. Kids have four legs, they eat grass and, I am told—when they are full grown—the lids of teapots, nails, and belt buckles; and the one word they are capable of saying is "Ma-a-a-!" Children have only two legs, but apart from this—from a kid's point of view—misadventure they have other and multiple talents. They speak a real language, they dance and sing, make up poems, wash the dishes (if urged strongly enough), suffer the pain of being young and, if lucky, rejoice in the same condition. They may, imitating the more jocular kind of grown-up, speak of themselves as kids, but we who have the responsibility of accompanying them on their way to maturity —I say this with fear and trembling— should accord them the dignity of their proper title, which is children.

It was not Four-legs who came ma-a-aing to me to ask for an interview for a children's newspaper but a group of lively Two-legs. "Yes," I said, "if you'll promise me not to ask how I came to think up Mary Poppins!" I am tired of that question, for I have been asked it throughout the world from West to East and back again. If I were in whatever African country that speaks Swahili—for my books are translated into that language—I am sure the question would arise there too. A Professor of Eastern Theology met my plane when I touched down in Canberra, New South Wales, and immediately put it to me. "I just don't know," I told him, mortified at not being able to give a reply. He beamed. "I knew it!" he said triumphantly. "Straight out of the Unconscious!" And hurried away, apparently satisfied. Well, *I* wasn't satisfied. I would rather have ventured the opinion that Mary Poppins had thought up me. It would have been somehow safer.

Anyway, the children, having honorably given their promise, honorably kept it. Instead, they plied me with beautiful questions, full of imagination. "Suppose," said one little girl, "that Mary Poppins were going up the steps of the New York Public Library, would she and the stone lions greet each other?" "Oh," I said, "I am sure they would," and thereupon made a vow to pat those lions in a friendly way every time *I* went to the Public Library.

"What about her umbrella?" asked a boy. "Did it have a secret mechanism that enabled her to fly?" He was clearly mechanically or electronically minded; and the question was a logical one, but not at all mythological. And as I told him, you have to think mythologically if you think about Mary Poppins.

No, it was a perfectly ordinary umbrella, the kind you put up to ward off the rain. I remembered it from my childhood when it was proudly wielded by a maid of my mother's when she went on her Day Out. I had never seen another like it until, on my last trip to New York, my publisher gave

me a long package in pink-and-white striped paper as a farewell present. The antique shops of the United States had been requested to find, if they could, an umbrella handle shaped like a parrot. And one of them did. Ribs and covering were added, and there was an umbrella of the self-same kind that Mary Poppins had—and *has!* Not a sniff of secret mechanism

about it, as you will see if you visit the Donnell Library. For, having given to the Donnell several of my Mary Poppins treasures, I thought the umbrella should be there too. The parrot on the handle probably communes with the wooden Dutch doll that I found for Mary Shepard, the illustrator of the *Mary Poppins* books, so that she could see exactly how I had imagined the chief character to be—stiff, straight, and black-haired, with rosy-pink cheeks and a turned-up nose. And, along with parrot and doll, you will be able to see the

Royal Doulton bowl which was given to me by a godmother when I was three and which formed the basis of the chapter called "Bad Wednesday." And the white china cat covered with blue flowers who was the hero of "The Cat That Looked at the King." I have been so often asked for that cat. "Won't you even *sell* it to me?" asked an importunate lady who came to my very door in New York. And, of course, the answer was No. That cat was my friend, he came from the potteries at Quimper in Brittany. How could one sell a friend?

Then, together with these treasures, you will find all the small works of art or craft that Miss Andrew sent back from the South Seas in the story called "The Faithful Friends" in *Mary Poppins in the Park*—a pair of Staffordshire pottery lions, each with his paw on the breast of a soldier; a little celluloid winged horse that I won in a shooting gallery at a country fair in England; a china circus clown; a paperweight with the words *Home Sweet Home* inscribed over a little house under the glass; a Chelsea china woolly lamb; two children inside an apple or a pear—I forget which —and a little wooden fox.

None of these things is intrinsincally valuable. They are worth, at the most, a few dollars. But to me they are more precious than rubies because so much of my life, and, indeed, Mary Poppins', is wrapped up in them. That is why I gave them to the Donnell Library—for one thing so that they could all be together, and for another so that from time to time, when I visit the United States, I can go refresh my memory.

After all, in England, I have the Park,

where all the adventures happen. It is just around the corner from me. So I like to think that, with this little Donnell collection, New York too has something of Mary Poppins.

The Trial of John Peter Zenger

CATHARINE EDMONDS

John Peter Zenger was thirteen when he landed in New York in 1710. He was lucky to have survived the hard Atlantic voyage, but all the suffering he had endured to face this wild, unknown country was better than enduring the ruthless tyranny, wars, and starvation in Germany.

In ten years he became a free citizen and skilled in the craft of printing. After serving as the official printer for the province of Maryland, he returned to New York and set up his own printing shop. He and his family flourished.

Meanwhile, William Cosby became British Governor of New York. He planned to replenish the fortune he had squandered in Europe by taking money from the colonists.

Chief Justice Morris would not comply with the Governor's dirty dealings. On one occasion Morris ruled directly in writing against the Governor. The printer Morris employed was John Peter Zenger.

Morris quickly became ex-Chief Justice.

He then ran against one of Cosby's candidates for the Provincial Assembly, furious that Cosby had already appointed this candidate to another office. Morris won by a large majority. Cosby tried to fix a re-election, but Morris won again.

A dangerous conflict now came to the fore. According to British law, criticizing the government was considered not just slander, but treason and sedition. The penalty was death. Backed by Morris, Zenger put out the first issue of the New York *Weekly Journal,* which described the corrupt election tactics and the importance of every citizen's freedom to criticize the government.

The Governor couldn't suppress the popular paper entirely, but he ordered four editions to be publicly burned as a warning. Hardly anyone showed up for the burning; not even city officials attended.

Zenger was then arrested and thrown in jail on the third floor of City Hall (later Federal Hall). He refused to name the authors of the articles. Two prominent lawyers, probably the authors, demanded his release, first on a writ. When that failed, they tried to raise bail, which Judge De Lancey, Morris's pro-Cosby replacement, set impossibly high. Zenger remained in prison for almost a year. Only one issue of the *Weekly Journal* failed to come out during this time.

On August 4, 1735, he was taken to the second-floor courtroom to be tried for publishing treasonous material. The hostile De Lancey was presiding judge and had succeeded in disbarring Zenger's two lawyers. Every legal precedent stood against the printer, now defenseless as well as alone.

Then a stately old gentleman stepped forward and announced his intention to defend the printer. He was none other than Andrew Hamilton (not related to Alexander), one of the finest lawyers in Pennsylvania.

Yes, Zenger had admittedly published these articles, his argument ran, but they were the truth—not libel or treason. He asked the jury to view this trial not in terms of one man's guilt or innocence, but as a precedent for the right to speak out against tyranny.

The prosecutor seized upon Hamilton's admission that Zenger was the culprit, and before the jury retired, Judge De Lancey *ordered* them to decide exclusively on the basis of whether the articles had been printed, which meant, of course, a verdict of guilty.

It took the jury ten minutes to decide. "Not guilty." The courtroom broke into cheering. It was a great day for a new concept of freedom, freedom of the press, which would later form the basis of the First Amendment of the Constitution—thanks to the eloquence of Andrew Hamilton and the unwavering courage of the quiet printer, John Peter Zenger.

The Children's Express

FRANCESCA LYMAN

You never know when you could be in a magazine. Any place, any time in New York City you could be approached and asked for an interview by a band of kids with tape recorders and cameras, wearing yellow T-shirts that say "CHILDREN'S EXPRESS News Team." Be ready for them, for they are feature reporters for *Children's Express,* the national news and feature magazine written by children. Your answers to their questions could be published in their "Roving Reporter" column.

Or maybe you would prefer to ask the questions! If you do, and you are thirteen or under, you can become a reporter. Besides interviewing kids on the street, there are many other stories you could do. Chris Clay, twelve, a seventh grader from New York, caught an interview with Jimmy Carter at the Democratic Convention. Before going to the convention, he and thirty other reporters did a special interview with Walter Cronkite, Dan Rather, Roger Mudd, and Edwin Newman to learn their trade secrets. The kids knew next to nothing about politics when they started, but they astounded the press when an eleven-year-old reporter scooped the convention with the news of Mondale as Jimmy Carter's running mate. In the course of covering both conventions and the inauguration, they got exclusive interviews with everyone—Miz Lillian, Rosalynn, and Amy Carter, Paul O'Dwyer, the late Mayor Daley and Nelson Rockefeller, Ramsey Clark, and many more.

Children's Express now has about 130 reporters on its New York staff alone. A national magazine based in New York, it is read by about 400,000 people—adults as well as children—throughout the United States and Canada. Stories are assigned in New York, and most of the support comes from the New York staff of kid reporters and editors. There are now teams in many other cities here and abroad, but it's still easiest to get to *Children's Express* if you live in the New York area.

Many places and events in New York have been sources for stories. From the center ring of the Ringling Bros. Barnum & Bailey Circus at Madison Square Garden, reporters spoke to circus children (more than forty) who are trapeze artists, bareback riders, and elephant trainers. They have also visited film studios to interview stars (Jodie Foster and Scott Baio, and the crew of *Bugsy Malone*), TV studios to talk to anchor people (NewsCenter 4), and the theater (Doug Henning of *The Magic Show*). In an interesting interview with Jimmy Breslin of the *Daily News,* CE reporters were told about John Steinbeck's being discovered by a New York publisher who found one of his books in a second-hand store. "Six publishing houses could turn it down and still somebody would find it in New York City. That's why this city is so great . . . if you're good you're always going to get discovered here."

Michael Schreibman, fourteen, was discovered by *Children's Express* at the Democratic Convention. He tagged along with the T-shirted crew and eventually became an integral part of the magazine. In fact, he created the role of assistant editor. Since he was already over thirteen, he couldn't be a reporter, so he evolved the editor role, and now is an associate editor, which means he trains other editors, as well as reporters, and is present at interviews if help is needed. He is also one of the magazine's principal photographers. For Michael, *Children's Express* is a means "for kids to be journalists." He enjoys the opportunity to get involved in national politics and to learn audio techniques. He says his greatest accomplishment with the magazine so far was "finding out four days in advance that Jimmy Carter would be at the UN, getting credentials, and then being able to cover him." He also commented on some of the controversial topics that the magazine is becoming involved in, such as stories on children who have children, kids being sent to mental institutions without cause, and a ten-part series on child abuse.

His advice to New York kids who are interested is to call in ideas, or send in written pieces. They can also get a bunch of friends together into a news team and conduct interviews. One story got into the magazine because a former child opera singer called up with the idea of interviewing the Metropolitan Opera children's chorus. Not only do kids initiate all the ideas, Michael says, but they initiate contacts, make decisions among themselves, and do all the work. You can't become a reporter unless you are willing to work very hard. A trip to the office will show you kids at the phones taking notes and making arrangements in a very professional way.

An important source for the magazine is unsolicited submissions. None of these has been used as a major story, but they are always used in some way, even if they are rewritten sometimes, or go into the "Caboose" section at the end of the magazine. No story is considered too small.

These are some things you can send in:

drawings	pen pals
photos	reviews of books, movies, events
inventions	
cartoons	stories about: children's achievements
jokes	
puzzles	what children do: performers, dog trainers, pilots, etc.
mazes	
magic tricks	
opinions	children in business
essays	product reviews about things to buy
recipes	
science reports	fashion and fads
hobbies	a day in the life of a kid
letters about problems	

If you are under thirteen, you can become a reporter for *CE*. To do this you must learn how to research story ideas, prepare for a story by clearing it with the New York office, and to use a tape recorder.

You can become an assistant editor (if you are fourteen to sixteen) and learn how to support the reporters, set up stories, and conduct interviews. Send for the "Assistant Editor Manual."

Even if you don't want credentials as an *Express* reporter, you are welcome to send in story ideas and writing, photographs or art. If you want your work returned, send a stamped, self-addressed envelope to Dept. ED, *Children's Express*, 20 Charles Street, New York, New York 10014. Reporters and writers will be paid from $5 to $15 for work published. Assistant editors will get $10 to $25 for published stories they've worked on.

THE GOVERNMENT PRINTING OFFICE

STANLEE BRIMBERG

Controlling Fleas, The First Spectrum of Hafnium, Painful Trapping Devices, Aunt Sammy's Radio Recipes, what do these things have in common? They are all titles of books available at the U. S. Government Printing Office at 26 Federal Plaza in downtown Manhattan, a useful place to know about.

Among the hundreds of publications for sale are: fact sheets about a hundred or so countries, health and nutrition guides, books about Indians, gardening, energy conservation, and clothing repair. There is a phrasebook for Tagalog, one of the official languages of the Philippines, a complete course in photography, and a recipe book for catfish.

There just may be a book on exactly what you need to know.

Visit this unusual bookstore and see for yourself.

The New York Public Library employs book detectives, to track down stolen books.

POPULAR ITEMS

Three of the subjects most frequently consulted in the New York Public Library Central Branch are drugs, astrology, and Shakespeare.

POTPOURRI

(concrete poem composed of typewriter characters depicting a park, a city skyline, the Goodyear blimp, and buildings labeled "tall," "macys," "busy," "circus," "madison square")

The Smiths

WALTER MYERS

There was a man named Jeremy Smith
Whose wisdom was not his fame:
He married a lass named Sally Smith
So she did not change her name.

Things worked quite well at first
As they learned to do things in twos
But then one day dear Sally asked
Which name did they use.

"It's Mr. and Mrs. Smith, of course
But whose name have we taken?
Is it yours, or mine, my love
And whose has been forsaken?"

"It's mine, of course," said Mr. Smith
"For I'm the man you know,
  And custom states my Smith must stay
  And yours, my dear, must go."

"Well, custom fie!" dear Sally said,
"We'll have to mend our ways.
  We'll use your Smith, and then use mine
  On alternating days!"

That worked for a week
But things are now confused
For they argue each day and quarrel each
    night
Over whose Smith last was used.

219

Old Father Knickerbocker

STEPHEN MOOSER

Diedrich Knickerbocker was reputed to be an old Dutch gentleman with a flair for history. As the story goes he checked into the Independent Colombian Hotel one day, stayed quite a while, and then departed suddenly without paying his bill.

The innkeeper, checking Knickerbocker's room, found a manuscript titled *Knickerbocker's History of New York From the Beginning of the World to The End of the Dutch Dynasty.* Shortly thereafter, in 1809, the innkeeper had the book published to help satisfy the bill. The book was a satirical look at early New York history and its first three Dutch governors in particular. It was an immediate success and the real author was soon unmasked. The perpetrator of the little hoax was none other than Washington Irving, who went on to write many other famous books including *The Legend of Sleepy Hollow.*

Forty years later Irving noted with satisfaction that New Yorkers were now proudly calling themselves Knickerbockers. When I see that there are now such things as a Knickerbocker Society, a Knickerbocker Insurance Company, a Knickerbocker Bread and a Knickerbocker Ice Company, I please myself with the persuasion that I have struck the right chord," said Irving.

And he's still striking the right chord. New York today boasts scores of Knickerbockers, including the Knickerbocker Awning Company, Knickerbocker Coffee Shop, Knickerbocker Funeral Car Corporation, Knickerbocker Sanitation Company, the Knickerbocker Wine Company, Knickerbocker Beer, and, of course, the New York Knickerbocker Basketball Team.

Song

RUTH KRAUSS

on paper
I write it
on rain

I write it
on stones
on my boots

on trees
I write it
on the air

on the city
how pretty
I write my name

WHAT'S IN A NAME?

The Manhattan Telephone directory lists 3,277 Smiths, 2,811 Browns, 2,446 Williamses, and 2,073 Cohens.

THE DREADFUL DRAWKCAB

EVE MERRIAM

It's live and evil,
it will step on pets,
set part of a trap,
stab at bats,
turn a star into rats.

Discovering Columbus Circle
This is where freedom of speech can be witnessed going at its fullest force.— Long may it rave! (a view from my window)

Don Freeman
1941

A FRACTURED
NEW YORK GLOSSARY

OLGA LITOWINSKY

NIGHT LIFE	The roaches in the kitchen when the light is out.
ST. PATRICK	The man who invented the green bagel.
BIKE	Something that disappears when you turn your back.
CAR	Something you can't find a place to park.
TAXI	Something that disappears in the rain.
BUS	Same thing only bigger, except on Fifth Avenue, where they disappear in bunches.
GEORGE WASHINGTON BRIDGE	Amazing achievement by early president.
BROOKLYN BRIDGE	Card game played in Flatbush.
RUSH HOUR	All day.
EMPIRE STATE BUILDING	The world's tallest building on Thirty-fourth Street.
FUEL EARL	Heating fluid sold in Brooklyn.
QUEENS	Wives of Kings
MANHATTAN	Name to be changed to Personhattan (legislation pending).
BRONX	More than one Bronk.
STATEN ISLAND	Dutch exclamation at first sighting: "Stat an island?"
BROOKLYN	Indefinable.
TAR BEACH	Apartment house rooftops—last resort in hot weather.

1

2

City Problems for which a
solution can be found . . . .

Poem

WALTER MYERS

Pittering, pattering, split and splat
The raindrops fall upon my hat
So quick as a bunny I stand on my hands
And now the rain goes down my pants

3

4

INVITATION
TO A DIFFERENT DAY

JEAN LITTLE

All you who live within New York
For whom it's simply "home,"
Try to think how you'd picture it
If you'd grown up in Rome

Or Tel-Aviv or Saskatoon
Or Perth or Monterrey,
And, somehow, you had won a trip
To New York for one day.

Now, walking down your street, pretend
That you're the one who came.
You've never seen New York before.
Does it look just the same?

One day to spend! Where will you go?
I wonder what you'll do
To celebrate this day on which
New York is really new.

Try something that you've never tried.
Sight-see, sound-hear! Explore.
Discover things you never dreamed
Were there to find before.

Adventures beckon everywhere.
It would be such a pity
If, just because it's home, you missed
The lure of New York City!

California Kids Look at New York

MYRA COHN LIVINGSTON

It came as a surprise to my classes in the four elementary schools of Beverly Hills, California, that I would ask them to write something about their ideas of New York City. A few had been born there, a few had visited; they sensed that sky-scrapers, the Empire State Building, the Statue of Liberty, and subways were part of what went on in a place three thousand miles away. They were invited to use their knowledge or imagination, and the following words and poems are what followed:

The streets are busy.
The buses have to run.
You've got to hurry to lose
    the crowd.
But still the people are the same.
We walk the same.
We talk the same.
So still we are the same.

> Jennifer Factor
> Grade 2
> El Rodeo School

Two girls, both fifth-graders, remembered New York:

When I think about New York City
I think of the outside of my old
    apartment in black and white,
But when I think about Central Park
And flowered carriages that take you
    for a ride,
I think in color.

> Nina Bari Cutler
> Grade 5
> Beverly Vista School

One contrasted her life in California to New York:

If I was in New York now,
I'd be sitting by the fire
    drinking hot chocolate.
I'm in California instead
    heating up from the warm air,
Trying to find an air-conditioner!

> Melissa Heather Weinstein
> Grade 5
> El Rodeo School

The Statue of Liberty was a favorite for many:

That big Golden Woman in the sky,
Her royal crown that sits upon her head
With a torch in one hand and a book in
    the other
Just stands there,
Never moving a royal inch from her royal
    platform.

> Jennifer Jessum
> Grade 3
> Beverly Vista School

A number of children had questions or comments about the Statue of Liberty:

Statue of Liberty,
Does your eye see things in the sky?
Your hand is so big.
Is it big as a house or a tree?
Do you touch the sky,
Or a plane in the sky?

> Andrew Zax
> Grade 2
> Hawthorne School

Hey you, there,
The one with the torch!
You're the cause of all our trouble.
You're the cause of all our smog.
Why don't you put your torch out?
You've got that book there—
Doesn't it say anything about pollution?
Doesn't it say not to pollute?
You're supposed to greet the people,
Not make them sick.
Just turn it off
Or *you* won't make it much longer!

> Daniel Loftman Hurewitz
> Grade 5
> Beverly Vista School

In cinquain form, many asked this question:

Doesn't
your arm ever
get tired, Statue of
Liberty, holding up your torch
so high?

> Melissa Heather Weinstein
> Grade 5
> El Rodeo

Skyscrapers and the Empire State Building were popular subjects for comparisons, questions, and comments in many forms:

Finger,
Yes you, you big
thing pointing at the sky
on top of the Empire State
Building,

Are you
telling me to
jump up to the sky
to see what the world looks like
from *there?*

> Carissa Wong
> Grade 5
> Hawthorne School

Empire State
with your needle
so sharp,

I've had my shots.

Can't you see
My shots are all over.
I don't want them again.
So keep your needle
Away!

> Lisa Shaw
> Grade 4
> Beverly Vista School

Stretching
skyscrapers are
children's arms reaching for
the high-shelved cooky jar, with their
moms gone.

> David Chao
> Grade 7
> Horace Mann School

A touch of humor permeated one quatrain:

New York City is lovely and has no crime.
The streets are clean and free of grime.
But that's a cinch for me to say—
I live in Calif-or-ni-ay!

> Nina Cutler
> Grade 5
> Beverly Vista School

Fond memories of New York prompted this:

As you go up—your stomach goes down,
Around, around and around again,
And when you stop—oh! the pain—
You're finally at the top.
You look out the window, 110 floors up.
You feel nauseous and kind of dizzy
And your head starts spinning
Until you look—
Until you look at the lady in the harbor
With her torch reaching the sky
And her proud greenish color
And you realize what a great city
You're in!

> Diana Kaufman
> Grade 5
> Beverly Vista

ST. PATRICK'S CHILDREN

New York City has a larger population of native-born Irish than the Irish cities of Killarney, Donegal, Galway, and Tralee put together.

GIMME SHELTER

How come brand-new bus shelters were built just when New York City was facing bankruptcy? Because the city didn't have to pay for them, that's why.

The idea was the brainstorm of a Paris businessman, William Bouchara, who decided to do something nice for his second favorite city. A private company builds and maintains the shelters, then rents advertising space. New York City gets 5 percent of the fees collected from advertisers, plus a permit fee for each shelter erected.

So, everyone's happy. Especially New Yorkers who wait for buses in the rain.

Patricia

A PROFILE OF A NEW YORK KID

Patty, thirteen, is the youngest of three sisters in an Irish family on Manhattan's Upper West Side, half a block from Central Park. She goes to St. Gregory's School and is in the eighth grade.

Twice, Patty's family went to Ireland to live and came back to New York. The last time was when she was nearly ten. She has lived in Wicklow and Galway, where playing was more fun, but Patty likes school better here.

Her abiding passion (as well as that of her sisters) is the rock group from Scotland, the Bay City Rollers. All three girls lost their voices at Madison Square Garden when the group appeared there, screaming and shouting with thousands of other avid fans.

Patty's hobbies include rock music, collecting half dollars and stamps, and reading. Her favorite magazines are *Sixteen* and *Tiger Beat*. Her most treasured possession? Her diary.

Performers from the Big Apple Circus show their stuff. Emigrés from Russia, teenagers from the Bronx, dancers from Argentina, and street performers from everywhere delight audiences in New York's only permanent circus, founded in 1977.

NEW YORK SEAWAYS

Island of Tears

BARBARA BEASLEY MURPHY

Ellis Island was designated an immigration station in 1890. More than half the immigrants entering the United States between 1892 and 1924 passed through its gates. It was an anxious passing.

Every day the place teemed with people. Only a short time before, they had had their first glimpse of New York's tall buildings and the Statue of Liberty. After the many days on a dark ship, the statue symbolized all their dreams. But first came Ellis Island.

The noise and commotion of the place were unbelievable. Many languages were spoken at once. Tags were attached to the immigrants' coats. Guards called out their numbers and shouted, "Keep moving," "Hurry up." In a group the immigrant was pushed along one of the dozens of metal railings that divided the room into several passageways until he reached the inspector who looked at hands, face, hair, and neck. Another inspector asked questions. "What is your age? What work do you do?" Then there was an inspection for diseases. Then an eye inspection. Anyone who didn't pass was marked for deportation. He had to return from where he had come, his dreams for a new life extinguished.

The final inspector asked, "Can you read and write? Do you have a job waiting for you? Who paid your passage? Have you ever been in prison? How much money do you have? Let me see it," and more. The buildings of Ellis Island echoed with shouting, crying, and laughing. After passing all the examinations, the immigrant was given a landing card. He was free to enter the United States and begin the process of becoming an American citizen.

Ahoy, Mate!

During the summer months you can take a cruise on a real gaff-rigged sailing ship. The ship is the schooner *Pioneer,* built at Marcus Hook, Pennsylvania, in 1885. The South Street Seaport Museum has re-outfitted the ship and for twelve dollars (half fare for children) you can help sail her around the harbor on a three-hour cruise.

If you prefer to be a landlubber you can tour the museum's permanently moored old sailing vessels docked at the Fulton Street piers. There are also museums, shops, and galleries filled with nautical mementos from yesterday. It all can be found at the South Street Seaport Museum at 16 Fulton Street, open daily from noon to 6 P.M.

Mini Liberty

At 43 West 64 Street, just across from Lincoln Center, is a 55-foot replica of the 151-foot Statue of Liberty. William H. Flatteau ordered the statue built in 1902 and had it erected above his warehouse on West Sixty-fourth. Like its big sister, the statue once had a lighted torch, a spiral staircase, and a hole in its head through which the city could be viewed. However, a big storm in 1912 blew off the torch and weakened the staircase so badly that people were no longer allowed to ascend into the lady's head. The statue, however, is still very much visible above Mr. Flatteau's old warehouse.

KNICKERS

BROOKLYN-BORN WARSHIP

The *Monitor,* famous warship of the Civil War, was launched from Greenpoint, in Brooklyn, on January 30, 1862.

Skyline Crossword

ACROSS

2. Grant's _____ is a historic landmark on Riverside Drive.
6. Nathan's of Coney Island is known for making the _____ _____ a national habit.
9. A pastry with a filling.
10. The city official who lives in Gracie Mansion.
11. Age, period.
12. A boy's name, for short, or a kind of turkey.
13. Latest radio craze.
14. Kind of music played on WABC-AM in New York.
17. The New York Telephone Company is often referred to as ____ Bell.
18. Short greeting.
20. One of the features at Radio City Music Hall.
22. Abbreviation for road.
24. The Verrazano Bridge connecting Brooklyn and Staten Island crosses New York _____.
25. Rule of government.
26. Nickname for New York City.
28. Skin of an orange.
30. Initials of famous building and organization.
32. The New York Mets are a baseball _____.
33. Center of the solar system.
34. Original settlers of New York.

DOWN

1. Lad, fellow.
3. What Beverly Sills sings at Lincoln Center.
4. Painter whose work hangs in the Museum of Modern Art.
5. Coney Island, Brighton, Orchard, Midland, Rye, or Jones.
6. Amateur radio operator or Christmas dinner.
7. The kind of store F. A. O. Schwartz is.
8. Abbreviation for Doctor.
10. Something that comes out at night.
13. A famous amusement area is _____ Island.
15. Oven for baking ceramics.
16. Most famous street in the world.
17. Short name for opera house in New York City.
19. Slang for all right.
21. Famous postcard view.
22. Torn and tattered cloth.
23. What little ones sit on.
25. Stone animals in front of the New York Public Library.
27. Name of New York City river.
28. New York Yankees home run king was Babe _____.
29. Speechless.
31. Printed sales pitch found on buses, subways, etc.

(SOLUTION, PG. 376.)

Rosenblum©1977

New York from the Harbor

SCOTT CORBETT

You have never really seen New York City's skyline until you have seen it from the harbor.

The last time my wife and I saw it properly was when we took a trip on a freighter. Freighters are cargo ships but some of them take passengers—never more than twelve. When we sailed from Pier 9A in Brooklyn in February, the water was full of cakes of ice. We sailed late at night, but in spite of the cold we stayed out on deck to look at the lights in the thousands of windows of the skyscrapers that make up the magical skyline of New York City. In front of them, out in the harbor, the Statue of Liberty held her bright torch high in the air.

After half an hour or so, a great string of lights swung above us, the lights of the huge Verrazano-Narrows Bridge. Beyond the Narrows lay the Atlantic Ocean—fortunately for us, it was in a good mood that night. We were off on a trip around the world.

We crossed the Atlantic Ocean and the Mediterranean Sea without stopping, then went through the Suez Canal. Our first port was Jedda, in Saudi Arabia, on the Red Sea. Then came Singapore, ports in Malaysia, Indonesia, and Borneo, then Manila and Hong Kong, Taiwan and Japan. Along the way we saw other impressive skylines, especially in Hong Kong, which has an astonishing number of tall buildings and one of the most dramatic and interesting harbors in the world; but nothing equals New York's skyline.

When we sailed from Yokohama in Japan, we traveled for twenty days at sea without stopping, until we reached the Panama Canal. On the other side of the Canal, our first port in the United States was Miami, which we reached exactly eighty days from the time we sailed from

New York. Around the world in eighty days!

A few days later, after stops at Savannah, Georgia, and Wilmington, North Carolina, we returned to New York. From a long way out at sea we could see the Verrazano Bridge arched across the Narrows, because this time we were approaching the harbor in the morning. We sailed under the bridge, and there ahead of us stood the Statue of Liberty, and behind her the world's most spectacular skyline.

You don't have to take a trip around the world on a ship, however, to have this experience. Just go down to the Battery some fine day and take the ferry to Staten Island, and you will see it all—the greatest single sight New York City has to offer.

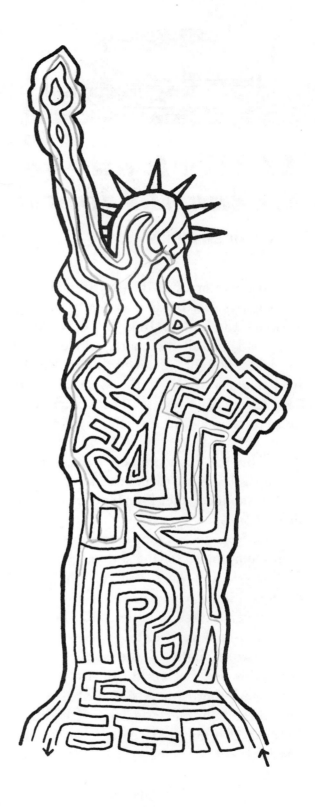

MISS LIBERTY MAZE

See if you can find your way up to the torch in Miss Liberty's hand and down again by a different path. (SOLUTION, PG. 376.)

At Work on the Statue of Liberty

NORAH SMARIDGE

In the winter of 1875, the French sculptor Auguste Bartholdi was ready to begin work on the statue. In a large workshop, he spread out all his charts and drawings. He had thought of everything. He had even made a study of the weather on the East Coast of America. The statue would have to stand firm in storms and hurricanes.

One by one, his workmen arrived—metalworkers, plasterers, carpenters by the dozen. They examined the four-foot model curiously.

"First," Auguste said, "we must decide what metal to use for the statue."

"Not stone," said one of the metalworkers. "Stone would be too heavy."

"Bronze?" asked another. But bronze is heavy too—and very costly.

Auguste thought of the statues he had seen all over the world. In Italy, he remembered, there was a statue of San Carlo Borromeo, standing by a lake. It had stood there for two hundred years, in all kinds of weather, so it must be strong. It was made of copper.

"We will make the statue of copper," he told the men. "And it will be 151 feet high." The men gasped. Auguste went on, "We will begin by making a model four times the height of my nine-foot working model."

When this was done, the thirty-six-foot model was carefully taken apart. Each section was made in plaster again and again, each time a larger size, until it was the right size for the real statue.

To make the parts, copper sheets the thickness of a silver dollar were pressed into wood patterns. Then they were hammered into shape by hand.

All this did not happen in a hurry. Twenty men worked ten hours a day for weeks to make parts for the right arm and the hand holding the torch. As they worked Auguste went from man to man, examining the parts closely. Everything must be exactly right. The statue must be strong enough to last forever.

"This is a long, hard job, sir," one of the men said one day. "What happens when all these copper parts are made?"

Auguste smiled. "We will fasten them onto a steel frame," he said. "Don't worry about that now. Gustave Eiffel is going to design it for us."

The newspapermen heard about what was going on and pushed their way into the workshop. Pointing to a heavy plaster cast lying on the floor, one of them asked, "What is that gun for?"

"It is not a gun," Auguste said. "That is the torch which Miss Liberty will raise in her hand."

The newspapermen poked and pried. "What are these five rifles? No woman can shoot five rifles at once."

Auguste laughed. "Those are Miss Liberty's fingers. And if you look over there you will see her hand. We have just finished it."

The newspapermen rushed back to their offices and began to write stories about what they had seen. "The thumbnail of the statue is a foot long . . . A boy could stand up in Liberty's thumb . . . The statue will have a steel frame, strong as a bridge."

In New York City, the special French newspaper had glaring headlines about Miss Liberty's progress:

LIBERTY IS SO BIG
YOUR HEAD ONLY REACHES HER KNEE

LIBERTY'S CALF
IS AS THICK AS A GIANT TREE

HER THIGH
IS AS BIG AS A CANNON

THE FOLDS OF LIBERTY'S GOWN
COULD HOLD BARRELS OF WATER

LIBERTY IS SO TALL
YOU CANNOT SEE HER HEAD

FULTON FISH MARKET

See how many five-letter words you can make from the bold letters above. Plurals, proper nouns, or more than one form of a word are not allowed. (SOLUTION, PG. 375.)

Please Be Magical

SHEILA MOON

Jic stuck the box into his pocket and wiped his face on his sleeve. "It's a hotter day than I had wanted, and scratchier."

"And stinkier," said his companion. "And I still don't know why we're doing whatever we're doing."

Sightseers shoved the boy and girl off the ferry and onto the path leading to the huge statue. Jic pulled the girl to the side and pointed to the city. "Look, Lonny, it's like everyone's burning trash at the same time! You can't see anything except through dirty air! That's why we're doing this!"

The crowds carried them on toward the stone entrance. Guides shouted information to large tour groups. Jic and Lonny pushed through and hurried to the elevator. "After this, we walk," Jic stated.

The moment the elevator opened they were out. "Is this where the stairs begin?" Lonny asked.

"Yes. Here we go. Fast, but not too fast because it's a long way."

They climbed and climbed and climbed. "It's a hundred and sixty-eight steps to her head," Jic said, over his shoulder.

"Okay, Mr. Smart. Then how do we get to her torch?"

"My dad knows a guy that works here. He's going to let us up. I hope." Jic looked at the jam of people pushing into the openings. He pulled Lonny around a corner to a door. He knocked.

TOYS

berthe

A man with a dark face and nice brown eyes opened the door. "Closed—Oops, it's you, Jic. Come in!" He shut the door behind them. "There are fifty-four rungs on this ladder, kids. I'm coming up behind you. You can't have long because it's really against the rules. Let's go." The three of them arrived at the top breathless, shaky-legged. "Do what you want to do quick. Only a few minutes, see."

Jic and Lonny walked to the window. Jic took out his box and set it on the ledge with great care. He turned to Lonny. "I've got twelve fireflies here. I gathered them on my uncle's farm yesterday. My dad said fireflies are magic—some Indians called their poems fireflies in the night." He paused, wondering whether what he was about to do and say was silly. He decided it wasn't. "There's a poem on this statue somewhere. It says the tired, the poor, and the homeless can come here and be free. The last line says, 'I lift my lamp beside the golden door.'" He sighed. "The door isn't golden any more, the tired and the poor can't breathe, and how can her lamp be seen in the smog?" He opened the box and turned the insects onto the ledge. Slowly he blew them into flight. Lonny took his hand, and they watched while the fireflies disappeared into yellow-gray air.

"Please be magical! Please!" Jic said softly.

"Yes, please do," Lonny added.

"Time to go down," said the man with the nice eyes.

As they sat together on the return ferry, they kept looking back. "I guess because she's a she," Lonny said thoughtfully, "she just might let the fireflies help her. Don't you think so?"

Jic nodded. "Let's say yes!"

Come All Ye Seafarers...

PAMELA MORTON

For all you seafaring boys and girls there is a part of the city which can become yours and which is one of the most exciting things to happen in New York in many years.

If you take a subway to Fulton Street in Manhattan and walk east to the river you will arrive at the South Street Seaport Museum. Tied up at a pier are ships which have been rescued from retirement and which are being restored so that we can see and feel what the great seaport of New York was like in the nineteenth century.

Next to the Fulton Street Fish Market, where fish are unloaded and sold in the early hours of the morning for all of New York, is a Gloucester fishing schooner, the *Lettie G. Howard*. Something is always happening on board, from splitting and salting fish to singing sea chanteys.

Farther down the pier is the *Ambrose Lightship*, the famous floating lighthouse which for many years guided ships safely toward the port of New York. On the other side of the pier there are two great rigged ships, the *Wavertree* and the *Peking*.

The Museum and the Seaport extend to seven blocks of buildings which are in the process of restoration. There is no end to the bustling activity which goes on every day at South Street.

SUPERTANKER FROM BROOKLYN

GEORGE SULLIVAN

Cutting torches crackle. Crane engines hum. Warning bells clang. Thick steel plates creak and groan as they are cut and bent into intricate shapes. Out of this bedlam at the former Navy shipyard on the shore of the East River in Brooklyn, the supertanker *Bay Ridge* is taking shape.

The *Bay Ridge* is the fourth in a series of such vessels being built by the Seatrain Shipbuilding Corporation at the Brooklyn site. They are among the biggest ships ever built in the United States, and the biggest ever to fly the American flag.

The *Bay Ridge,* like its three sister ships —1,094 feet in length—is so big that three football games could be played end to end on its deck. The ship's cargo tanks are capable of carrying one and a half million barrels of petroleum, enough to fill a fifty-mile line of tanker trucks, or power the au-tomobiles and heat the homes of such cities as Green Bay, Wisconsin, or Bethlehem, Pennsylvania, for an entire winter.

The *Bay Ridge* is being put together in a dry dock, a structure that resembles a huge concrete bathtub, the bottom of which is sixty feet below water level. Powerful cranes hoist completed ship sections into place. When the ship is completely assembled, the dry dock will be flooded like the lock of a canal and the *Bay Ridge* will float. After several months at an outfitting pier, the ship will be nudged by tugs out into the East River, and will then steam out toward the open ocean for several days of trial runs. Soon after, the ship will go into full operation.

OPPOSITE PAGE: The supertanker, *Bay Ridge,* in dry dock in the former Brooklyn Navy Yard.

New York City by the Sea

LAUREN L. WOHL

It's easy to forget, when you're standing in the middle of Manhattan surrounded by skyscrapers, concrete, and asphalt, that New York City is actually surrounded by water and that some of the city's most exciting features are a direct result of this geographical fact. There's an area in Brooklyn, for example, that puts this fact to the utmost advantage. It's called Sheepshead Bay, and it's a nautical paradise.

There isn't anything relating to the sea that you can't do in Sheepshead Bay. One of the largest charter fishing fleets on the East Coast makes its home there. These boats can be taken out for single-day fishing excursions. They offer a variety of luxuries from on-board restaurants and snack bars to heated fishing rails for those colder mornings. The catch ranges from fluke, blackfish, porgies, and sea bass to blues and flounder, depending on what's running in season. Boats leave on regular schedules each morning (starting as early as 5 A.M. and as late as 10 A.M.). They cruise out to areas where experienced sea captains with names like Rocky and Tootsie know "the fish are biting," and return to the piers beginning at 3 P.M. It's exciting to watch the fishermen disembark with their burlap bags full of the day's catch. Regular crew members offer their catch for sale, and buyers can find real bargains on fresh fish.

There are also boats for private charter, boats which can accommodate whole families or small groups of people. And for the less adventurous, there's always fishing off the piers and the wooden pedestrian bridge which connects Sheepshead Bay to Manhattan Beach. Pier fishing techniques range from simple drop-lines to poles to rods and reels. Using bait such as clams, shrimps, spearing, and small lures, pier fishing can bring in snappers and, on occasion, flounder. There's also crabbing, using simple traps, and at night, with the aid of a flashlight and scoop net, the fishing goes on.

The needs of fishermen, whether it's simply bait or the whole gamut of equipment, can be completely met in any one of several fishing, tackle, and bait shops which border the pier and surrounding areas.

And if a day's fishing proves not too fruitful, Sheepshead Bay offers restaurants galore. There is the world-famous Lundy's, of course, but there are also many other restaurants featuring oyster bars, clam chowder, and fresh fish—what else? In the mood for just a snack? There are plenty of quick-eateries as well.

Sheepshead Bay also boasts a couple of ferry boats. One brief trip goes around the bay, stopping at nearby Breezy Point to let passengers off for a day at the beach. Another ferry offers a three-hour lectured tour of the Gateway National Recreation Area Park now being established by the federal government.

What's more: Sheepshead Bay is beautiful. You'll enjoy just walking around it, smelling the sea air, viewing the boat-spotted horizon, seeing authentic old salts care for their boats with expertise and love, being a part of New York City by the sea.

THE BOROUGHS
OF NEW YORK

THE BIG AIRPORTS

John F. Kennedy International Airport is operated by the Port Authority of New York and New Jersey. It is located in the southeastern section of Queens County on Jamaica Bay and is fifteen miles by highway from midtown Manhattan. It covers 4,930 acres and is nine times the size of La Guardia Airport. About $60,000,000 was spent by the City of New York on its original construction and to date the Port Authority has invested approximately $673,000,000 at the airport.

About 39,400 people were employed at the airport in 1977.

The runway system consists of two pairs of parallel runways and there is a fifth runway for private and commuter airplanes. The total length of the runways is nine miles.

There are nine passenger terminals in the center of the airport surrounded by a dual ring of aircraft taxiways. About 145 aircraft gate positions serve the various terminals. There is a ten-story airport control tower, a central heating and air-conditioning plant, the Tri-Faith Chapel Plaza, and parking for over 6,600 autos.

The Air Cargo Center consists of twenty-two cargo handling and cargo service buildings, an Animalport operated by the ASPCA and a U. S. Post Office Airport Mail Facility.

There are thirteen aircraft hangars and a 32-million-gallon aircraft fuel storage facility. There is a Port Authority office and maintenance building, a police building and a medical building.

The International Hotel at the airport

contains 520 rooms. Three rental car service buildings are located at the airport. In addition you will find a Citibank and six food production centers. The airport has over thirty-two miles of roadways.

Located in the Borough of Queens in New York City bordering on Flushing Bay and Bowery Bay is La Guardia Airport. It is eight miles from mid-Manhattan and occupies 650 acres.

The City of New York spent $40,000,000 on its original construction and the Port Authority has invested about $219,735,000 in the development of the airport. In 1977 there were 8,078 persons employed at the airport.

There are two main runways, each seven thousand feet long, and a general aviation runway, two thousand feet long.

Sky Words

LAURIE NORRIS

On a clear day, have you ever been surprised by mysterious writing that appears in the sky? Magically, giant letters that seem to be written by an invisible hand are suddenly filling the empty blue sky with a message.

These letters are really a type of smoke created by planes with special equipment. If one pilot in a fast, easily maneuvered plane is printing or writing words in a continuous stream as you would write with a pen on a piece of paper, the message is sky writing. When the letters are formed horizontally in puffs of smoke, five airplanes are traveling across the sky in a parallel formation, and a computer is printing the letters for them. This display is called sky typing.

For both writing and typing in the heavens, the process is similar. When the day is clear and the sky is bright blue, the planes fly very high into the atmosphere, up to an altitude of at least ten thousand feet where the air is extremely cold. Flying over a hundred miles per hour, the airplanes pump a nonpolluting liquid containing paraffin or oil into this atmosphere as a vapor. The steamlike vapor turns into ice crystals that form the white writing we can see from the earth. Depending upon weather conditions, including the velocity of the wind, the letters can be seen for five to twenty minutes or even longer by many people in a thirty-square-mile area on the ground. Gradually, the letters fade and the message disappears.

Sky writing, which was invented in England about 1920, depends more upon the pilot for its form than sky typing. It may become a lost art; there are fewer than half a dozen sky writers left in the United States. Younger pilots can learn the secrets of this skill only from them. (In some parts of the country, many kids younger than fifteen have never seen sky writing, but only sky typing.) Sky writers draw pictures, also; for instance, on Valentine's Day, a heart has appeared in the sky.

Sky typing, an American invention that is only about twenty-five years old, is gaining popularity. Both displays are known as aerial advertising, and they spread messages for politicians, candy companies, airlines, and ordinary people who want to say something like "Happy Birthday" in a special way.

The mile-high letters can form a message six or seven miles long, and the prices are high, too. A message of twenty letters costs at least four hundred dollars. Most messages run twenty to twenty-five letters long. Check the Manhattan Yellow Pages under "aerial advertising" if you would like someone to put a message in the sky for you.

The next time you admire a clear sky the color of a bluebird, wait. You just might be able to read it!

Rachel

A PROFILE OF A NEW YORK KID

Rachel is in the sixth grade at P.S. 196 in Forest Hills, Queens. She likes art and composition best, and math least, and may be a teacher herself when she grows up. A career as a decorator would be all right with Rachel, too.

At the moment, Rachel's favorite person, the one she would love to spend an afternoon with if she had a dream come true, is Jacqueline Smith, of "Charlie's Angels." However, the person who makes her laugh the most is Peter Sellers.

For fun, Rachel likes to sleep over at a friend's house, or play in the park, or meet her friends at the pizza parlor. If she could stay up all night some time, she would spend the time this way: fix up her room a little, draw something on her shirt, watch a little TV, read a book, and fix a grapefruit for breakfast.

The Names of the Five Boroughs

Manhattan was the Indian name for "island surrounded by hills."

Richmond was named after the Duke of Richmond.

Brooklyn is named for a village in Holland called Breuckelen.

Queens is named after Catherine, the English Queen.

The Bronx was named after Jonas Bronck, a Dane who made the first settlement there for the Dutch West India Company.

MULTIPLICATION

"New York City" meant only the island of Manhattan until 1898, when the other four boroughs became part of it.

METAMORPHOSIS

Flushing Meadow Park, in Queens, was first a swamp, then a garbage dump, and then a park. The United Nations General Assembly met there before their permanent headquarters was completed on the East River. In 1939 and in 1964 the Park was the site of the New York World's Fair. The Hall of Science, part of the 1964 Fair, remains today, a museum of science and technology.

Wooden sidewalks along Flatbush Avenue, Brooklyn, in 1880.

WHEN THE CITY OF BROOKLYN WAS SEVEN YEARS OLD

In 1841, when Brooklyn had a population of 35,500, there was only one major thoroughfare, Fulton Street (known today as Cadman Plaza West), which petered out into a country road. The Heights were merely a bluff, Court Street was unknown, and Sands Street was where the aristocrats lived. City Hall stood at the corner of Cranberry and Henry streets. Williamsburgh was looking upon Brooklyn as a dangerous rival while Bedford had hopes of its own. A great newspaper was born that year in Brooklyn—the *Eagle*.

There were only two thousand miles of railroad in the whole United States at that time. Times were changing fast. Sealing wax and goosequill pens were going out as envelopes and steel pens were coming in. The first steamer from England had arrived in the Port of New York three years earlier, and there was talk about building iron ships. John Tyler was President, Samuel Morse was about to lay his first telegraph wires, and candles were steadily being replaced with fish-oil lamps even though some people were saying that gas was the light of the future.

O.L.

246

LIMERICK

CATHARINE EDMONDS

There was a young man from Astoria
Who loved a young neighbor named
Gloria.
Then he moved to Manhattan,
His fortunes to trap, and
Said, "Don't wanna see any more o' ya."

الهنلتيكس افنيو

(Atlantic Avenue)

BARBARA HENNESSY

"Atlantic Avenue" in Brooklyn is "Main Street" for New York City's Near Eastern (Syrian, Lebanese, Yemenite, Palestinian, etc.) population. If you're searching for fruit leather, frankincense, or a beautiful backgammon set, Atlantic Avenue is the place to go. The two-block area between Henry and Court streets houses bakeries, restaurants, groceries, record, and dry goods stores.

Browsing from shop to shop, you will see racks of baked goods like baklava (a flaky, many-layered honey and nut cake), spinach pies and khubz, circular loaves of pita bread. The smells of herbs and spices —cumin, fennel, cardamon, coriander, mint, cinnamon, caraway—fill the air. Barrels of imported olives, dried apples, rice, fava beans, and nuts—pistachios are an Arab favorite—line the walls.

If you're looking for sweeter things, sample the apricot delight called mush-mush, the sesame crunch or the halvah. Walking down the street, you are liable to hear the distinctive sounds of Arabic music filtering out of the doors of the many inexpensive restaurants. Their menus offer dishes of saba glaba and tawook mishwe (roast lamb) as well as the more familiar shish kebab. Atlantic Avenue is as full of surprises as Aladdin's lamp.

Poor House

In 1826 two civic-minded gentlemen, Joseph Sprague and Alden Spooner, bought Fort Greene and presented it to the town of Brooklyn to be used as the site for a poorhouse.

WALKING ON WATER

In 1781 the Hudson River froze solid and people walked across. The British brought supplies to Staten Island by horse and sleigh.

MOODY LADY?

The town of Gravesend was established in what is now known as Brooklyn in 1645. It was headed by a woman, Lady Deborah Moody.

Outside My Front Door in Brooklyn

ELEANOR ESTES

Early one morning I opened the front door of our little house in Brooklyn to let the cats out. They tore across the street so fast they didn't see the slate-gray pigeon.

"He might be hurt," I thought. I clapped my hands to see if he could fly. He flew in a straight line up above our little house and then he flew back down to my front porch. Why doesn't he fly away? I wondered.

"Shoo! Go away, pigeon," I said.

But he wouldn't go.

"Pigeon," I said. "Please go away. Go over to Myrtle Avenue where there are lots of pigeons."

I gave him some bread and he ate it, so I knew he wasn't sick.

When I peeked through the curtains he was still there.

At around three o'clock a friend of mine drove up with her five children.

"Hey, everybody," I said, "I have a visitor . . . a pigeon. Anybody want him?"

They all wanted him except their mother. "Is he tame?" asked Jonathan.

"Tame!" I said. "I'll show you how tame he is. Watch!"

I clapped my hands and the pigeon flew way way up above the roof . . . and he flew back down again. We did this several times.

Jimmy said, "Are you a Houdini?"

"No," I said. "You try it." Jimmy tried. Same thing. All the children had a turn.

They were very excited and wanted to take him home with them and teach him to fly away. I fetched a shoe box, put the pigeon in it, and my friends went off. As they left their mother muttered, "We already have gerbils, two dogs, some worms, birds, fish, some crickets in a cage . . ."

In a little while the children came back. "You know?" they said. "He doesn't fly away. He just sits on our front porch and he flies up and he flies down but he doesn't fly over to the Engineering School or even to here. Why? He isn't caged. He could go anywhere he wants."

"Even across the Atlantic," said Tommy.

Next morning when all the children were at school, my friend and I decided to take Pidge, as the children had nicknamed him, to the zoo in Prospect Park to find out what to do.

A young man there said, "Oh, you have a coopie there . . . a coop pigeon."

"He won't fly away," we said.

"No," said the man. "He's trained *not* to fly away. He signals his flock to come back to their own rooftop after their exercises. He is a beacon . . . guides them to their landing board."

"How did he get onto my front porch, then?" I asked. "There isn't a covey of pigeons on my roof and I don't raise racers."

"I don't know how he got there," said the keeper. "But we can put him in the cage with the city birds. He is the only coop pigeon we have and we'll put a label on the cage . . . Coopie. He'll be happy."

It was a high cage. Pidge could fly way way up and fly back down again. "We'll bring the children here later to watch him fly up and fly down," I said.

I wondered as we drove home about the pigeons that Coopie was supposed to be the beacon for . . . had they gotten back to their own roof?

"Perhaps they will all be sitting on my front porch when we get home," I said.

They weren't. But something else was . . . a fine-looking black and white terrier with a brand-new red collar around his neck and no license. That was Robbie, that dog on my front step. Some other time I'll tell you about him. Right now, I have to go because I think I hear something scratching at my front door.

THE LOST VILLAGE OF BROOKLYN

BARBARA SEULING

Students at Central Brooklyn Neighborhood College discovered an honest-to-goodness "lost village" as a class project. They had put together assorted clues, such as conversations with grandparents, an old map with the name "Weeksville" on it, although it couldn't be found and no history book mentioned it. Diligently they studied census and property records, tracked down families who lived in the area, dug up photographs, documents, artifacts, a church, a couple of houses, and even signs of old roads belonging to the village.

They learned that, from around 1835 to 1870, the town of Weeksville was the name of a community of free, middle-class black people. The area is now known as Bedford-Stuyvesant.

Hunts Point

MICHAEL DORMAN

Kids who live or visit in the South Bronx—particularly the Hunts Point section—may not realize it but the ground on which they play stickball, ring-a-levio, and Johnny on the pony has a rich history dating back to its ownership by various Indian tribes.

The Indians called the area Quinnahung. They played a game with a stick and a ball that was not much different from current kids' baseball or stickball. They also played tracking games similar to hide-and-seek along the banks of the Bronx River, near what is now Edgewater Road.

The land now called Hunts Point was bought from the Indians in 1666 by English colonists. They established farms there, and built several large mansions. A family named Hunt, for which the area is named, ultimately sold parcels of the land to many other colonists. During the Revolutionary War, members of the Hunt family were leaders of the Minutemen and other organizations opposing British rule. In retaliation for their activities, a British ship sailed up the East River to the point where it joins the Bronx River and bombarded the Hunt mansion with cannons. The Hunts were forced to flee, but the mansion survived the attack. Some of the British cannonballs remained embedded in the mansion's walls until the early 1900s.

General George Washington's troops, retreating from British soldiers after the Battle of Long Island, fought skirmishes with the enemy in Hunts Point along the Bronx River banks. Relics of those battles can still be found in the mud beside the river, which local kids today call "The Creek." If you want to find some Revolutionary War souvenirs, that's a good place to look.

Another interesting spot where you can look for reminders of Hunts Point's history is the Joseph Rodman Drake Cemetery at the intersection of Hunts Point and Oak Point avenues. Revolutionary War soldiers, other early settlers, and black slaves owned by pioneer residents are buried there. Joseph Rodman Drake, for whom the cemetery was named, was a famous poet who was only twenty-five when he died in 1820. Among his best-known poems was a tribute to the American flag that began:

When freedom from her mountain height
Unfurled her standard to the air,
She took the azure robe of night
And set the stars of glory there.

Drake also wrote frequently about the glories of Hunts Point and other sections of the Bronx—glories that can be reborn among today's kids. As Drake put it in one poem:

Yet I will look upon thy face again,
My own romantic Bronx,
And it will be
A face more pleasant than the face
of men.

CITIZEN PAINE

Thomas Paine lived in Brooklyn at Sands and Fulton streets.

The Brooklyn Children's Museum

What building houses a windmill, a calliope, a giant plastic molecule, a stream, and a real waterfall? The answer is the brand-new Brooklyn Children's Museum in Brower Park in the Crown Heights section of Brooklyn. There's been a children's museum in Brower Park since 1899 (it was the first museum ever just for children), but there's never been anything quite like the million-dollar educational funhouse that's there today. Visitors can see natural history exhibits, all kinds of machines— there's even a greenhouse, and there's a playground on the roof!

The Brooklyn Children's Museum is more than just a room of exhibits, it's an experience, and something you should see. Best of all, it's free.

HOW TO GIVE A BRONX CHEER

1. Push tongue so that it extends beyond lips.

2. Keeping mouth closed around tongue, blow.

SUNKEN TREASURE

STEPHEN MOOSER

Loaded with four million dollars' worth of gold, the British ship *Hussar* sailed proudly from New York Harbor in 1780. Just beyond Hell Gate, the ship ran into rocks and sank. Although many people tried to recover the gold they were unsuccessful.

Then, in 1900, men who were searching for a yacht that had recently sunk in the East River recovered the *Hussar's* anchor. Hopes of finding the treasure ran high. However, none of the treasure came to light.

The place to look, if you'd like to try to find the gold, is right across from North Brother's Island at the tip of the Bronx.

HIGH POINT

Staten Island boasts the highest point on the Atlantic coastline between Maine and Florida—Todt Hill, 410 feet above sea level.

LEFT OUT

Staten Island is the only borough of New York City without a subway.

"Stand beside her and guide her with the light from a bulb."

Unconscious humor is delightful, and each school semester brings a fresh harvest of gorgeous boners. Teachers treasure their pupils' choice *faux pas* and every family has its flub and fluff heirlooms. They kindly send them to me to illustrate. So do students with the healthy ability to laugh—at their friends' boo-boos! (Somehow the most outrageous flubs are always made by some other kid in class.)

Here are a few endearing, and perhaps enduring, fluffs by New York children about New York.

J.R.

"The Sanitation Department takes the garbage out to sea on cows."

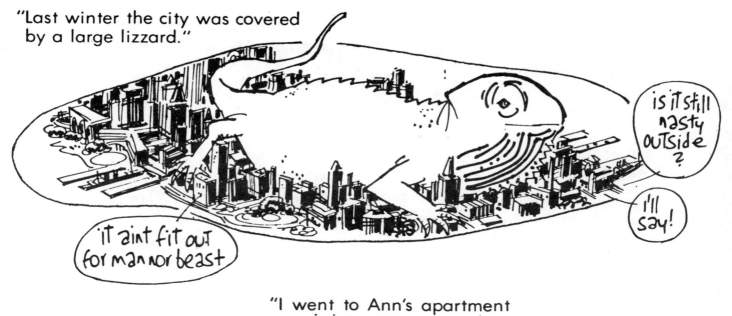

"Last winter the city was covered by a large lizzard."

"I went to Ann's apartment on the IRT subway."

My brother-in-law . . . has a lovely place [on Staten Island] and every kind of fruit on it, and there is a fountain in front with pretty fish in it. The farmer's name is Andrew, and when he goes to market, Ellen and I go with him in the buggy; and we always ask him to take us past Polly Bodine's house. She set fire to a house and burned up ever so many people, and I guess she was hung for it, because there is a wax figure of her in Barnum's Museum . . .

From *Diary of a Little Girl in Old New York, 1849–50*

The Little Boat That Built a Fortune

STEPHEN MOOSER

In the late 1820s many New Yorkers began moving out of Manhattan in order to get away from all the "hustle and bustle of the big city." Some of these people settled on Long Island, others in the Bronx and even on Staten Island out in the bay. An enterprising young man named Cornelius Vanderbilt thought that a profit could be made in operating a ferry to Staten Island. He purchased a boat and at once began not only to make regular runs to the island but regular profits as well. His little shipping operation earned him the nickname "Commodore." The Commodore, however, had interests beyond the ferry business and in 1862 he began to acquire railroads. His railroad operations were even more successful than his shipping business and at the time of his death in 1877 he was one of the richest men in the world. One of the Commodore's railroad companies was responsible for the building of Grand Central Station. If you wish to see a statue of Mr. Vanderbilt you need only look up onto the side of the station and there he is, gazing off down Park Avenue. Of course, you will also want to take a ride on the Commodore's ferry boat, which still makes regular runs from the tip of Manhattan to Staten Island. For the 25¢ fare you'll get a close-up look at the Statue of Liberty as well as some striking views of the Manhattan skyline.

THE SUBWAYS

The First Subway

New York's first subway opened on February 27, 1870. It ran under Broadway between Warren and Murray streets for a distance of just over a hundred yards. The subway consisted of one twenty-passenger car pushed along by compressed air, much like the pneumatic tubes still found in some department stores. The subway was expensive for those times, costing twenty-five cents a ride. It operated until 1873 and was considered more an amusement than a serious means of transportation.

When the subway was not in use (which was often) the subway tunnel was opened to pedestrians.

The subway, as we know it today, opened in 1904. Its first route was under Broadway and ran most of the length of that street, sometimes above ground, but mostly below. At its deepest point, Broadway and 191st Street, the subway is 180 feet, or nearly twelve stories, under ground.

MULE TRAIN

Many mules, used in the construction of the first subway tunnels, died of exhaustion and were buried in the tunnels.

The Underground Museum

OLGA LITOWINSKY

Near Borough Hall in Brooklyn, on the corner of Boerum Place and Schermerhorn Street, is an unusual subway entrance. Large white arrows on a bright yellow sign point down a clean flight of steps. Could this really be a subway entrance? It once was, back in 1936, when the HH shuttle ran between the Hoyt-Schermerhorn and Court Street stations. Today, the Court Street station has been scrubbed, but is otherwise unchanged, except for the signs of its new

KNICKERS

double life. Movies requiring a genuine subway location are filmed here (*The Taking of Pelham 123*, *The French Connection*, and *Death Wish* are three recent examples), and the station also houses the New York City Transit Exhibition.

At the foot of the entrance steps are two ancient oak benches flanking a potbellied stove. A few feet away are the turnstiles (1931 model) which lead to the exhibits. As you wander on the upper level of the station you can see various pieces of subway equipment, such as semaphors, third rails, and kerosene lanterns.

Particularly interesting is the subway mosaics display. Many of these date back to 1904 when every station on the IRT Line was embellished with an identifying mosaic symbol. (The real thing can still be seen in some stations along the IRT line. For example, there are mosaics depicting caravels at Columbus Circle, beavers at Astor Place, and steamboats on Fulton Street. It's fun to spot these unusual works of art still in their original homes, and the display at the museum will sharpen your eye for them.)

Streetcar and subway car models from 1884 to 1950 come next. Then the size and complexity of the world's largest underground mass transit system is made apparent immediately by a large-scale model laid out on a huge relief map made of cork. There is also a display dedicated to the Transit Authority Police.

"You can catch all the trains you missed" by walking down a flight of steps to the lower level. Stationed on the tracks are a number of different kinds of subway cars—including two red electric locomotives and a bright yellow freight car. Most of the cars are open, and you are free to walk through and touch. "The A Train" of Billy Strayhorn's jazz classic (made popular by Duke Ellington) is on display, with its original rattan seats and ceiling fan. Back around 1930 this was the fastest train underground. A 1927 BMT train carries a vintage subway map. It too has rattan seats and ceiling fan, and is a handsome train indeed.

Across the track is a brand-new F train with bright orange seats, wood-grain Formica paneling, and stainless steel handles. The air conditioning is unobtrusively installed in the ceiling—quite a difference from the old cars.

Back on the upper level, you can buy a genuine old handstrap, a gold-painted souvenir spike, or a real rolling black-and-white cloth sign painted with the names of stations. The best buy, of course, is your very own red leatherette subway seat! There are many other items for sale, including books, old subway maps and posters, as well as tote bags imprinted with your favorite subway line.

Since the atmosphere in the museum is nothing if not genuine, there is a Nedick's selling hot dogs, drinks, candy, and Cracker Jack. If you've come with a group (the exhibit has been approved by the Board of Education), you'll probably be eating your brown-bag lunch in a special area provided with genuine "antique" beat-up wood benches.

Nearby, behind a mock-up of an RR train, is a theater, furnished with old subway seats, where "flicks" devoted to the story of New York transportation are shown. On the wall are old subway placards and a handsome oak time-clock, which can still be punched. After watching the transportation movies, you can get behind the controls of the RR mock-up and take the train as far as your imagination will allow.

As one young visitor said, "It would be fun to imagine riding in some of these cars." If you want to relive the past, you can hop aboard the Nostalgia Train which runs every weekend and holiday. Using old cars (the oldest goes back to 1914), the B train leaves at 1 P.M. from the IND stop at Fifty-seventh Street and Sixth Avenue in Manhattan. A short while later it pulls into the museum, where it makes a layover of an hour and a half so that passengers may tour the exhibits. Then the train heads out to either Coney Island or the Rockaways, making a twenty-minute rest stop at the end of the line. Back aboard, the passengers return to Manhattan after pausing at De Kalb Avenue to let off Brooklynites. The trip takes about four hours, and it's a great way to celebrate a birthday or any other underground bash.

THAT'S A LOT OF TOKENS

The cost of a new subway car is $106,000.

SUBWAY NUMBERS

The New York City subway system has 726 miles of track, about 8,000 trains, and transports about 3 million people a day.

RIDDLE

LILLIAN MORRISON

Here come tiger down the track
ROAR—O
Big white eye and a mile-long back
ROAR—O
Through the darkest cave he run
ROAR—O
Never see the sky or sun
ROAR—O

Answer: the subway train

FLYING UPTOWN BACKWARDS

X. J. KENNEDY

Train shrieks, squeezing round a bend:
Sharp chalk on gritty blackboards.

People talk or read or stare.
Street names flash like flashcards.

Hope this trip keeps going on
Flying uptown backwards.

EYE OPENERS

New York, I Love You

NANCY LARRICK

It was my first day in New York on my first job. I didn't know anyone and didn't expect a friendly greeting. But Jimmie, the elevator operator showed me I was wrong.

"What do you think about the World Series?" I had to confess that I knew nothing, hadn't even seen the game the night before. Jimmie's eyes popped, and as he began to fill me in, he revved up the elevator, and went past my floor and on to the top of the building, still talking about the teams, the pitchers, the umpire, the score, and what this evening's game would bring. As we drifted back to the eighth floor, Jimmie said, "Now you can go to work."

While Jimmie talked me into a warm friendship with New York, Mr. Vitello, who operated the corner newsstand, was doing it the quiet way. One evening as I came home from work, I heard "Hey!" and from back of the newsstand, Mr. Vitello brought out my bag of laundry, left at the laundromat next door on my way to work that morning. "He went home," was all he said.

The other day I bought half a dozen loaves of freshly baked bread on Bleecker Street. As the baker put the bulging brown bag in my arms, he murmured, "Hold it like this. It keep you warm."

When I went to the television repair shop on Seventh Avenue to pick up my

259

midget Sony, I expected to give my name and claim check. But before I could open my mouth, the girl said, "We been trying to get you on the phone to say it's ready."

"How did you know me?" I asked.

"You brought it in seven weeks ago," she said.

And as I walked across Fifth Street toward Third Avenue, I heard a husky voice: "I love you . . . Sure I love you . . . Yep, you can kiss me . . ." I turned and saw this love scene at the corner filling station: a beautiful German shepherd dog stood with his forepaws on the shoulders of a rumpled workman. As the tender words flowed on, the dog licked the man's neck and ears and nuzzled against his cheeks. Trucks, taxis, and cars roared up Third Avenue. The wind blew dust and litter in my face, but the gentle voice persisted: "I love you . . . Yep, you know I love you . . ."

The Hole That Led to Nowhere

KEN RINCIARI

The hole that led to Nowhere
can be seen on 49th Street,
New York City,
unless it has been filled up
by this man
who works for us.
His name escapes,
But never mind,
His number is
49.

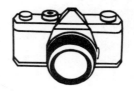

You Are a Camera!

LAVINIA RUSS

How would you like to tell the story of the New York you know? You don't have to tell it in words; you can tell it in pictures.

There's nothing to it. All you need is a camera, a love of walking, and a curiosity about people and places. (A sense of humor doesn't hurt, either.)

You probably have the camera already. If you don't have one yet, don't feel you have to save all your allowance to get one. There are good, inexpensive cameras on the market that do an excellent job.

Job is not the right word for the pictures you will be taking. There is only one right word, and that word, in capital letters, is DISCOVERY. For when you begin to see New York through the lens of your camera, you will begin to discover things, people, and events you would never have noticed with your naked eye.

You will really *see* the people on your street and in your neighborhood, funny people, sometimes sad people, always different people.

You will become an expert recorder of serendipity, which means "the faculty of making fortunate and unexpected discoveries by accident." If you live in the

Village, say, you will notice and photograph unexpected combinations—like the old lady listening with rapt attention to a rock group playing by the fountain in Washington Square. You will surely want a picture of the man who dresses up like a pirate and walks down Eighth Street with a dignified air. You will find and photograph the flowers in the lovely quiet garden by St. Luke's Church, only a brick wall away from the noise and the hurly-burly of the traffic on Hudson Street.

New York City is like a Harlequin's costume. It's made up of different diamond-shaped sections of different colors. Downtown is Chinatown and the Italian section, and all the way down Manhattan is the Battery with its narrow streets and its buildings that reach up toward the sky. Uptown, on Fifth Avenue, are the great stores, the people staring in at the windows, and a woman in a mink coat, digging into a trash basket to find today's *Times*. There is a girl in a brilliant Japanese kimono walking with fast little steps to keep up with her companion, a boy dressed like Daniel Boone. There is a violinist on a corner, playing to earn the money for his music lessons.

Photograph all of them that interest you. And photograph the streets, as well as the people that are on them, so that when you are grown up and your children ask you, "Pa, what was New York like when you were a kid?" you can say, "Get down my portfolio," and show them!

A Walk in New York

DOROTHY E. SHUTTLESWORTH

If you walked along a New York Street
Who would you most like to meet:
A person selling candy bars
Or a creature just arrived from Mars—
A jumping, leaping kangaroo
Pursued by a keeper from the Zoo—
A boy with a yo-yo on a string
Or a girl peeping through a carousel ring?
Would you like to see a red-nosed clown
And know the circus was in town?
How about joggers who would take
You jogging with them around the lake—
And sailors and pilots and many more
Who could whisk you away to some
                    foreign shore?
Such travel could surely be quite nice,
But before you go, do think twice:
Where would you find anything to beat
The fun of a walk on a New York street?

I went with my father to Brady's Daguerrean Gallery, corner of Tenth Street and Broadway, to have our picture taken.

My father was seventy-four, and I was seven. It is a very pretty picture, but people won't believe he isn't my grandfather. He is sitting down and I am standing beside him, and his arm is around me, and my hand hangs down and shows the gold ring on my fore-finger. He gave it to me at New Year's to remember him by . . .

FROM *Diary of a Little Girl in Old New York, 1849–50*

Subways Are for Shooting

STANLEE BRIMBERG

Take your camera underground.

For portraits, you couldn't find more interesting faces anywhere. And where else will you get perfect strangers to sit still for you?

But be sensitive. If someone looks panicky when you raise your camera, back down. You'll have other opportunities. New York is full of hams.

For stills, try the Lexington Avenue line. South Ferry and many other stations along that route are decorated with beautiful mosaic pictures and patterns. Shoot the trains entering the station. Shoot the graffiti.

If you have an adjustable camera, follow your light meter. On simpler cameras, load up with Tri-X or other "fast" black and white film. Flash and tripods are not allowed. If your first results are a little dark, go to an outdoor station.

A great one is the Smith–9th Street station on the "F" and "GG" lines. At ninety feet above the ground, it is the highest station in the city. From it, you can shoot the Manhattan skyline, the Battery, and magnificent sunsets over New Jersey.

Before you start, you must get a permit from the MTA. Go to 370 Jay Street ("F" or "A" trains to Jay Street, or IRT trains to Borough Hall). If you're under seventeen, bring a parent to witness it. It's free.

Should you like a little more privacy for your shooting sessions, you'll be happy to know that the MTA will let you shoot to your heart's content in an empty station. You only need to pay for the personnel needed to maintain the station when you're in it. Remember *The Taking of Pelham 123?* It was filmed in the Court Street station in Brooklyn. The company used the station for up to fifteen hours every day for four months. The MTA's bill for personnel was a measly quarter of a million dollars.

Things to Spot in New York City

BARBARA BEASLEY MURPHY

13,000 Street Vendors: A frankfurter wagon costs anywhere from $780 to $1,300 and holds as many as 360 franks.

TV and Radio people: New York City has 14 TV stations and 60 radio stations. Many broadcast from the top of the World Trade Center.

Window Cleaners: Over 800 window-cleaning services are listed in the Yellow Pages.

9,000 Pickpockets are reported annually.

1,500,000 School Kids attend the city's elementary and high schools.

60 Horse-drawn Carriages drive in Central Park.

97 Mounted Police belong to the NYPD.

14,000 Sanitation Workers: They carry off 7,000,000 tons of refuse and wash 75,000 miles of streets each year. (Did you ever thank one?)

12,172 Motorcyclists are registered.

Rabbis and Pastors: New York City has over 2,250 churches and 1,200 synagogues.

2,250,000 Trees: Each New Yorker then has the use of a quarter of a tree.

Publishers: 1,175 publishing companies employ over 60,000 people making New York City the publishing capital of the world.

2,095 Firemen work in Manhattan alone.

98 Judges preside in New York.

325 Magicians from New York City belong to the American Society of Magicians.

20,000 Underground Workers use 683 manholes to get underground. (Check out manhole covers; they're not all alike.)

1,670 Pro Athletes live at least part of the time in New York City. (They give autographs when you ask.)

Garment Workers: 43 percent of New York City workers are employed in the garment industry.

20 Major Parades: Macy's Thanksgiving Day Parade is the biggest.

11,787 Medallion Cabs: The average cab lasts 2 years.

Printers: 30 percent of the city's workers are employed in printing, the city's second largest industry.

437 Dancers: Dancers Equity lists 437, but doesn't count belly dancers.

3,221 Conductors are employed by the Metropolitan Transit Authority.

Writers: 21,200 reporters; 4,600 authors.

93,000 Actors and Actresses work in New York.

83 Theaters for plays are in operation.

400 to 600 Shopping Bag Ladies are served bread and coffee free at the St. Francis of Assisi Church.

Jazz Musicians: Many play but most have to work at other jobs, too. Hear them free at St. Peter's Church on Sunday evenings at five.

United Nations Representatives from 151 countries.

Street Music

CATHARINE EDMONDS

At Fifty-fifth Street and Fifth Avenue, there is the sound of a violin over the rumbling traffic. Sometimes the roar of an accelerating bus drowns out the delicate strains. The violinist is a young woman from Erie, Pennsylvania, nineteen or twenty years old, in a plaid shirt and jeans. She plays Brahms from memory, her music stand closed down in front of her over a small colander half full of dollar bills and coins. The sign leaning against the stand reads: "Juilliard student needs tuition to continue studies."

Farther uptown is a wind trio—two clarinets and a bassoon—three nicely dressed young men from New York, California, and Alabama. They play from memory every weekend on Fifth Avenue or in Central Park, three hours or more at a time. They play to live; they're out of school now, having studied their instruments for ten to fifteen years, and play concerts and with other groups individually. They call themselves the Mostly Mozart Trio. An open clarinet case lies on the sidewalk with clarinet pieces obscured by bills and coins. Set up against the upright lid are photos of them in eighteenth-century "Mozartian" costumes—tailcoats, ruffles, and silk stockings. Under the tall archway of a store, their music carries softly over the noise.

At the north fountain in front of the Metropolitan Museum, a redheaded young man from Connecticut who is studying at Juilliard to become a percussionist plays Bach fugues on a marimba with two soft mallets in each hand. The marimba looks like a xylophone with wooden keys, and has an ethereal, happy sound. It's his "summer gig" to play here, Brian says, sometimes for six hours straight. He also studies tympany, drums, vibraphone, and xylophone, and plays in the Juilliard orchestra.

A cab driver waiting by the curb cheers at the end of the fugue. A thin, wild-haired man walks over with his racing bike. "Do you play jazz?"

Brian taps out a crazy, intricate run.

"Lemme get my horn. I'll be right back!" The man tears off on his bicycle.

In Central Park, a man is quietly playing a concert harmonica, slouched on a bench. On a bench in the Mall, there are three conga players, a bongo player, two flutists, and a man playing sticks on a soda bottle. The large crowd around them dances and bobs about. The players are serious, mesmerized as they beat and beat.

Just out of earshot is a private little folk group made up of two guitars, banjo, mandolin, and a clarinet. One guitarist sings loud country.

On another bench is a man with a guitar, next to him a mandolinist. Someone plays a tambourine. The guitarist sings out the verses of a jaunty Beatles' song, and a large crowd, dancing and clapping, sings back the chorus.

These are only a few of the musicians on the streets of New York. You can also find a bagpiper, an autoharpist, or a country fiddler. They are usually out on a nice summer day. Look in Washington Square Park, all over the Village, the Delacorte Theater, the Schaefer Festival, Grand Army Plaza, near the Alice in Wonderland statue in Central Park. And there's always Michael the violinist hamming it up before curtain and at intermission around the Off-Broadway theaters.

Street music is a special part of New York, and the people love it. Amid the noise of traffic, car horns, fire engines, subways, planes, and people bustling, there is nothing quite so exhilarating as the sound of beautiful music.

SEATING PLAN

The architects of Lincoln Center, in studying human dimensions for the installation of theater seats, discovered that the average American's hips had grown considerably wider in the last fifty years.

TALL PLACES

My Personal Friend, the Elevator

CONSTANCE C. GREENE

I live in an apartment house and when I step inside the elevator and push the UP button, I feel as if I'm boring into the center of the universe, the place where I live, where I am calm and safe and where no one can touch me. I like to watch the light travel from one to seven, which is my floor. I like the whooshing sound the elevator door makes as it slides open. Then I step into the hall, smell what we're having for dinner, and put out my arm to hold the door open to prevent it from closing. When I do this I feel powerful, as if I were master of the earth and monarch of all I survey. This also tends to irritate people who are trying to use the elevator themselves. But I am there with my arm out, in command of my space ship.

An elevator is a very intimate thing. I have made many friends while riding inside. Old people, middle-aged, and people my own age. Also dogs. There are quite a few dogs in our building. Some of them are nervous when they ride the elevator. They whine and tremble and one dog I know, sad to say, mistook the elevator wall for a tree. If John, our super, ever discovered the dog who committed this indignity, he would probably prohibit that dog from ever using the elevator again.

An elevator is something that people who live in the country are not familiar

267

new york
city

man-hat-in

or....

man in hat.

with. You might almost say they are deprived. My cousins, who live in a one-family house surrounded by grass and trees and even a rose garden, think an elevator is the coolest thing imaginable. When they come to visit, they're pests about riding up and down. Last time they were here their father finally had to yell at them. Especially Charlie, who is ten and a terror, and who says he's going to be an elevator operator when he grows up. I suspect by that time there won't be any such thing as an elevator operator. It'll all be done by computers.

When I go to their house, I must admit I enjoy taking off my shoes and running barefoot through the grass, picking the flowers, although my aunt would prefer leaving them waving in the breeze for the neighbors to admire, and weeding out the dandelions.

The country is nice and we always have a good time there. Still, when we get home and I hop into the elevator and push that button, I feel good. I'm home at last.

GOING UP?

Skyscraper Elevator Passenger: This must be a fascinating job.

Elevator Operator: Oh, it has its ups and downs.

SPEEDING UPWARD

Elevators in some skyscrapers can travel as fast as twenty miles per hour.

sometimes living in new york makes me feel
part of something really Big.

Take a ride on the new-york-city-mobile, Beeb! Beeb!

269

High Places

JUDY DONNELLY

In 1641 the five-story city hall was the tallest building New Yorkers had to look up at or down from. For the next two hundred years buildings were not much taller, except for church steeples. Of course, taller buildings meant more stairs to climb—until the 1850s, when elevators were invented.

In 1889, New Yorkers were awed when the 50 Broadway Building rose up on the horizon. It was 11 stories high. Everyone was afraid it would collapse. Their fears were quieted when the architect moved into the top floor to show his confidence that his building would stand.

Around the turn of the century buildings rose higher and higher. One "tallest" building after another appeared: the 26-floor gold-domed World Tower, the Park Row Building, the Singer Building. In 1899 the Metropolitan Life Insurance Building—700 feet or 50 stories—held the title until the firm made the mistake of refusing Mr. Woolworth a loan. Miffed, he told his architect to build a taller skyscraper. In 1913, New Yorkers thought Woolworth's new building was about as tall as a building would ever be: 60 stories or 792 feet and one inch. They were right—until 1929. That year two architects, former partners, each began work on his own "world's tallest building." When one announced the Chrysler Building would tower to 925 feet, the rival architect at 40 Wall Street made his building 2 feet taller. But he had been tricked. Working secretly inside the Chrysler Building, engineers constructed a stainless steel spire which made the building 1,048 feet tall. The triumph was brief. Only a few months later the Empire State Building was completed. At 1,250 feet, it was unchallenged as the world's tallest from 1931 until the World Trade Center towers were finished in 1971. (These have now been topped by the Sears Tower in Chicago, which is 1,454 feet tall.) For the time being, the ten tallest buildings in New York are:

World Trade Center (1971)	1,350 feet	(110 stories)
Empire State Building (1931)	1,250 feet	(102 stories)
Chrysler Building (1930)	1,048 feet	(77 stories)
60 Wall Tower (1932)	965 feet	(67 stories)
40 Wall Street (1929)	927 feet	(71 stories)
Citicorp Center Building (1978)	915 feet	(59 stories)
RCA Building (1939)	850 feet	(70 stories)
Chase Manhattan (1960)	813 feet	(60 stories)
Pan American (1963)	808 feet	(59 stories)
Woolworth (1913)	792 feet	(60 stories)

And if all the buildings in Manhattan were to vanish one day, the highest point on the island would be a small ridge near 181st Street and Fort Washington Avenue.

The Flatiron Building

JAMES CROSS GIBLIN

For over seventy years artists have painted it, photographers have taken pictures of it, and visitors to New York City have looked up in awe at the Flatiron Building.

It was called the Fuller Building when it was erected in 1902, but it soon acquired the nickname of the "Flatiron Building" because its triangular shape resembles the flatirons that people used to press their clothes at the beginning of the century. The building stands on Twenty-third Street in Manhattan where Fifth Avenue and Broadway cross each other as they head north, forming a triangle.

Although the Flatiron Building contains only twenty stories, it was once one of the tallest in New York City—and one of the first to be called a "skyscraper."

A building that scrapes the sky. That's a poetic way of describing what the dictionary defines as "a modern building of great height constructed on a steel skeleton."

The earliest tall buildings were of stone masonry construction with thick walls on the lower floors to support the upper ones. This pattern was followed by one in which an iron frame supported the floors and the masonry walls bore their own weight. Finally, engineers invented a metal frame sturdy enough to support both the floors and the walls.

Many people think New York City was the birthplace of the skyscraper, but actually the first building in which the new metal frame was used went up in Chicago in 1883. From then until the end of the nineteenth century, one skyscraper after another was built in Chicago. Then in 1902 the Flatiron Building, constructed on a metal frame, helped to bring the idea of the skyscraper to New York.

Not everyone liked the Flatiron Building. The English artist Sir Philip Burne-Jones, who visited New York in 1902, called it "a vast horror."

However, the American journalist John Corbin admired its dramatic thrust and said it dominated the nearby avenues like "an ocean steamer with all Broadway in tow." The French composer Camille Saint-Saëns thought it made a "fantastic and marvelous spectacle." And the famous British author H. G. Wells expressed the feelings of many people, past and present, when he wrote in 1906: "I found myself agape, admiring a skyscraper—the prow of the Flatiron Building to be particular, ploughing up through the traffic of Broadway and Fifth Avenue in the late afternoon light."

As far as height goes, the Flatiron Building was soon eclipsed as taller and taller skyscrapers were built throughout the city. But today the Flatiron Building still ploughs up through the traffic of the avenues, as H. G. Wells wrote, and still commands the attention of New Yorkers and visitors alike.

What makes the Flatiron Building so special? Is it the slender, graceful form that makes it appear to be taller than it really is? Or is it the handsomely decorated façade with flowers, faces, and the heads of lions carved in its gray limestone surface? Perhaps it's these—and perhaps it's something more. Like the Colosseum in Rome or the Arc de Triomphe in Paris or Buckingham Palace in London, the Flatiron Building is a reminder of our history, architectural and otherwise.

New York City is not kind to its older buildings. Each year more and more are torn down to make way for new, larger, and often uglier structures. So far, fortunately, the Flatiron Building has survived. Today we can still see it rise majestically above the treetops of neighboring Madison Square Park in summer, or loom suddenly through the snow and fog of a January evening. And as we look at it, we can imagine the excitement it must have caused back in 1902 when the whole notion of the skyscraper was new and strange.

MASTER SWITCH

On April 24, 1913, President Woodrow Wilson pressed a button in the White House in Washington, D.C., which turned on the lights for the first time in the Woolworth Building, opposite City Hall Park in New York City, celebrating the tallest building in the world at sixty stories high.

THE HUMAN FLY

BARBARA SEULING

At the crack of dawn, on Thursday, May 26, 1977, a young man crept up to the 110-story building of the World Trade Center and began climbing up. Higher and higher he climbed, like something out of a comic book or a science-fiction movie. There was no rope pulling him up, no scaffold for him to rest on. All that he had was some climbing equipment he had made himself, and more courage than any thousand people below.

The fellow was George H. Willig, a toy-maker from Queens. George was an avid mountain-climber and part-time inventor. He had scaled many a mountain in his twenty-seven years, but nothing gave him quite the challenge that the smooth façade of the tallest building in New York did. Outside the building are narrow tracks used for window-washers' equipment. George invented climbing equipment that fit into these tracks and locked in place as he climbed, supporting his weight as he ascended.

As he climbed higher, people below, on their way to work, noticed him up on the building. The crowd got larger, the police and fire department were called, and George climbed faster. At first, emergency teams thought George was crazy, and set out to rescue him. A scaffold was lowered from the roof. When George saw the scaffold, he swung over to the next window-washing track to get out of reach. He was determined to make it to the top on his own.

The rescuers began talking to George as he climbed, and discovered he had guts, but he was not crazy. They actually began rooting for him, and stopped trying to talk him out of it. As a matter of fact, the two men from the police emergency squad, expert suicide rescuers, exchanged notes with George and got his autograph as he rested at about the seventy-fifty floor along the way.

After three and a half hours of climbing, George reached the top. A roar went up from thousands of delighted spectators below. Emergency workers and newsmen cheered and applauded. The Port Authority police slapped three summonses on George and arrested him.

In 1974 a French high-wire artist sneaked past guards and walked across a cable strung between the two towers of the World Trade Center. A year later, a sky diver parachuted from the roof to the ground, 1,350 feet below. But George Willig—the human fly—was the first to WALK up the city's tallest building.

WAY DOWN SOUTH

The Chase Manhattan Bank Building, the southernmost skyscraper on the island of Manhattan, has sixty-five stories, five of which are underground. There are eighty-eight hundred windows to wash. There are forty-seven elevators. In one of these, you can reach the sixtieth floor in thirty-two seconds. On the ground floor concourse there is an atomic clock which is powered by gamma rays. Two million checks are processed at this bank every day, worth about two billion dollars. In the fifth basement is the largest bank vault in the world. Each of its six doors is twenty inches thick, and its length is that of a football field.

Manhattan's Furriest Buildings

THOMAS G. AYLESWORTH

The original King Kong at the height of his acting career. He is on top of the Empire State Building and the Chrysler Building, with the funny spire, is just to the left—in between the Empire State and the airplane in the foreground.

The World Trade Center is the highest building in New York. It is also the second highest building in the world. It has twin towers of 110 stories and it rises 1,350 feet into the air—almost a quarter of a mile.

Ever since its dedication in 1973, people have been using it in strange ways. They have stretched a tightrope between the towers and walked from one to the other. They have parachuted off the roof. They have climbed up the side like mountaineers.

But they all may have gotten the idea from a giant gorilla—that's right, King Kong. In 1976, millions of people all over the world cheered when they watched the super-ape scale the wall, and cried when he fell to the street below.

Why did he pick the World Trade Center to climb? Oh, there was a lot of stuff in the movie that made us believe that he was homesick for a couple of twin cliffs on his native island. But the truth probably is that the director and the producer of the film wanted him to be on top of the highest building in the city.

You see, they were copying the old man —the original King Kong. Had he lived, he would have been celebrating his forty-third anniversary as a movie star when the new film came out.

He, too, climbed the highest building in New York (which was also the highest building in the world at that time). It was the Empire State Building, on Fifth Avenue, between Thirty-third and Thirty-fourth streets. And it was only two years old when the first King Kong got to the top in 1933.

At that time, it was 1,250 feet high. When Kong was on the roof, he was at a height equal to more than four football fields laid end to end. No wonder he was killed by the fall. By the way, the Empire State Building is taller now. They have added a 222-foot television and radio transmitting tower.

One thing should be made clear. There is no truth to the rumor that the first Kong did not die. He was *not* lured from the top of the Empire State Building when the U. S. Marines put a giant banana on top of the Chrysler Building on Lexington and Forty-third.

But it may be that the two King Kongs chose their own buildings, after all. Who of us, even if we are giant gorillas, could resist such a view from the top? On a clear day, from either building, you can see for eighty miles in any direction.

why go to the laundry-mat when you can just as easily hang them on the sky line.

Tilting in the Wind

BARBARA BEASLEY MURPHY

Do skyscrapers tilt in the wind? Yes! And it sometimes makes people sick.

At Fifty-fourth Street and Lexington Avenue you can see the world's eighth tallest building, the new Citicorp Center. It seems to stand on tiptoe with its crown 915 feet above the street. The first floor begins where the ninth floor usually does. This amazing office tower was designed by Hugh Stubbins, who was sensitive to the discomfort suffered by some people who work high up in tall buildings. When the building sways on gusty days, some of them actually feel airsick. They can't take dramamine; it would make them sleepy. So Stubbins worked with engineers who discovered a way to cut down on the movement of the Citicorp Center building.

MTS Systems Corporation designed machinery for a new device called the TMD. The initials stand for *tuned mass damper*. (On ordinary days the folks at MTS make machinery to simulate earthquakes and shock-test army tanks.) The TMD, a four-hundred-ton concrete block, is installed at the top level of the building. It moves out of phase with the tower's motion during high winds. A series of pistons and spring mounts secure the block to the building. Should the building move, the block remains stationary for a moment, then moves in the opposite direction, sliding on a film of oil on a steel plate. The effect dampens the sway by approximately 40 percent. If you need one for your tower, you can buy a TMD for approximately one million dollars.

The best way to get around in New York is by OX.

277

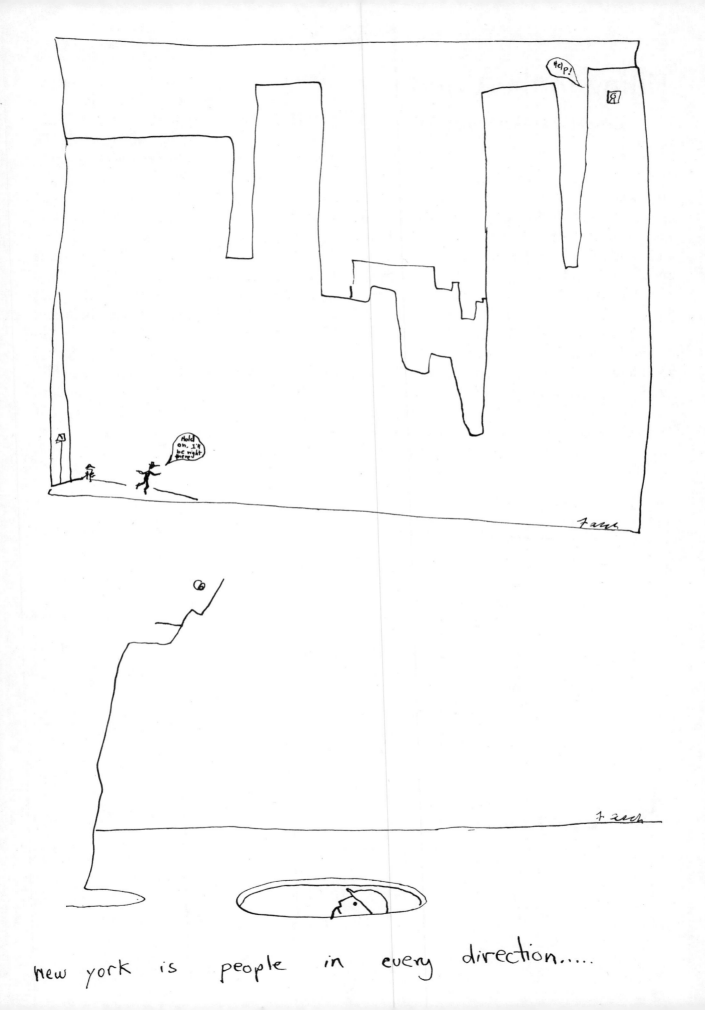

new york is people in every direction.....

sometimes looking up
feels like everything else
is looking down.

.... and every direction in people.

9 million from 0 to 100 equal 20 life times a day. Sometimes around sundown, when everyone is rushing home, you can feel it.

THE TALLEST HOTEL

New York City's tallest hotel is the Americana, with two thousand rooms on fifty floors.

WINDOW WASHERS EXTRAORDINARY

The washing of skyscraper windows is often done by Mohawk Indians, who are generally not susceptible to dizziness.

when I get tired of watching T.V. I look out the window, It relaxes me. I look at the people and they look back at me, sometimes. The T.V. never looks back.

HOLIDAYS

Celebrations Around the Year

BARBARA SEULING

JANUARY

In Times Square, New Yorkers gather in throngs to welcome in the New Year. When the ball slowly drops on top of the Allied Chemical Building, indicating the passing of the old year, an incredible cheer goes up from the crowd. Network cameras capture the moment for TV viewers across the country.

FEBRUARY

The first full moon after January 21 signifies the beginning of the Chinese New Year, and in Chinatown fire-breathing dragons and lions wind through the narrow streets in celebration. Masked dancers accompany the beasts, and fireworks ward off evil spirits. At Madison Square Garden there is usually an ice show at this time.

MARCH	There are more Irish in New York City than in Dublin, Ireland, and on St. Patrick's Day, the seventeenth, they all come out to march in or watch the parade. Marchers come down Fifth Avenue past St. Patrick's Cathedral, which is dedicated to the patron saint of the Irish. Spirits are high, and green is everywhere.
APRIL	Spring comes to the city in many ways. The Botanical Gardens in both Brooklyn and the Bronx are abloom with spring flowers and special shows. On Easter Sunday, the Easter Parade fills Fifth Avenue. (Sometimes this happens in March.) And the baseball season opens at Shea Stadium in Queens for the Mets and at Yankee Stadium in the Bronx for the Yankees.
MAY	New York, the "melting pot," is never more visible than at the Ninth Avenue Festival, held the second week in May. Food specialties of many nationalities are spread out from Thirty-ninth Street to Fifty-sixth, outside the shops and cafes. There are Chinese dumplings, Hungarian sausages, Argentinian steaks, Vietnamese rice dishes, Greek baklava, Italian zeppole, Filipino pineapple slices, French pastry, Arab falafel, and more. Bring along some Alka-Seltzer and try to sample them all.
JUNE	Beaches in four boroughs are open to celebrate the summer: Coney Island and Brighton in Brooklyn, South in Staten Island, Orchard in the Bronx, and Rockaway in Queens. If you're stuck in Manhattan and want to swim, there are pools at the YMCA, health clubs, and hotels, and in Central Park.
JULY–AUGUST	In Central Park three different plays are performed each summer at the Delacorte Shakespeare Theater. On the Sheep Meadow and at Wollman Rink, classical, jazz, and rock concerts are given. Take along a picnic and some friends and enjoy music under the stars.

SEPTEMBER   When Little Italy celebrates the Feast of San Gennaro, the patron saint of Neapolitans, Mulberry Street turns into a carnival and the street is lined with booths featuring games and prizes and Italian food specialties. At the Atlantic Antic, a street fair in Brooklyn, the flavor is strictly Middle Eastern. Look for the camel, imported for the occasion.

OCTOBER   The Columbus Day Parade is a celebration of Italians by Italians, but everyone joins in the fun. The Grand Marshal could be Yogi Berra. The central feature could be old-fashioned fire engines or the West Point cadets or an Italian soccer team. Judges grade the high school bands as they pass by the reviewing stand, and the winning band is awarded a plaque.

NOVEMBER   Macy's Thanksgiving Day Parade, the most festive of all New York City parades, with its giant balloons, fantastic floats, superstars, and Kris Kringle himself, marches down Broadway on Thanksgiving morning. It ends up at Herald Square when Santa Claus wishes everyone a Merry Christmas and disappears down a chimney in Macy's window.

DECEMBER   New York City has its own special Christmas tree, in Rockefeller Center. It is usually a sixty-foot Norway spruce, and there is a gala celebration under the tree when the lights are lit for the first time. Tree decorations, carolers, and ice skating below give the city a sparkly glow.

When I grow up I think I shall have a beau, and his name is Sam B. and he lives across the street, for he sent me a valentine he painted himself, and it is a big red heart with an arrow stuck through it, and one of my school friends says that means he is very fond of me, but I don't see much sense in the arrow . . .

FROM *Diary of a Little Girl in Old New York City, 1849–50*

CHRISTMAS CHEER MAKES A NEW YORKER FAMOUS

BEBE WILLOUGHBY

"'Twas the night before Christmas, when all through the house/Not a creature was stirring, not even a mouse" is the first line of a poem we hear every Christmas. Did you ever wonder who first described Santa as having "a broad face and a little round belly that shook when he laughed like a bowl full of jelly"?

In 1822 Clement Clarke Moore read it to his six children on Christmas Eve as they all sat around the fireplace in the big house near Chelsea Square. It was a holiday present. Legend has it that he composed it that afternoon as he rode to town in his sleigh to get the Christmas turkey.

The poem was first published in a newspaper on December 23, 1823, under the title "An Account of a Visit from St. Nicholas," as the editor had named the ballad. In 1837 Moore included it and several other poems in an anthology called *The New York Book of Poetry*. In 1848 the poem was first published in book form and was called *Santa Claus*. Theodore C. Boyd, a New York artist, designed woodcuts for this edition that influenced our conception of Santa Claus and his reindeers even today.

Moore wrote what has become the most popular American Christmas poem. An unusual and talented man, he was Professor of Oriental and Greek Literature at the Episcopal General Theological Seminary, at 175 Ninth Avenue. As a poet, scholar, writer, educator, church layman, and musician, he was active in church and cultural affairs of New York.

Clement Clarke Moore died five days before his eighty-fourth birthday. Every year on Christmas Eve a winter wreath is placed upon his grave in Trinity Cemetery at 155th Street near Riverside Drive, and "A Visit from St. Nicholas" is read aloud. What he gave to the Christmas holiday spirit will make him remembered always.

Christmas Eve

JOHANNA REISS

It was Christmas Eve
The Broadway bus seemed empty
and silent
except for the wind that howled through
and except for the few passengers huddled closely in the front:
a lady in fur, shivering in spite of it,
a man next to her, hands under his armpits.
Bitterly cold. Only the boy across from me didn't feel it,
Too busy with his guide book to New York
which he kept upside down on his lap
Reading from it anyway, then closing his eyes, moving his lips,
memorizing.
Silence.
Except for the wind that blew in from the windows in the back
opened by a man, long scarf wrapped around his neck.
There, opening another one, laughing strangely as he did.
The woman in fur and the man with the hidden hands looked on,
Saying nothing
Frightened
As the bus driver pulled up his collar
and the student still memorized upside-down information in New
    York
and Santa Clauses outside rang their bells,
Going around with tin cups
wishing all of us a merry Christmas.

Caving In

PYKE JOHNSON, JR.

There are those who love the city's cold.
This feeling, I don't share it.
For winter I've not love, but hate.
(It shows perhaps I'm growing old.)
Yet I've decided how to bear it—
Next year I'm going to hibernate.

Succot

EDITH BING FIRESTONE

One of the most colorful and symbolic Jewish holidays—Succot—occurs each year in the fall, two weeks after Rosh Ha'Shana, the Jewish New Year. Succot is a harvest festival, commemorating the forty-year period when the Jewish people wandered in the desert after they were freed from slavery in Egypt, nearly thirty-five hundred years ago. In the desert, the people lived in small, temporary huts called Succot. Today, Jews celebrate this holiday by building and decorating their own Succot, in which they eat their meals during the seven-day festival.

The other major symbols of the holiday are the Lulav and the Etrog, used during religious services in the Synagogue during the recital of "Hallel"—selections from the Psalms. The Lulav consists of a palm tree frond, encased in a small woven palm handle with holders on one side for two branches from a willow tree, and on the other side, for three branches from a myrtle bush. The Etrog is a citron, a tangy, spicy-scented fruit related to the lemon, but usually larger and with a bumpier skin. The Lulav and Etrog, held together in one hand, are waved toward the four corners of the earth (East, West, North, South) and up and down, to indicate that the presence of God touches all spheres of the earth.

After the holiday, you can make a pomander ball out of the Etrog by sticking it with cloves. Some people make Etrog liqueur or jam to enjoy the whole year through and to remind them of the holiday. And, you can save the Lulav to place on the roof of your Succah (singular of Succot) next year.

If you've never seen or been in a Succah, start by going to your local synagogue. If they build a Succah, volunteer to help make decorations. If they don't maybe you can organize enough friends to build a Succah for the community. In Manhattan, it is hard to find many Succot because there are so many apartment buildings, but several large synagogues in midtown have them. Temple Emanu-El (1 East 65 Street) welcomes guests and conducts tours of their Succah. The Park East Synagogue (163 East 67 Street), The Jewish Theological Seminary of America (3080 Broadway), The Jewish Center (131 West 86 Street), and Congregation Shearith Israel (8 West 70 Street) all maintain beautiful Succot which are open to the public. Many also cater meals during the holidays; if you call in advance, you may be able to make arrangements to eat in one. There are several New York neighborhoods with high concentrations of Orthodox Jews, and you'll be able to spot lots of Succot: Boro Park, Flatbush, and Williamsburgh in Brooklyn; Kew Gardens Hills, Kew Gardens, Forest Hills, and Rego Park in Queens.

SHOPPING FOR SUCCOT

EDITH BING FIRESTONE

A few days before the holiday starts, several stores on the Lower East Side (take the subway to Essex Street) sell the Lulav and Etrog. There will be a lot of bargaining going on as everyone tries to find the nicest-looking Lulav, the biggest, prettiest, and sweetest-smelling Etrog, and the best price. You'll even find some peddlers hawking the willow branches, called Aravot, and the myrtle branches, called Hadassim, from the street corners. Wait until just before the holiday to buy these leaves as they spoil quickly. Keep the Aravot and Hadassim on the lowest shelf of your refrigerator wrapped loosely in damp paper towels or newspapers in a plastic bag. The Lulav keeps very well with its stem in a vase of water. Keep the Etrog wrapped in the flax in its little white cardboard box—just as you buy it.

For decorations, a trip to the flower market, above Twenty-third Street along Sixth Avenue, may yield ideas. Some dealers sell plastic flowers and leaves, and you may find old, dusty items for half price. All that is needed to restore the leaves to new is a dunking in soap and water.

Macy's Parade

BARBARA SEULING

New York City does things bigger and better than anyone—Macy's Thanksgiving Day Parade proves it.

Dozens of marching bands from all over the country—even Hawaii—fly in to take part in the spectacle. The parade starts out from Central Park West and Seventy-seventh Street at 10 A.M. on Thanksgiving morning and marches down Broadway, ending up at Macy's Department Store on Thirty-fourth Street, just about noon, so everyone can get home to Thanksgiving dinner.

Celebrities such as Evel Knievel, Laverne and Shirley, Barry Manilow, and Paul Williams ride the decorated floats. Miss America might ride Cinderella's coach while Roberta Peters sings from one made up like a paddle-wheel showboat. Magnificent Clydesdale horses pull the Old Country float, while Bavarian dancers do the "slap" dance alongside. In and around and between the floats are tumblers, a thousand clowns, funny cars, and the greatest feature of all, the giant balloons.

The balloons are kept on high by thousands of gallons of helium, and held down by dozens of handlers. Favorites are Snoopy, the Happy Dragon, Dino the Dinosaur, Underdog, Smokey the Bear, and an old favorite, Mickey Mouse, who has been in the parade since 1934. It takes thirty-six handlers tugging at his strings to keep Mickey upright. The balloons, flying up among the skyscrapers, are quite a sight, even for New York City!

Since Thanksgiving Day signals the beginning of the Christmas season in New York, the last float—a beauty—bears Santa Claus pulled in his sleigh by eight tiny reindeer. Santa stops at Macy's and wishes everyone a Merry Christmas, then climbs down a chimney in Macy's window.

St. Nicholas

BURTON FRYE

Nieuw Amsterdam stood where Wall Street, Trinity Place, and Rector Street are now. Dutch boys and girls clogged in their wooden shoes over the cobblestones in summer, and in winter went ice-skating on ponds that are now part of Central Park.

Every year they celebrated the joyous festival of St. Nicholas.

Nicholas was a bishop. He was devoted to people and did many good deeds; for instance, he gave oranges in silk stockings to devout sisters of charity every year. He was such a good man that he was quite often able to perform miracles. His most famous achievement was to rescue two little boys who were trapped in a pickle barrel.

The Dutch children of Nieuw Amsterdam loved St. Nicholas. By and by, children from all over the world lived in New York City. Today, they all share the heritage of good St. Nicholas. You do too! You don't? Yes, you do. Only, now, you call him SANTA CLAUS. (Say SAN NICHOLAS, over and over, and faster and faster, until it comes out "Sana Claus"!)

There's even a street named for him in Spanish Harlem! For seventy years, there was a children's magazine called *St. Nicholas,* which published poems, stories, art, and music by and for children, and, today, you can see, in the New York Public Library, copies of the magazines or read Henry Steele Commager's two delightful St. Nicholas anthologies (Random House, 1950) and *St. Nicholas, the Early Years* (Meredith Press, 1969).

Chinatown

Chinatown began back in 1858 when a man by the name of Ah Ken and his family moved into a small house on Mott Street. Other families followed and today there is a community of some 10,000 Chinese living in an area bounded by Baxter and Canal streets, the Bowery and Chatham Square. There is much to see, do, taste, and smell in Chinatown. On the first full moon after January 21, Chinatown celebrates the Chinese New Year with a parade of fire-breathing dragons and dancers accompanied by the pop-pop-popping of thousands of firecrackers.

There's an excellent museum at 8 Mott Street which features exhibits relating to Chinese customs and culture. The museum is open from 10 A.M. to 10 P.M. daily. Admission is fifty cents (seventy-five cents on Sundays and holidays).

When there is real good sleighing, my sister hires a stage sleigh and takes me and a lot of my schoolmates on a sleigh ride down Broadway to the Battery and back. The sleigh is open and very long; and has long seats on each side, and straw on the floor to keep our feet warm, and the sleigh bells sound so cheerful . . .

FROM *Diary of a Little Girl in Old New York,* 1849–50

A NINETEENTH-CENTURY CHRISTMAS PARTY

August 6, 1850, entry, *Diary of a Little Girl in Old New York*, by Catherine Elizabeth Havens

I must now write about our Christmas party. Every year before school closes for the holidays my sister gives me and my schoolmates a party. I wish I had curly hair, but I haven't; and so the night before the party Maggy puts up my hair in curl papers and keeps them pinned in until the party, and it is horrid to sleep on them for they are so hard and lumpy and hurt my head, and then as soon as we get warm playing our games, the curl all comes out and my hair is as straight and stringy as ever. Ellen has lovely dark, curly hair. By and by, while we are playing our games the sliding doors into the dining room are shut, and the lights turned up bright there, and then we know the supper is getting ready. The lights shine so pretty through the glass panes, and show the birds of Paradise on the palm trees, and then the girls all gather near the doors so as to get in quick when they are opened. One of the girls has a pocket tied around her waist under her dress, and as soon as she gets her plate with figs and nuts and raisins and mottoes handed to her, when she thinks nobody is looking she turns up her skirt and dumps it all into her pocket, and then looks as if she had not had anything. No boys are invited to the party and only two gentlemen. One is Mr. Hoogland, our writing teacher; he wears blue spectacles, and the other is a second cousin of ours who has attacks, my sister says, but he has never had one at the party. I wish he would, as I have never seen anybody have an attack, but of course I don't want him to suffer. The table looks so pretty at our party. My mother and my sister and Maggy fill the dishes with mottoes and heap them up high, so that there will be plenty for all my schoolmates, and last of all comes the ice cream and cake. Then all the girls say good evening to my sister, and thank her for the party, and go home, and no more lessons till after New Year's day.

CHRISTMAS AT THE BRETT DOLL HOUSE

ALFRED TAMARIN AND SHIRLEY GLUBOK

For 150 years a family of dolls has lived in a miniature house in the Museum of the City of New York. The little family still has much of the original furniture, and through the years has acquired more treasures. The house contains musical instruments, fine silver candlesticks and china dishes, a stove with pots and pans, and even tiny pets. At Christmastime the house is decorated with a tree and stockings are hung over the fireplace.

Peter

A PROFILE OF A NEW YORK KID

Peter, a sixth grader at the Ethical Culture School on the Upper West Side of Manhattan likes to work with his hands, and builds rockets and airplanes in his spare time—"Just as long as they can fly," he says. When he isn't working with his hands, he works with his feet—skiing is his favorite sport.

What about eating? He says that's one of the best things about New York. French and Chinese are his favorite foods. "Sometimes I go with my family to the Chinatown Fair on Mott Street. You can get the best food in the world there," he adds. Anything you hate, we ask? "I won't eat shad roe," he answers. "Of course I personally have never tasted it, but my mother hates it and that's good enough for me."

Any career plans? Peter isn't quite sure, but thinks he might be either a musician or an actor some day. "A lot of people like that live in my neighborhood," he explains. Peter's neighborhood is near Riverside Park in the West Nineties.

And what makes your neighborhood special? "Well," he says, "it's the kids. The kids make it special. Some are nice, some are snobbish, some are dirty, but most are all right."

THE BLIZZARD OF '88

In 1888 a terrible blizzard struck New York. Snow piled up in thirty-foot drifts. Everything came to a halt. But the people didn't let all that snow get them down; they just made jokes about it. At Third Avenue and Thirty-first Street somebody put a sign on top of a huge snowdrift. The sign said:

TAKE SOME!

At 105th Street somebody put a sign on another huge drift. It said:
WANTED—A CASHIER FOR THIS BANK

Another sign said:
THIS LOT TO BE RAFFLED
JULY 4TH. CHANCES $10

On Barclay Street:
WANTED: ONE THOUSAND MEN TO CHEW SNOW

And, on Fifth Avenue:
SNOW FOR SALE!
COME EARLY AND AVOID THE RUSH

CITY ANIMALS

```
                                                              ogoodo
                                                          ogoodyearodo
                                                        ogoodyeargoodo
                                                       ogoodyeargoodyear
                                                        ogoodyeargoodo
                                                         ogoodyearodo
                                                           ogoodyearo
                                                            theblimp
                                                            theblimp
                                                             floats
```

CITY CATS

There are perhaps a hundred thousand stray cats living in New York. Many of them can be found near the docks searching for rats. Others get their meals in the alleys behind restaurants and markets where they can be seen pawing through the garbage for a few choice morsels. There are even cats who spend their whole lives underground. They live in the subway tunnels and stations. Sometimes subway workers leave them something to eat, but most of the time they are on their own.

A few cats have part-time homes in markets and other small businesses, but most have to fend for themselves on the streets, which is a hard life. The SPCA says that apartment cats in New York live to an average of twelve years but that cats on the street only live to an average of two.

a cool New York Cat

The Penguins
and the Truck Driver

ELIZABETH LEVINE

A truck driver was supposed to deliver fifty penguins to the Bronx Zoo. On the way, his truck broke down. He hailed another truck passing by, and asked the second driver if he could do him a favor and take the penguins to the zoo. The second driver said, "Sure, I'm going that way, anyway."

A few hours later, the first driver's truck was fixed, and he decided to go to the Bronx Zoo to see how the penguins were doing. When he was near the zoo, he saw the second driver walking away with the fifty penguins marching right behind. "Hey! What's going on?" demanded the first driver. "I told you to take these penguins to the zoo for me."

"Well, I did," said the second driver, "and then we still had time left, so I thought I'd take them to a movie!"

PLEASED TO MEET YOU

NORAH SMARIDGE

A tiger with a hungry smile,
A large and scaly crocodile,
A grizzly bear with big, sharp claws,
A lion with enormous jaws
Would not be very nice to meet
If you were strolling down the street.

But when you see them in the zoo
Just smile, and ask them "How d'you do?"
Since they're locked IN and you're locked OUT
There's nothing to be scared about.

Seuling

How Animals at the Bronx Zoo Created the Superhighway

STEPHEN MOOSER

LIMERICK

BARBARA SEULING

There was a weird child at the zoo
Who made faces one day at the gnu,
Said the gnu to the child,
"Should we meet in the wild,
I'll eat you, so help me; now SHOO!"

LAWN MOWER

The first animal imported to Central Park for children's rides was the camel. When it wasn't carrying children around, it was hitched to a mower and used to cut grass.

If I told you our modern highway system, with its high-speed turnpikes and freeways, was started by some animals at the Bronx Zoo would you believe me? Probably not. Well, it's all true, and here's how it happened.

In 1906 some animals at the Bronx Zoo got sick and died unexpectedly. At first zoologists couldn't figure out what had killed the animals. But a few months later they stumbled on the answer—the animals had all drunk water that had been poisoned by the nearby polluted waterway known as the Bronx River. For years people had been dumping their garbage onto the

banks of the Bronx River, and thinking little of it. They thought the river would carry away the garbage, and for a while it did. But over the years the dumping increased, and so did the pollution. Finally the water got so bad that it poisoned the animals in the zoo.

Now it didn't take people long to realize that if the water was bad for animals, it would be bad for humans too. Something had to be done to stop the dumping, or before long people were going to start getting sick, and maybe dying.

It was finally decided that the roads to the river's edge would be eliminated. The old dumps would be turned into a long park. So that people could enjoy this park a long, winding roadway would be built down its middle. The park planners envisioned the roadway being used by people on bicycles, horseback, and even behind the wheels of the newfangled automobiles that had just begun to appear on New York's streets.

The road that was finally built was called the Bronx River Parkway, and it was like no other road that had ever been built. There were only a few places where vehicles could get on or off the roadway. Intersecting roads either passed under or over the Parkway.

Does this kind of road sound familiar? It should. It's the basic design of all our modern superhighways. If it wasn't for turnpikes and parkways cars would have to stop at almost every intersection. Trips that now take minutes, would take hours. If you like getting places quickly and comfortably then you should thank those poor animals who gave up their lives so long ago at the Bronx Zoo. They made it all possible.

The World of Birds

BARBARA BEASLEY MURPHY

Recently a group of New York City students came out of a terrific snowfall into a tropical rain. They heard birds screech, titter, and coo. They saw them swoop from branches and vines to forest floor and soar up to cliffs. The students stared through the fine warm raindrops. Yet everyone, birds and students alike, seemed to take it very naturally. They were in the World of Birds at the great Bronx Zoo.

The World of Birds is a planned introduction to wild birds. In the wonderful new exhibit building you can go from sloping hillsides to wooded swamps, from Australian scrub to New England forest, and from jungle floor to treetop vistas. Several of the naturalistic displays are seen at more than one level. Yet you enter the building, pass through it, and return to the starting point without ever having to backtrack or climb a flight of stairs. Nowhere in the world are birds exhibited better, more beautifully, or more meaningfully.

Many of the birds are not even in cages! Their soaring flights, dazzling colors, and unceasing activity are easy to see. On special days you can accept the zoo's invitation to visit the world *behind* the World of Birds. A keeper will show you the incubators where wild bird eggs are waiting to be hatched. You can hold in your hand an egg the size of a baseball. It will feel warm as a toasted bun, smooth as a rain-washed pebble. Inside the beautiful egg is a miniature ostrich. Visit the baby bird nursery and see who's just been hatched. It may happen before your very eyes. See where birds are kept who are ill or injured from fights with other birds.

Out in the exhibit area again you may see the spectacular basket nests of the cacique and, if your eyes are sharp, the delicate cups of webs built by hummingbirds. Or the dance of the manakins, dazzling acrobatic maneuvers for courtship. Read the signs and funny pictures by cartoonist Tomi Ungerer. Discover that many birds navigate as sailors do, by sun and stars, that the Arctic tern undertakes an annual round trip of twenty-two thousand miles from the Arctic to the seas that fringe the Antarctic, that an azure jay once lived to the grand age of nearly thirty-nine in the zoo! Find out why the owl's flight is silent . . .

The World of Birds. If it belonged to a bank, they'd keep it in a vault; it's one of New York's most beautiful and surprising treasures. And it's free once you pay a small admission to the zoo. Bring your camera. Everybody does.

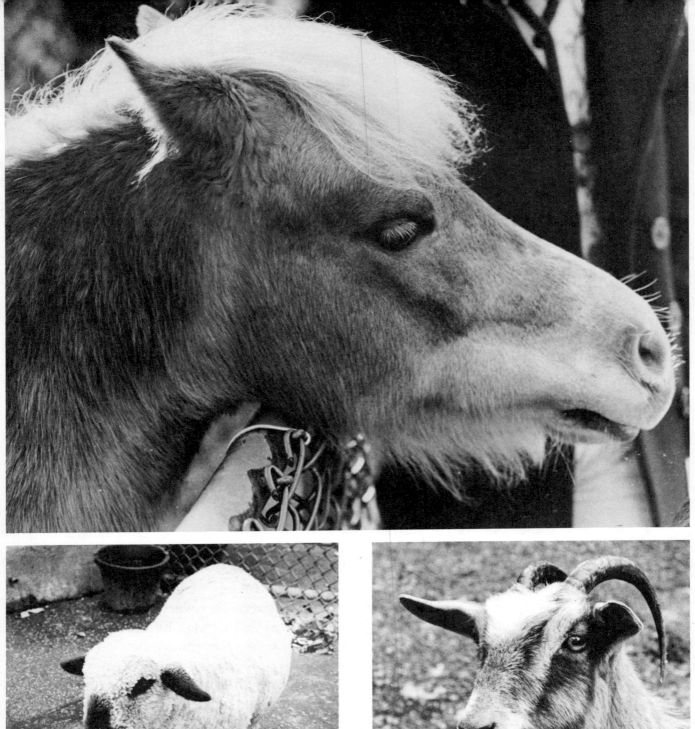

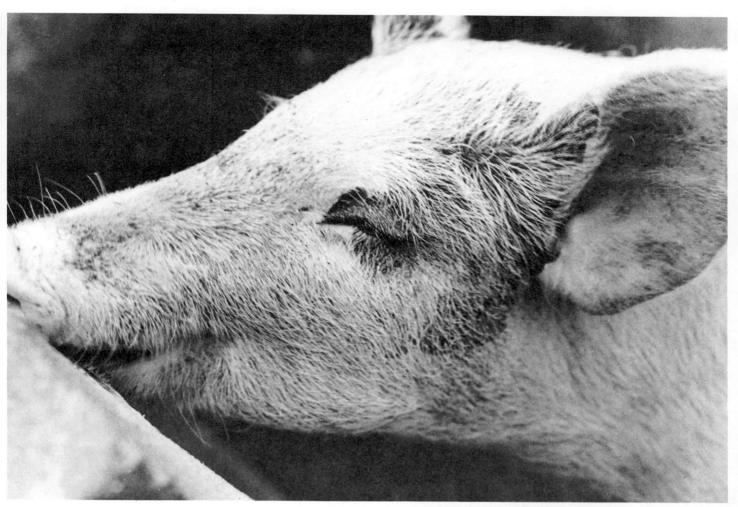

HERE ARE SOME FRIENDS
YOU MIGHT MEET
AT THE CENTRAL PARK
CHILDREN'S ZOO

by WINNETTE GLASGOW

Saving the Bison

ALICE SCHICK

New York City seems an unlikely place to save a wild animal from extinction, especially the largest animal on the American continent. Even back in 1895, wild city places were few and far between. And the American bison, which had once ranged throughout most of the United States, had never lived in New York.

These facts did not discourage William T. Hornaday, the first director of the Bronx Zoo. Hornaday had been concerned about the bison for a long time. Sixty million animals had been reduced to eight hundred, and those eight hundred were so scattered that the species was in serious danger of extinction. Hornaday believed it was just as important for an American zoo to preserve endangered native animals as

to display exotic foreign creatures. So he set out to save the bison.

When Hornaday made this decision, the Bronx Zoo did not yet exist. There were no animals, no buildings, not even a location for the zoological park. Hornaday had been appointed director shortly after the New York Zoological Society was organized in 1895, and part of his job was to select a site, get the zoo built, hire a staff and acquire animals.

In looking over possible sites for the zoo, Hornaday kept in mind his plan to gather a breeding herd of bison. The place he chose, Bronx Park, had a twenty-acre meadow in the southeast corner—a perfect place for bison.

Hornaday still needed animals. He wrote letters to men in Massachusetts and New

Hampshire, who kept bison herds on their estates. When they refused to send animals, the zoo director was forced to look farther afield. Eventually, Hornaday was able to buy several bison for $500 a cow and $400 a bull. The zoological society considered these prices outrageous, particularly since there were so many other animals to be bought, but the director insisted they were fair and refused to bargain.

For the zoo's official opening in November 1899, there were seven bison, the promising beginning of a large herd. But something went wrong. Grazing on the meadow grass, the animals sickened and some died. Hornaday moved the animals while the grass was burned and the topsoil removed. Still the bison died.

Hornaday would not give up. He bought more bison. At last some of the animals adjusted to living conditions at the zoo and began to breed regularly. When the American Bison Society was formed in 1905 to establish bison herds in government preserves, Hornaday became its president. Because of the success of his bison breeding program, the Bronx Zoo was able to send twenty-nine animals to the first two government preserves in Oklahoma and South Dakota.

Today the American bison is no longer threatened with extinction. There are about twenty-five thousand animals on preserves and in zoos, including the Bronx Zoo. If you visit the southeastern corner of the park, you can see some of the descendants of Hornaday's bison—the wild animals saved in New York City.

Hot Dogs!

A couple of winters ago, when dogs walked down the wet and icy sidewalk in front of 347 Convent Place in Harlem, the hair on their backs went shooting up. It wasn't that the dogs had seen a ghost, but rather that they had walked across a stretch of pavement that had accidentally been electrified. Apparently the insulation on a cable beneath the sidewalk had rotted away and the leaking electricity and wetness charged the pavement. No people were affected because their shoes offered sufficient insulation from the weak electrical current beneath their feet. Dogs, however, will be happy to know that Con Ed has since repaired the break, so a stroll down Convent Place is no longer a hair-raising experience.

Bird Watching, Anyone?

BARBARA BURN
AND EMIL P. DOLENSEK

You don't have to leave New York City to see wild birds. All you need is a bird guide (there are several good ones at the library), a pencil to list the birds you see, and a lot of patience. Wild birds don't like noise or sudden movements, but if you sit still and are very quiet, they will probably not even notice you are there. A pair of binoculars is useful but not necessary.

The best places to see birds are in relatively large wooded areas, which can be found all over the city. One dedicated birdwatcher claims to have seen over three hundred different species of birds in Central Park alone. In the Bronx, you can try Pelham Bay Park (including the Thomas Pell Sanctuary), Van Cortlandt Park, or the Botanical Garden. Brooklyn has Prospect Park, of course, Queens has Flushing Meadows, and you mustn't miss the Jamaica Bay Wildlife Sanctuary on Cross Bay Boule-vard. There is also a bird sanctuary in Staten Island, but since birds can't read signs, there's a pretty good chance of seeing one almost anywhere.

If you'd like to see some exotic species without sitting outdoors in a park, you can always visit some of the marvelous pet shops in the city. The following shops specialize in birds of all kinds—from tiny canaries to enormous parrots:

Fish and Cheeps, 104 Second Avenue

Belmont Bird and Kennel Shop, 30 Rockefeller Plaza

Crystal Aquarium, 1438 Third Avenue (between Eighty-first and Eighty-second streets)

Crazy World of Pets, 216 Avenue A (at Fourteenth Street)

Blumstein's Department Store, 230 West 125 Street

Snakes

GEORG ZAPPLER

The Staten Island Zoo has one of the largest snake collections in the world.

Every kind of rattlesnake that lives in the United States—there are about forty varieties—is kept at the zoo. There are also many other kinds of snakes, poisonous as well as nonpoisonous. The large constrictors, the boas and pythons, some of them twenty feet long, are the most impressive.

Did you know that the first constrictors were around by the end of the Age of Dinosaurs? These snakes do not kill their prey by squeezing it to death the way most people think. Instead, they keep tightening up their coils around the victim every time it expels air to take a breath. Eventually the chest cavity is so constricted that no new air can be taken in.

Poisonous snakes came on the world's scene long after the dinosaurs were gone. There are numerous different species, but in all of them salivary glands have changed to poison sacs that empty their venom through grooved or hollow teeth.

For Junior Herpetologists

**BARBARA BURN
AND EMIL P. DOLENSEK**

People come from all over the world to see the snakes, lizards, and alligators in the reptile house at the Bronx Zoo. But there are other good places to visit if herpetology (the study of reptiles) is your particular interest. The Staten Island Zoo has one of the largest and best collections of rattlesnakes in the country (call 442–3100 for information), and various pet stores throughout the city have good reptiles for sale and for browsing.

The Fang and Claw at 304 West 14 Street is not very large, but its owner, Aldo Pasera, is a knowledgeable dealer who can tell you about the exotic specimens he has on display as well as about species that are common in this country. If you prefer amphibians—frogs, toads, and salamanders—your place is Small Worlds, which is on 107 East 88 Street, in Manhattan. The whole shop is an environment filled with creatures who don't seem to mind being stared at—including a frog named Bully, who will come when called and speak on command.

 # City Wildlife

MARY BLOOM

New York is a city of pets—over a million dogs, hundreds of birds, many thousands of cats. City dwellers bring pets of all kinds into their homes. Some say it's to make them feel they are in the country without leaving the city. Others try to learn more about the world we live in through their animals. Apartments are shared with bees, parrots, coyotes, mice, skunks, bobcats, monkeys, lizards, toads, snakes, and many more.

A five-year-old boy in Brooklyn shares his room with Millie, a pet millepede. She is a friend who plays hide-and-seek under his pillow and tickles him when she crawls up his arm. A young teenager keeps a tarantula which she feels is beautiful and interesting to study, and she has learned many things about herself and her fellow man by observing the social behavior of insects. In school, one boy who lives in Manhattan had a science project which turned into a very good friend. He studied chicks hatching in an incubator, and became attached to his egg, which later grew to be a large rooster that lives in his apartment but does not crow early in the morning because he stays up late watching television with the family.

There is a gorilla in a home in Brooklyn, a kangaroo in Manhattan, and at least one mule on Staten Island, so if you are walking on Broadway and think you heard a lion roar—guess what, you probably did!

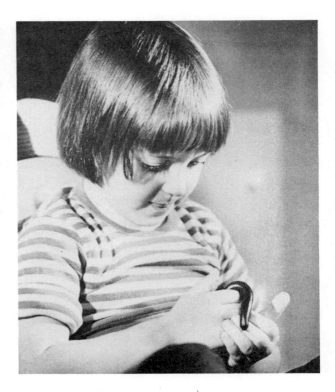

"The jaywalker is a very rare bird."

"New York was named after the Duck of York."

"I rode an alligator to the top of a skyscraper."

"My uncle works for the Rabbit Transit Company."

NEW YORK CITY STARLINGS, OR WHY DID SHAKESPEARE DO IT?

BETTY BOEGEHOLD

In March 1890 a Shakespeare lover named Eugene Scheifflin let a flock of starlings loose in Central Park, eighty in all, whose descendants were soon to engulf all America like a tidal wave. Scheifflin wanted to acquaint America with every bird mentioned in Shakespeare's writings. History doesn't tell us much about the other birds he imported, but it does record (perhaps with a shudder) that, not content with his first boo-boo, he repeated it the next year, releasing forty more starlings to join their happy companions.

The starlings adopted New York enthusiastically, soon spreading out to every borough. Then, like pioneers, some headed west; and fifty years later, a cloud of starlings spread over the whole continent.

Like most New Yorkers, starlings prefer city and suburban life. Aggressive, adaptive, and smart, they've learned to eat anything from good grain to junk food. They prefer man-made structures to wild woods or soaring mountains, from building ledges and warm-air outlets to bridges and viaducts. The resident New Yorkers are joined in winter by their northern relatives, swelling the flocks to between a quarter to half a million birds. They've also adopted the commuting habit—in reverse. Setting out at dawn, they scatter to forage in the suburbs; then from all points of the compass they gather in huge flocks to wing back to their city residences. The bridges over the Harlem River make luxury living quarters: a half mile of intersecting traffic arteries, a jumble of concrete ramps, posts, and steel girders—and all of it almost void of human beings. Under these soaring structures is a perfect bird sanctuary protected from snow, wind, or rain—perfect, that is, for birds like starlings, who don't mind exhaust fumes, polluted air, and noise.

Starlings are pretty noisy themselves, especially settling down at night, yakking over the day's events to their neighbors, while decorating the landscape with tons of bird droppings. Humans roaring by in cars and trucks don't hear or see them, but bridge and girder painters, struggling to chip away the thick dried guano, are resentfully aware of the starling invasion.

Starlings are amazingly inconspicuous, considering their numbers, their raucous whistling and aggressive ways. Most people don't even recognize the strong-beaked, short-tailed stumpy black birds—iridescent with purple and green by summer, speckled with white in winter—as they waddle over city grass. For all their aggressiveness and indifference to human proximity, they are wary birds and hard to approach. But they are equally hard to drive away permanently. Like human city dwellers, they have learned to cope with almost any condition. Without any federal handouts or protective services, the starling has made it in the Big Apple. And some of us, like Shakespeare, have to admiringly salute this spunky fellow creature who, like it or not, has chosen to cast its lot with us.

An Egret's Secret

THE JAMAICA BAY WILDLIFE REFUGE

FRANCESCA LYMAN

Not many New Yorkers know about the Jamaica Bay Wildlife Refuge. This peaceful refuge, the largest wildlife refuge of any city in the world, lies just across the bay from Kennedy Airport. Its 18⅔ square miles of sandy islands, tidal marshes, dunes, and freshwater ponds are kept in their natural state. Looking out from the shore of the West Pond, where snowy egrets are wading, you might think that the Manhattan skyline on the horizon was a mirage.

Geographically New York City is situated directly under the Atlantic Flyway, the bird highway that extends up north into Canada and south to Florida. It also lies just under the turnoff to the western states and prairies. Jamaica Bay is a very popular stop for all kinds of migrating birds—some that stop for just a few days (Canada geese, sandpipers, and others); some that stay all winter (brant, pintail, hawk); some that stay all summer (egret, heron, ibis, tern)—as well as permanent residents (mallard, duck, killdeer, sparrow, gulls).

Besides geography, there is another reason why so many birds stop here. The variety of natural habitats—wooded gardens, freshwater ponds, tidal marshes and mud flats, and the saltwater bay—is suitable to all types of waterfowl, land birds, and shore birds. Each year about 750,000 birds come here, of which 450,000 are within a list of 312 species.

Twenty years ago, Herb Johnson, a horticulturist, was hired by the City of New York to create an artificial environment for birds to nest in. Out of the sand and salt water, he dredged, filled, and landscaped the area. He planted trees and shrubs that the birds could feed on—rose hips, bayberries, autumn olive, holly, and Japanese black pine. Many of these plants are labeled for the public. Since 1974, when the refuge passed into the hands of the National Park Service, the place has been carefully maintained by rangers.

You can get a permit to visit the refuge any weekend, but it is recommended that you call first and make a reservation. The Park Service offers slide shows, bird walks, and nature walks to hundreds of people every Saturday and Sunday.

You can ask your schoolteachers to bring your class on field trips during the week in which you can take part in the special environmental workshops. The rangers will present you with various ecological games and activities, such as the wildlife treasure hunt, in which you look for clues—sign of an animal (feather, hair, tracks), food sources (berries, roots, seeds) and habits (pecks on the tree trunks, nests). You will also learn about really looking to find out about the adaptations of different birds to their particular habitats: why a marsh bird has a long neck, a bill, and long legs, why a hunting bird needs a curved beak and talons, what the best kind of swimming feet are. In the upland tracts, there are wooded glades where you can learn to identify bird calls.

Besides birds, the other types of wildlife you might see are turtles, muskrats, cotton-tail rabbits, and frogs.

It is easy to get there by subway from the city. From Manhattan it is a forty-five-minute ride on the express train during rush hours (IND A-train to Rockaway to the Broad Channel stop)—and closer from Brooklyn and Queens. From the Broad Channel station you walk about three quarters of a mile west on Cross Bay Boulevard.

When you go, take scarves and hats because it's often windy. Bring binoculars if you have them. It is well worth the trip.

NEW YORK CITY HAS THE MOST

BARBARA BEASLEY MURPHY

New York City is famous for having the most of many things. It has the longest subway tracks, the loudest talkers, the highest tree (on top of one of the tallest buildings), the richest kid, the most dirty words on buildings, etc., etc.

This is about the fattest woman. Call her Irma. She lives on Tenth Street in the Village. Irma was invited to brunch in someone's garden. He was rich and famous. Someone like Walt Frazier or Robert Redford or Farah Fawcett. But not any of them. Call him Irving.

It was the first warm day in May. Irma took a Checker Cab to Irving's party. (Checkers are the biggest.) His maid let Irma in the front door and showed her out the back into the garden. It was the tiniest

garden in New York. Full of tulips, blooming forsythia, and the rich and famous of Greenwich Village. Irma, whose legs bothered her, looked for a seat.

Irving welcomed her and said he'd find her one. Together they edged through the milling throng.

"Irma, wait till you see my miniature poodles. Ping and Pong. They're a matched pair, very rare. The most expensive dogs sold."

"Oh, I'd love to see them. They sound adorable."

"They're the most adorable dogs in New York City," Irving said. (You don't have to believe *everything* you hear in New York.) "Look, Irma, there's a seat under the forsythia."

It was a white wicker settee.

Irving said, "The maid will bring you a plate of Eggs Benedict in a minute. As soon as I get a chance, I'll show you the pups." He turned around to greet another guest.

Irma squeezed past a movie star and sank into the settee. It wasn't very comfortable. To see anybody or eat anything, she had to push the forsythia branches out of the way. All the guests talked to her and told her their stories. Irma laughed and ate and had a good time.

In mid-afternoon Irving carried out one of the miniature poodles on his hand. "Everybody! This is Pong. Isn't he cute? I can't find Ping. She's shy and won't come out at parties."

Pong yipped and wagged his tiny tail.

Everyone said, "That's the most adorable dog in New York."

When Irma stood up, she found the other one. On the chair where she'd been sitting. It was unconscious.

Aghast, Irma scooped it up, opened her purse, and tucked it inside without closing the bag. The pup was still warm. But Irma wondered if the heat was just from her own body. She thought she'd faint.

Irving came to escort her to the door. "Irma, dear, I'm so glad you could come. You make a party so much fun."

"Oh, Irving, it was lovely. Thank you for inviting me. I . . . I . . . just don't know how to tell you . . ."

"You don't have to say a word. It wouldn't have been fun without you." Irving opened the door and closed it behind her.

Irma stood there heartbroken, the tiny dog a weight in her purse. Then she started to run, huffing and puffing, the pocketbook slapping her side. At the corner she found a phone booth, fumbled for a dime, and dialed the ASPCA.

"Please be there," she prayed.

A woman answered.

Irma said, "Oh, help! I've got a nearly suffocated puppy in my purse. Please tell me what to do!"

"First of all, Lady, take the dog out of your bag." Then the woman proceeded to direct Irma. "Now we'll do artificial respiration."

With the receiver hung over her shoulder, Irma knelt and kneaded the puppy's little chest rhythmically, according to the woman's directions.

Finally the puppy feebly wagged its tiny tail.

With a shout of joy, Irma thanked the ASPCA and, cradling the puppy, rushed back to Irving's.

If you just ask, she thought, people in New York are the most helpful in the world.

Animal Emergencies

WHAT DO YOU DO IF YOU FIND A SICK BIRD?

Call 369-3520

(ASPCA—Emergency)

WHERE DO YOU REPORT DOG LITTER?

Call 966-7500

(Environmental Protection Agency)

WHERE DO YOU REPORT CRUELTY TO ANIMALS?

Call 876-7700, Ext. 169

(ASPCA—Humane Division)

WHAT DO YOU DO IF YOU FIND A LOST DOG?

Call 860-3431

(ASPCA)

Lost and Found

CANINE DEPARTMENT

BARBARA BURN AND
EMIL P. DOLENSEK

Losing a dog can be a very distressing situation—for the owner and for the dog. The best way to avoid this, of course, is to make sure that the dog can't get away.

A person should always use a leash when walking his dog. (No dog should be allowed to run free; if it doesn't run away, it is likely to get into a fight with another dog.) In case of mishap, however, the dog should wear a collar with an identification tag along with its regular license (which is obtained from the ASPCA at 441 East 92 Street for $8.50 a year). One should also teach a dog to come when it's called.

If your dog disappears, the best thing to do is call the ASPCA (876-7701), whose job it is to round up all loose dogs (and cats). Ask if they have picked up a dog matching the description of yours. Even if they say no, go to the shelter nearest you (there's one in Manhattan, one in Brooklyn, one in Queens, and one in the Bronx) and look for yourself. At the same time, make up a sign with the dog's name, description, and your name and the telephone number (offer a reward if you can afford it). In describing the dog be sure to include color, size (in pounds), hair length, tail length, type of ears, and any markings. (A photograph is a good idea, if you have one.) Get local shops, veterinarians' offices, and shelters to put the signs up on their bulletin boards (check the Yellow Pages for names and addresses of vets and shelters).

If all else fails, you can try calling radio stations to ask them to advertise your dog or put a classified ad in your local newspaper.

Most important, keep making trips back to the ASPCA and the shelters near you. The law says that these organizations need hold dogs for only forty-eight hours before destroying them, so you must act promptly. (Not all dogs are killed, of course, but the statistics are discouraging. Only seven thousand dogs out of a hundred thousand find new homes through the ASPCA each year.)

If you have found a dog, simply do all of this in reverse. Call the ASPCA if the animal has a license number and try to find the owner. Check local bulletin boards and newspapers. If you decide to keep the dog, be prepared to give it up if the real owner finds you. If keeping the dog is impossible, you had better call the ASPCA to come and get it.

If you see a lost dog but can't catch it, the ASPCA will do it for you. Don't try to touch any dog that seems shy or agressive or sick. Stray dogs can be ill, starved, or hostile and dangerous to people, so if the ASPCA hasn't shown up after a few hours, you might call the police department as well.

Animal Doctors

**BARBARA BURN AND
EMIL P. DOLENSEK**

A veterinarian is a medical doctor who has had four years of graduate school, passed a state exam, and received a special Doctor of Veterinary Medicine degree to practice on animals. In addition to giving regular examinations, shots to prevent certain diseases, and advice about proper feeding and care, veterinarians also do surgery, take X rays, and make many kinds of tests in order to diagnose illness. Although in school a vet will learn about horses, cattle, and other animals including dogs and cats, most of the city's vets are small-animal doctors, specializing in pets. Some veterinarians, however, treat other kinds of animals. At the Bronx Zoo, the veterinarian must deal with several thousand different species—mammals, reptiles, and birds, including some as small as a newly hatched duckling and others as large as whales and elephants. The veterinarian for the police department must take care of horses and dogs (the narcotics squad uses dogs in their work), and some private vets take care of exotic pets, such as skunks, monkeys, and ocelots, even though it is illegal to keep these without a special permit.

There are two large animal hospitals in New York City—the ASPCA hospital on East Ninety-second Street, and the Animal Medical Center on East Sixty-third. The latter, called the AMC, is open around the clock, twenty-four hours a day every day, and is the best place to go in case of an emergency (call 838-8100). Several different doctors work in these hospitals and the AMC even has specialists for animal eyes, animal neurology, pathology, dermatology, and orthopedics.

CITY PETS

GEORGE SELDEN

I'd like to say a few approving words
About our city dogs and cats.
I mean, about the boy or girl who guards
Our animals—and make them into pets.

I once knew someone who adopted *rats!*
(And that seems very strange to me.)
But he—my friend—he had no doubts, regrets—
He just had human sympathy

For all four-legged things that whine—lonesome—
And know that their only rewards
Are words of love: the greatest words
From kids who give their pets a life, and home.

No Pets

ROBERT BURCH

I've never understood why not everyone cares for animals. Well, I suppose almost everyone does. I've met only one man whom I suspected did not. He was the superintendent of a very big building in which I had a very small apartment in New York. His last name was Cross. Some of the tenants called him "Super." I called him Super Cross.

I had seen him briefly when I rented the apartment, but for some reason he was not around when I moved in. Two days later, while I was working on a story, someone knocked at the door. Before I could answer it the lock clicked, the knob turned, and the door swung open. Super Cross stepped inside. He said, "Don't bother to get up; I've let myself in," as if I couldn't see that he had. "Just checking!" he added, smiling at me.

"Checking what?" I asked. "To see if the key worked?"

He laughed. "No, to see if everything's all right."

"Everything's fine," I said. "Will you have a seat?"

"Can't spare the time," he said as he sat down. "Got work to do." He sprang to his feet. "Those are fish in that tank back of you!" he said.

"Yes, so they are," I said, wondering what he found so unusual about them.

"But no pets are allowed in this building," said Super Cross, crossly. "I made that clear to you: no pets!"

"Yes, you did," I agreed. "But surely fish are not included."

"The rule is: *no pets!*" said Super Cross. "Didn't you understand that?"

"Yes, certainly. But I thought you were talking about things like dogs. I had no idea you meant fish too."

"Well, I did!" he snarled. Then, as if he were doing me a big favor, he said, "You can keep them, I guess. But it's still against the rules!" He started toward the door but was looking at me so angrily that he failed to watch where he was going. He almost knocked over a bird cage. He wheeled back around and glared at me as if the cage had hit him instead of the other way around. "That's a bird!"

"Where?" I said, hopping to my feet and looking out the window. I didn't see anything, and it came to me what Super Cross was talking about. He was staring at the bird in the cage. "Oh," I said, "*that* bird. Yes, well, actually, it's a canary, but you're right: a canary *is* a bird."

"And it's alive, isn't it?"

"I should hope so!" I said. "There'd be no need to keep it in the cage otherwise. I mean, if it were dead it couldn't fly away even if it wanted to."

"Well, you're not supposed to have canaries!"

"Oh, I only have one," I said. He looked less annoyed until I added, "The others are parakeets and finches. And a parrot that can say, 'Hello, darling! Hello, darling!' Would you care to hear him?"

Before Super Cross could answer me, Ridley, my beagle hound, trotted across the rug and sat at my feet.

"Whose is that?" shouted Super Cross.

"Mine," I said.

"But a minute ago you said you thought "no pets" meant dogs."

"Yes, but I thought that meant *big* dogs . . . you know, great Danes, or boxers, or Irish wolfhounds, and what's that really big one—the giant?"

"Great Dane," he said.

"No, I named great Danes." I scratched my head, trying to think. "Saint Bernard!" I said happily. "That's it! It came to me! Funny how words sometimes escape us, isn't it?"

He didn't look as if anything had ever

been funny to him. He just stood there, his face turning red and appearing to grow larger as if steam were being pumped into it. Neither of us said anything until the rooster suddenly crowed in the next room. Super Cross regained his voice instantly. "Don't tell me you've got a flock of chickens in there?"

"Well," I said, "I wouldn't call three hens and a rooster a flock, would you?" I explained to him that they were livestock instead of pets and how I was reared in a small town in Georgia with lots of farm animals around and that it was "down home" to have a few with me now. Also, the price of groceries being what they were, it was a saving to grow my own eggs.

"I don't care! I don't care, get rid of them!" he shouted. "When those chickens scatter feed there'll be vermin in this building, do you hear? And that's something I've never had in a building that I look after. There'll be mice and roaches!"

"That's fine," I said soothingly, trying to calm him. "The mice will eat the roaches, and everything will be just fine."

"I'm trying to tell you," he shouted, "I don't have mice!"

"Oh, I didn't mean *your* mice," I told him.

He seemed puzzled, and then he looked

as if he understood but couldn't believe it. "You mean you've got mice running around here all the time?" His voice was shaky, and instead of his face being red now, it grew pale, and he breathed in short gasps.

"Heavens, no!" I said, which somehow reassured him. When he was breathing in a normal fashion, I added, "Not all the time. Only in the afternoons, when I put

the cat in the bathroom. Then the mice get to play everywhere else. Can you think of a better solution?"

Instead of saying whether he could or could not, he held his arms up and shook them, a strange expression on his face, and ran out screaming.

Eventually I had to move, but I really needed more space anyway. The last I saw of Super Cross he was showing my apartment to an attractive woman from Australia who kept opening the pantry door and looking inside. I could tell by the way she was studying it that she was trying to decide whether it was big enough to house koala bears. Or maybe a kangaroo.

LITTLE WILLIE WILLIAMSON

WALTER MYERS

Little Willie Williamson
Was quite the baddest thing
Caught a worm and called it Sam
And tied it with a string

Walked it down the Boulevard
And bought it a balloon
Fed it corn and popsicles
And drinks in a saloon

Then he put it on his nose
And as it slid down to his chin
He opened his mouth as wide as he could
And watched the worm slide in

LOOKING FOR LOOK-ALIKES IN WASHINGTON SQUARE PARK

LOWELL SWORTZELL

Do you think dogs look like their masters? Or masters like their dogs? These questions really bother me. You see, I am a very large white poodle and considered by most dogs and their masters to be quite good-looking. When walking in the park people come up and say, "Pretty boy" or "Splendid fellow," and I give them my paw and we shake on it. Of course, I know they are just being nice and don't necessarily mean it any more than they do when greeting each other with shouts of "You're looking great" or "Wow, get a load of you!" I learned to handle compliments as a puppy, and even though I am a French poodle I don't let that sort of thing go to my head.

But the other day when we were sunning, some ladies on the next bench remarked that dogs and their owners grow to look alike. And then they talked about their friend Millicent Andrews and her little Winnie and not being able to tell them apart. They found this very funny and laughed a lot.

I chuckled softly to myself and looked up to see if my master was amused. Then it hit me. My smile disappeared and I shook all over. Was I going to look like *that*? Or was he going to look like me? Or like Millicent Andrews and Winnie were we already indistinguishable?

I haven't been the same dog since. I stared at my master as if I had never seen him before. "Wow, get a load of you!" I murmured half-heartedly, and sat with a very long face. My ears are bigger, God knows, and my nose more a part of me. But maybe around the eyes, I wondered, is that where it begins? My lashes curl while his don't do much of anything. Yet there could be a resemblance. Yes, our eyes are the same color. For heaven's sakes, why haven't I noticed that before! The change has begun. Perhaps my ears aren't as big as I thought. Maybe my nose looks fixed, too!

Since that day I've been watching every dog and owner in the park, and while this pastime hasn't solved my own frustrations, it has been lots of fun. Look-alikes are everywhere: a bushy-haired man in a red checkered shirt leads Sam, a bushy-headed English sheep dog, sporting a red kerchief round his neck; a very friendly lady talks to anyone who will listen while her two escorts sniff about for companionship; a ballet dancer floats through the walkways with her cloudlike Afghan; an old lady surrounded by friends and their dogs presides from the same bench every morning with the help of Sara, her really regal poodle. I like Sara and try to say hello every chance I get.

When approaching any of us, you should ask the master if we like to be petted. We have down days and sometimes just aren't in the mood. However, a dog biscuit or two (I prefer the spinach-flavored ones) will make most of us more than agreeable. Our masters love to talk about us, sometimes even before they are asked.

Be certain to learn our names. You won't believe what some dogs are called these days. But since my name is Crême de la Crême (Cream of the Cream), maybe I shouldn't bring up the subject of unusual or funny names. Just call me Crême for short.

My master takes me to the park between seven and eight every morning, and again in the early evening. Look for us. We like to greet new friends. Oh, yes, in case you have trouble in telling who is who, I'm the one with four feet.

Animal Pests

BARBARA BURN AND EMIL P. DOLENSEK

Many people think of squirrels, pigeons, cockroaches, rats, and English sparrows as terrible pests who run around carrying diseases, causing damage, and giving humans a lot of trouble. But instead of thinking of them as pests, think of them as human inquilines. In other words, think about the fact that these animals are entirely dependent on us for their life cycles, and, if it weren't for humans, wouldn't exist in such large numbers or perhaps at all. They live in places we have made (parks, build-ings, rooftops, etc.) and eat our food (which we throw away or hand out to them). So the next time you see a pigeon, don't blame it for being what it is; blame yourself and treat it with a certain amount of respect.

Remember that it is illegal to be cruel to animals, and that anyone who intentionally harms an animal is in trouble. The law was designed to protect horses, cats, dogs, and other animals that we use and enjoy, but it also applies to wild animals, which certainly deserve the same right to live their lives without interference as any other creature. This does not apply, however, to animals that are dangerous or harmful to us—such as wild rats, cockroaches, and wild dogs that are aggressive to people. Cockroaches can be taken care of with spray bombs in the home, but the other creatures should be reported to the police or to a local authority so that they can be eliminated professionally.

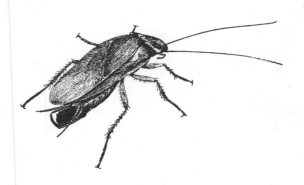

IN THE NEIGHBORHOOD

Coney Island

PHIL SEULING

The Astro Tower is so tall that it is the first visible point of land for travelers coming to New York by sea. The Cyclone is the most famous roller coaster in the world. The boardwalk is more than three miles long. More than six million hot dogs are sold each year by *one* store. All of these marvels are in one small seashore area of Brooklyn. The name of the place has become a national expression for hot dogs, or for any big, colorful, spicy, cheap attraction. The place is Coney Island.

Back in the late eighteen hundreds, Coney Island featured giant amusement parks glittering with paint and tinsel and lights. Dreamland Park, Luna Park, and Steeplechase Park were, at different times, palaces of fun for millions of New York people. Today the giant parks are gone, and it was once thought that Coney Island would gradually fade away. But Coney Island today attracts millions of visitors each summer, just as it has in the past.

The people come to ride the zooming rides. They want to smell the sand, the french fries, the salt air. They want to be on the biggest Ferris wheel in the world, the Wonder Wheel, or one of the many roller coasters. They laugh at the fun houses and water flume rides. The sounds of shooting galleries and loud music and carousels keep the spirits up. There is nothing gloomy about Coney Island.

The bathing beach extends for miles, and it is a long distance from boardwalk to water's edge. In the summer, newspapers often show helicopter photographs of crowds numbering more than a million on the beach.

321

Urban Homesteading

PAMELA MORTON

Some New York kids have all the luck. They grow up on a block where new adventures are happening all the time.

Skie and Taina, Dori, Lillian, Amparo and Pito are among such lucky ones. They live in a building on East Eleventh Street which they and their parents have rehabilitated. Where once there stood a burned-out vacant building which had been vandalized for years, there is now a handsome building with eleven apartments and a park and a playground which have been made from the empty lot next door. With a loan from the city and technical assistance from a community group called Adopt-a-Building, they have done all the work on their apartments themselves, and now are becoming the owners of those apartments. The process of obtaining ownership is called "sweat equity." It means that by the "sweat of your brow" you bring an abandoned building to life and usefulness again and that the work you do constitutes your buying it.

If you were invited up to the roof of 519 East 11 Street, a surprise would await you. There, turning in the wind, is a very tall windmill. It is part of the building's exploration into alternative energy sources. The windmill generates enough energy to light the hallways and the basement. Another remarkable sight is the solar collectors which gather enough solar heat to provide all the hot water for the building.

The enthusiasm and hope generated by the rehabilitated building is contagious. Other buildings on the block are being homesteaded now. And a community garden with family vegetable plots has started nearby. Young people who grew up on the block have organized after-school and summer programs for the children. They call their association Nosotros and they are making things happen. There are summer picnics and block parties with relay races and dance contests. Dori and Lillian are working on their clown costumes and *everyone* is getting out his Eleventh Street T-shirt because you just never know what might be going to happen next on this block!

THE LONGEST BOARDWALK, THE LARGEST BEACH

Coney Island has the largest beach and the longest boardwalk in the world.

Heather

A PROFILE OF A NEW YORK KID

Heather, 14, goes to John Dewey High School in Brooklyn, where she studies (and loves) marine biology. A real Coney Islander, she was born and raised a block from the boardwalk and beach, and four blocks from the famous New York Aquarium. Heather loves her neighborhood. "Even in winter it's not dead," she says. "There's no end to the crowds and the movement." Once, when she was younger, Heather and a friend saved up and went on the Cyclone seven times in a row. She can name every new ride that is installed in Coney Island, and tries them all out herself right away.

Heather is an outgoing type, friendly to everyone. Her idea of misery? "Eating alone in the school cafeteria," she replies. Heather's best feature is that she doesn't give up easy; she always gives things another try. She likes people; that's why she likes New York and feels it is the best city in the world. "There's never a shortage of people," she says, "you know, funny people, like on the subway. People make me laugh."

The Narrowest House in the City

ANN McGOVERN

Hey, look at me! I'm as big as a house!" a man said, standing outside my house. He was speaking the truth.

Was the man a giant? No, he was a regular-sized person, standing outside my house with his arms stretched out. From the tips of his one hand to the tips of his other, he was exactly the size of my house.

For many years, I lived in the narrowest house in New York City, in New York State, and, for all I know, in all of the fifty states. It stands on Bedford Street, in Greenwich Village, and is so tiny that if you blinked as you passed by, you might miss it altogether. Inside it measures eight feet, seven inches at its widest, and two feet at its narrowest, where the steep staircase ends on the top floor.

Living in the little house was like living in a doll house. It had five rooms, three floors, a basement, and a tiny garden. My favorite place was the top floor, which was long and very narrow. That was my living room, library, and writing room. It had two tiny fireplaces and a skylight for the sun. The table where I wrote my books looked out over the tiny garden. Of course I could grow only tiny flowers in the garden, for the garden was doll-size too.

On the middle floor there were two bedrooms but they were so small that only one bed could fit in each room. My bed was built inside the room and when I moved out, the bed had to stay behind because it wouldn't fit through the tiny door. The first floor was made up of the tiny kitchen and dining room. A trap door in the middle of the kitchen floor opened to tiny stairs, leading down to the basement.

The house is over one hundred years old. Before there was a house at all, the space was just a path between two houses. Then, some say, it was a blacksmith's shop, and later a community kitchen for the houses around it. Although the main entrance to the house was on Bedford Street when I lived there, the door that led to the garden in the back was the main entrance when the house was built. There was a terrible sickness raging in the city at that time, and the people who built it thought it was healthier to enter the house through the garden.

The floors in the old house were very crooked and on a slant, so much so that whenever I fried an egg or made a pancake, it slipped to the edge of the pan and came out shaped like a half-moon.

Many famous people have lived in the house over the years. The great actor John Barrymore was said to have lived there and, years later, Marlon Brando. The wonderful artist and writer William Steig also lived there once, but I think it is best known as the home of Edna St. Vincent Millay, the poet. Sometimes it's called the Millay House.

I liked to think about the ghosts of all the people who lived there, especially Edna St. Vincent Millay, whose poems I love to read. Often on days when it rained hard and was dark inside, with the wind sweeping in through the cracks in the windows and whistling down the fireplace, I felt exactly as she must have when she wrote the first and last stanzas of her poem, *Wraith:*

> "Thin Rain, whom are you haunting,
>   That you haunt my door?"
> *Surely it is not I she's wanting . . .*
> *Someone living here before!*
> "Nobody's in the house but me:
> You may come in if you like and see."
>
> Curious, how she tried the window,—
> Odd, the way she tries the door,—
> *Wonder just what sort of people*
> *Could have had this house before . . .*

———◆●●———

WHAT HAPPENED TO FOURTH STREET?

SYDNEY TAYLOR

One day Fourth Street lay sprawled in the gutter, as usual, when an old newspaper came floating by. That's how it chanced to come upon an article written by a chap named Horace Greeley, with the headline "Go West, Young Man!"

"Go West!" Fourth Street exclaimed. "Greeley must be talking about me! He says 'go forth'—that's my number!"

All that day Fourth Street waited impatiently for night to fall. Then, promptly at the stroke of midnight, when everyone else was fast asleep, it made its move. Slowly, cautiously, it tiptoed across Seventh Avenue.

"Lucky for me there's no moon tonight,"

Fourth Street said with a chuckle. "Not a soul will see me. I'll be way ahead of all the rest of the numbered streets around here."

Inch by inch Fourth Street crept along through the darkness. At last, when morning dawned, it looked around. Goodness gracious! It had started out to go west all right but in the pitch blackness it had somehow wandered off to the north as well. It had crossed Eighth Street, then Ninth Street, even Tenth, Eleventh, and Twelfth—all the way up to Thirteenth Street.

A policeman passing by was the first to notice Fourth Street stretched out groggily across Thirteenth Street where it had bumped its head against a solid row of houses. He immediately called up the Mayor and the City Council.

"Come and see what has happened to Fourth Street!"

By the time the Mayor and the City Councilmen had arrived, the whole neighborhood was crowded with people all staring and talking at once.

"This will never do!" the City Councilmen said to one another.

"See here, Fourth Street," the Mayor demanded, "you'll just have to go right back to where you came from!"

"Yes, yes! Go back to where you belong!" the people all shouted.

But groggy or no, Fourth Street was also stubborn.

"No! I am now the first west numbered street. I am here, and here I'll stay!"

The people pleaded; the Councilmen scolded; the Mayor stormed.

"If you don't do as I say," the Mayor finally threatened, "I'll have you locked up!

No traffic will be allowed to go in, out, or around you. Do you hear?"

But Fourth Street was adamant. "I will not budge!" it growled.

Well—that did it. There was nothing anyone could do. Everybody, even then, knew that the city budget was very low. (Ask your mom and dad about budge and budget.)

And so to this very day, Fourth Street has stayed where it is. A lucky thing, too. Had it managed to move on to Fourteenth Street it would have been a real calamity. Fourteenth Street is a main artery of New York City with lots of trucks and buses rushing back and forth, so Fourth Street would surely have been run over by now.

Now if you don't believe this tale, that's your affair. But please, for your own satisfaction and mine, next time you're in the Greenwich Village area, take a stroll down West Fourth Street. See for yourself if it's not the absolute, 100 percent truth!

Striver's Row

Striver's Row is the name given to a group of elegant homes between Seventh and Eighth avenues on 138th and 139th streets in Harlem. The homes, which were built between 1890 and 1891, were designed by the famous architect, Stanford White.

The Row earned its unique name because it was said that the people who bought these homes were "striving to get up in the world."

I roll my hoop and jump the rope in the afternoon, sometimes in the Parade Ground on Washington Square, and sometimes in Union Square. Union Square has a high iron railing around it, and a fountain in the middle. My brother says he remembers when it was a pond, and the farmers used to water their horses in it . . .

FROM *Diary of a Little Girl in Old New York, 1849–50*

AROUND THE WORLD IN ONE DOG WALK

MADELEINE L'ENGLE

Most people have to fly millions of miles to get acquainted with the people of different countries. Not on the Upper West Side of New York. When I leave my apartment to take my dog for a walk I go by a Taiwanese shop, which is next door to a kosher butcher. Everybody on the block loves the Taiwanese baby who toddles from store to store. Our section of the city has the largest group of Orientals, next to Chinatown. My dog and I walk by the Buddhist Temple, with its huge and magnificent statue of St. Shinram. We hear a lot of Spanish spoken, and I am slowly learning some Spanish from the children who want to pet *el perro*. I speak French with a neighbor from Haiti. And all around me I hear German spoken, and Yiddish, and even some Hindustani.

When I shop for food I can buy all kinds of things which in most communities are unavailable: all kinds of oriental delicacies; exotic fruit drinks from Germany and Austria; black-eyed peas and collard greens from the south; chutneys and all the spices for curries. It's one of the most cosmopolitan neighborhoods in the world.

Cosmopolitan, yes; and realistic. We're not sheltered on the Upper West Side from the seamier sides of life. There are apartment buildings for middle income people next to Single Room Occupancy buildings. There are old people living alone who find their only sociability in sitting on the benches on the islands in Broadway when the weather is temperate. There are people on welfare. People on drugs. All kinds of people, from all races and all colors and all backgrounds.

Because I have a dog I am able to make far more friends than I would be if I were walking alone.

Heard on the Sidewalks of New York

Oh, Marguerite, go wash your feet.
The Board of Health is across the street.   (SONG)

On the mountain stands a lady
Who she is I do not know
All she wants is gold and silver
All she wants is a nice young man.
So jump in my (*friend's name*)
So jump in my (*friend's name*)

On the mountain stands a lady . . .   (JUMP-ROPE RHYME)

One potato
Two potato
Three potato
Four
Five potato
Six potato
Seven potato
More.

One, two, three. You're out!   (CHOOSING GAME)

I won't go to Macy's
any more more more
There's a big fat policeman
at the door door door
He will pull you by the collar
And make you pay a dollar
I won't go to Macy's
any more more more   (GAME PLAYED BY SLAPPING HANDS)

One, two, three alairy
My first name is Mary
My second name is Anna
That's the way you spell banana   (GAME PLAYED WITH BOUNC-
ING BALL)

A my name is *Anna*   (GAME PLAYED THROUGH THE
And my husband's name is *Alfred*   ALPHABET WITH A BOUNCING
We come from *Argentina*   BALL, TURNING THE LEG OVER
And we bring back *Apples*   AT EACH NAME, WHICH THE
PLAYER HAS TO FILL IN. IF YOU
LOSE CONTROL OF THE BALL OR
CAN'T THINK OF A NAME THAT
FITS, YOU LOSE YOUR TURN.)

Strawberry shortcake cream on top
tell me the name of my sweetheart
(a, b, c, etc.)
          (JUMP-ROPE; THE INITIAL YOU
MISS THE ROPE ON IS THE INI-
TIAL OF YOUR SWEETHEART)

Teddy bear, Teddy bear
Touch the floor, floor, floor
Teddy bear, Teddy bear
Shut the door, door, door
Teddy bear, Teddy bear
Go upstairs, stairs, stairs
Teddy bear, Teddy bear
Say your prayers, prayers, prayers
How many prayers did he say?
(1, 2, 3, etc.)

(JUMP-ROPE RHYME; OBJECT
TO SEE HOW HIGH YOU CAN
COUNT BEFORE YOU MISS)

Victor

A PROFILE OF A
NEW YORK KID

Victor has curly hair and big brown eyes. He is eight years old, and lives on Manhattan's southeast side in a big complex with a plaza. "I hate not being able to play baseball in the plaza, but we go over to the Veterans Hospital and play there. I love baseball."

He loves to play hide-and-seek, too, and to visit his father's restaurant, La Scala. If he could take his best friend anywhere in the world, he'd go to Grossinger's in upstate New York: "That place is a lot of fun —they have swimming, skating, skiing. Everything's right there."

Victor spent two days with his friend Adam, whose father works at ABC-TV, at the World Trade Center for the "ABC 76–77 Funshine Saturday," a weekend of cartoons and programs for kids. They had private showings of "Electra Woman," "Dynomutt," "Dr. Shrinker," "Scooby Doo," and other season previews. They had lunch at the World Trade Center restaurant, and met "Mr. Puff 'n' Stuff" himself.

Victor has done some other interesting things, too. He took tap dancing lessons with Charlie Lowe, the famous Palace Theater vaudeville star. And one day some "movie people visited my school and chose two of my friends to be in a movie, one as a turkey and one as a pilgrim. They made a hundred dollars. I was almost in a movie, too. My cousin Frank played the delivery boy. I was on the set all day when they were filming it—*Audrey Rose*. It's a horror movie. I'm not in the movie, but it was a lot of fun with all the lights and cameras." His favorite movies are *Airport 1977* and *Rocky*.

MORE
CITY PROBLEMS
FOR WHICH
A SOLUTION
COULD BE
FOUND

SHEILA GREENWALD

Stages run through Bleecker Street and Eighth Street and Ninth Street right past our house, and it puts me right to sleep when I come home from the country to hear them rumble along over the cobblestones again. There is a line on Fourteenth Street too, and that is the highest uptown.

FROM *Diary of a Little Girl in Old New York, 1849–50*

The Ninth Avenue International Festival

HANNAH SOLOMON

Imagine a feast, served to a quarter of a million paying guests in a space a mile long, consisting of foods from places as far apart as Poland, the Philippines, and the Pennsylvania Dutch region of the United States. Got that? You have just imagined the Ninth Avenue International Festival.

Ninth Avenue north of Thirty-seventh Street is lined with restaurants, groceries, greengroceries, delicatessens, butcher shops, and bakeries representing a wide range of nationalities. People shop there all year round, the way everyone used to shop before supermarkets took over—going into each little store for its own specialty. But for one weekend a year, the avenue is closed to traffic from Thirty-seventh Street to Fifty-seventh. Vendors dispense regional specialties from stands which line both sides of the street. There is also entertainment—international offerings in music, dance, and recreation. You might hear Irish, Italian, or Greek music, or domestic rock, or all of the above; see clowns and mimes; try out a trampoline. The scheduled events take place on three separate stages, and unscheduled events just happen everywhere. Most of the entertainment is scheduled for Sunday; on Saturday, famous chefs and cookbook authors demonstrate their craft in streetside booths.

In addition to a chance to see some of

the quarter million New Yorkers and tourists who visit the festival having a good time, this is a good occasion to eat yourself silly, provided you have some dollars to spend. (Few of the eats for sale are priced below a dollar.) If you're adventurous, you can make a meal (or several meals) of foods you've never tasted before. You might choose from Philippine dishes like pancit (a fried noodle and vegetable mixture) and banana fritters; kebabs, kokoretsi (a grilled sausage made from lamb liver and sweetbreads), and baklava (many-layered pastry with honey and nuts) from Greece; whole roast pig (sold sliced, in sandwiches), green coconuts (the top is sliced off so you can drink the water; if you return the nut to the slicer, he will cut it open so you can eat the inside), and empanadas (meat turnovers) from the Caribbean; funnel cakes (batter poured through a funnel into a sizzling skillet, fried crisp, served with sugar) from the Pennsylvania Dutch country; and a range of Italian specialties, including slices off a

six-foot hero sandwich. Other countries represented include China, Thailand, Mexico, Argentina, Vietnam, and Poland. Share new foods with friends or family; that way everyone can try more new things. If you want to stick to old favorites, you'll find hot dogs, corn, watermelon, ice cream, cotton candy, and other familiar festive fare.

The festival, sponsored by the Ninth Avenue Association of New York, was first held in 1974. It is generally the middle weekend of May; check local newspapers and magazines for an announcement of the festival date and schedule of events.

AWAY FROM IT ALL

In the 1830s, people were being lured up to Forty-second Street from lower Manhattan to settle uptown and enjoy the pure, clean air.

BUSINESS AS USUAL

Astor's Little Joke

John Jacob Astor made a fortune in New York real estate in the early 1800s. He was one of the richest men of his time. One day some people came to ask him if he would donate money to a charity. He said he would be glad to and gave the people a check for fifty dollars. The leader of the group had hoped this wealthy man would have been more generous. He gathered up his courage and said:

"We hoped you would give us more, Mr. Astor. Your son gave us a hundred dollars."

"Ah," said Mr. Astor. "My son has a rich father. Mine was very poor."

THE NEW YORK STOCK EXCHANGE

STEPHEN MOOSER

In the late 1600s the country's first stock-brokers began to meet under a buttonwood tree on the site of what is now 60 Wall Street. This casual little stock exchange lasted for a hundred years until Alexander Hamilton, the nation's first Secretary of the Treasury, decided that the United States should go into the bond business. Hamilton suggested that the U. S. Government take over the debts that the states had run up during the Revolutionary War. Since the government was broke itself, Hamilton suggested that bonds be sold to the public through the good offices of the buttonwood brokers. The brokers got together and drew up agreements, including a rate of commission they would charge in their role as middlemen between the government and the public.

Eventually the brokers, who now called themselves the New York Stock Exchange, moved out from under the buttonwood tree and into a building of their own. In 1903 they moved into the present building at 20 Broad Street just south of Wall.

THE LAW

It is *illegal* to leave a naked mannequin in a store window in New York City.

FOR A QUICK EXIT

NORMA FARBER

For going up or coming down,
in big department stores in town,
you take an escalator.
(They come in pairs.)
Or else an elevator.
(Also stairs.)

I wish storekeepers would provide

      a
        s
          l
            i
              d
                e
                  !

Success Story

BARBARA SEULING

In the middle of the nineteenth century, a boy was born in a brownstone house on West Twentieth Street in Manhattan. He received most of his schooling there, because Teedie, as he was called, was sickly for most of his early childhood, and couldn't attend an outside school with his brother and sisters.

Teedie's father told him that he had a fine mind, but not the body to go with it, so the boy began to build himself up physically with a strenuous exercise program. His father helped by installing gym equipment on a small porch outside the boy's bedroom window. By the time he reached his teens, young Teedie was as strong as any normal boy.

West Twentieth Street was slowly becoming a commercial neighborhood, and when the boy was fifteen the family moved uptown to a new house. Years later, equipped with a fine mind and a healthy body, Teedie was sworn in as the twenty-sixth President of the United States, Theodore Roosevelt.

BEWARE OF DOGS

At night, after Macy's doors are closed, fierce Doberman pinschers are let loose to roam the store looking for burglars.

LIMERICKS

CATHARINE EDMONDS

There once was a banker from Wall
Who stood on the subway too tall.
At each little bump,
His head got a lump,
Till he lost all his teeth at Canal.

There's a little old lady named Stella,
Who pokes people with her umbrella.
She flails with a fuss
On subway and bus,
Screaming, "Back off, ya creep, or I'll fell
ya!"

Hot Dog Hero

BARBARA SEULING

When Nathan Handwerker arrived in America from Poland around the turn of the century, he took a job at Feltman's, a junk food palace in Coney Island, where a sausage on a roll was the featured item. All the time he sliced rolls and made deliveries, Nathan dreamed about owning his own place. Two of Feltman's singing waiters, Jimmy Durante and Eddie Cantor, encouraged him, and suggested that when he opened his own stand, Nathan sell his hot dogs cheaper than the outrageous price at Feltman's—ten cents.

Nathan saved every penny, and eventually accumulated enough to rent a small stand on Surf Avenue, a block from the famous Coney Island Boardwalk and beach. On April 28, 1916, the stand opened, featuring five-cent hot dogs. Charlie Feltman may have invented the hot dog, but Nathan Handwerker made it a national institution. The little stand grew, and so did the hot dog habit.

Today Nathan's famous hot dogs are sold in stores all over the city. They are even served in the Brooklyn Museum. But once, people made the long trip to Coney just for one of Nathan's hot dogs.

Fiddle-Faddle

EVE MERRIAM

Riddle me no,
riddle me yes,
what is the secret
of Success?

Said the razor, "Be keen."
"String along," said the bean.
"Push," said the door.
"Be polished," said the floor.
Said the piano, "Be upright and grand."
"Be on the watch," said the second hand.
"Cool," said the ice cube.
"Bright," said the TV tube.

"Bounce back," said the yo-yo.
"Be well bred," said the dough.
"Plug," said the stopper.
"Shine," said the copper.
"Be game," said the quail.
"Make your point," said the nail.
"Have patience," said the M.D.
"Look spruce," said the tree.
"Press on," said the stamp.
"Shed some light," said the lamp.
"Just have a good head," the cabbage said.

Some Shops to Visit

BEBE WILLOUGHBY

One of the most wonderful things about New York is shopping. Below we've listed some fun places to visit, shop, and just plain look. By exploring New York you'll find more.

Beautiful and unusual toy-like fantasy objects are created by WILLIAM ACCORSI (473-8346). His store is located at 71 Irving Place. Carved Christmas tree figurines, castles made from building blocks and airplanes from clothes pins are only a few of the objects designed and created by this talented man.

GO FLY A KITE (988-8885) is located at 1434 Third Avenue. It is a colorful store specializing in beautiful and unusual kites.

Imaginative toys may be found at CREATIVE PLAYTHINGS (759-8884), 1 East 53 Street. They are mostly for younger children.

THE TEACHER'S STORE (674-7225) is located at 260 Park Avenue South at Twenty-first Street. It is filled with a wide range of educational kits, games, and instructional toys.

Are you fascinated by toy trains? A visit to MADISON HARDWARE COMPANY (777-1110) at 105 East 23 Street should satisfy you. There are trains of all ages and gauges. Sets run from $19.95 to $200. (A set includes locomotive, tracks, transformer, and cars.) There are also wonderful landscape items and unusual cars such as a Fort Knox car complete with gold bars to add to your set.

If you are an equestrian you probably already know about MILLER'S (691-1000) at 123 East 24 Street and KAUFFMAN'S (684-6060) at 139 East 24 Street—both have beautiful items for riding enthusiasts.

TANDY LEATHER COMPANY (947-2533) is located at 330 Fifth Avenue. They sell leather kits to make belts, moccasins, handbags, and vests.

THE FLEA MARKET at 252 Bleecker Street has a variety of old stuff, new stuff, and everything in between. It's a fun place to wander in. Its hours are Thursday, Friday 10 A.M. to 10 P.M. and Saturday noon to 7 P.M.

The world's largest cheese store with over a thousand different kinds of cheese is called CHEESE OF ALL NATIONS (732-0752). It is located at 153 Chambers Street and there are free samples included with a visit. Upstairs is a delightful cheese restaurant serving only cheese dishes.

DOLLS AND DREAMS at 454 Third Avenue (685-4277) offers irresistibly soft stuffed animals—owls, monkeys, kangaroos, dogs, lambs, and penguins to name a few. There is a special reading corner for children and many different kinds of toys and games. They have beautiful dolls designed by the famous doll-maker Sasha Morgenthaler, with faces that seem to change expressions.

ASTRO MINERALS at 155 East 34 Street (889-9000) is filled with many expensive gems and minerals which young geologists will enjoy. A set of drawers is stuffed with minerals that cost a dollar each. Rocks are sold by the pound in some instances, and the store has jewelry. If you wish to make your own jewelry, it sells polished stones for twenty-five cents.

Located at 513 Third Avenue is FISH TOWN U.S.A. (889-3296). It is like another world, dark with glass cases all along the walls. Prices vary from inexpensive fish at thirty-nine cents each to rare fish at two hundred dollars each. Aquarium equipment is available also.

OLD FRIENDS at 202 East 31 Street (686-4291) is a small store filled with memorabilia from Disney. See Donald Duck, Mickey Mouse, and all of their friends.

There are six AZUMA stores throughout Manhattan: 415 Fifth Avenue (889-4310), 666 Lexington Avenue (752-0599), 25 East 8 Street (673-2900), 1126 Sixth Avenue (682-0640), 251 East 86 Street (369-4928), and 387 Sixth Avenue (989-8690). The stores are filled with goodies—posters of Robert Redford, Farrah Fawcett-Majors, models of Spiderman and Batman. There are mirrors, candles, cards, and pillows, and even some Indian clothings—a large conglomeration of gifts and home furnishings.

An entire shop devoted to soap in the Village at 51 Grove Street is called THE SOAP OPERA (929-7756). They have unusual types of soap and even some soap that looks like candy.

THE GINGERBREAD HOUSE (989-9080) at 9 Christopher Street has creative toys, games, and books for children. There is lovely doll house furniture and a motorized train that lets a little boy off for school and then picks him up.

CHILDCRAFT (674-4754) at 155 East 23 Street offers an adventure in creative toys that is both stimulating and educational. There are word games, alphabet games, miniature animals, doll house furniture, and electronic games, to mention only a few of the items they carry. There's an adult corner for your parents if they are traveling with you.

Do you ever dream of making your own jewelry? An interesting place to visit is SHERU at 49 West 38 Street (730–0766). This is the largest bead store in the city. They carry all sorts of trimmings, bracelets, kits for jewelry making, ribbons, shells, and much more.

MINI MUNDUS (288-5855) at 1030 Lexington Avenue is for doll house lovers and collectors. It's a small store of miniature furniture, accessories, and dolls.

The NEW YORK DOLL'S HOSPITAL at 787 Lexington Avenue (838-7527) was established in 1900. Here antique dolls are bought, sold, and repaired. "I've never lost a patient and this is the only hospital that people come to with a smile," says its owner.

NOTE: Be sure to phone before visiting these shops. New York is an ever-changing city.

We get our stockings and flannels at S. and L. Holmes' store, near Bleecker Street. They are two brothers and they keep German cologne . . . I like best to go to Arnold and Constable's on Canal Street, they keep elegant silks and satins and velvets, and my mother always goes there to get her best things . . .

I have a green silk that I hate, and the other day I walked too near the edge of the sidewalk, and one of the stages splashed mud on it, and I am so glad, for it can't be cleaned.

On Canal Street, near West Broadway, is a box store, where my mother goes for boxes. They have all kinds, from beautiful big band boxes for hats and long ones for shawls, down to little bits of ones for children, and all covered with such pretty paper.

FROM *Diary of a Little Girl in Old New York City, 1849–50*

Markets

Diamonds	Forty-seventh Street between Fifth and Sixth avenues
Fish	Fulton Street near the East River
Flowers	Twenty-eighth Street between Broadway and Seventh Avenue
Furs	Twenty-fifth to Twenty-eighth Street off Seventh Avenue
Garment Center	South of Fortieth Street, between Broadway and Ninth Avenue
Stocks and Bonds	Wall Street
Trimmings (buttons, beads, fake flowers, lace, glitter, appliques, etc.)	Thirty-eighth Street between Fifth and Sixth avenues

DIAMONDS AND RUBIES

If you like pretty rocks, then Forty-seventh Street between Fifth Avenue and the Avenue of the Americas is the place for you. This street is known as Diamond Row and the windows of the small shops along this street are jammed with diamonds, rubies, emeralds, and other precious stones. Eighty percent of all the diamonds in America are bought and sold along Diamond Row. The gems are expensive, but the looking is free.

Kiss Me, I'm Left-handed

BARBARA SEULING

Are you left-handed? Do you grapple with a pair of scissors because they are made for right-handed people and cut the wrong way for you? There is a store—the only one of its kind in these parts—which specializes in left-handed items. It's called The Left Hand, and it's up on the tenth floor of 140 West 22 Street in Manhattan. They have guitars, junior and regular; drawing and writing tools; notebooks; playing cards with the numbers printed in all four corners; dog-grooming brushes; catchers' and fielders' mitts; child-size and adult scissors; watches; potato peelers; fishing reels; golf and tennis equipment; archery sets; address books and rulers going from right to left; a daily organizer with the pen attached by string to the *left* side, and even a boomerang manufactured with the proper angle for lefties.

A catalog of these and many other items costs one dollar, but you get it back if you make a purchase.

Shopping at La Marqueta

RACHEL COWAN

Stretching along Park Avenue from 111th Street to 116th Street, under the railroad tracks, is a giant indoor market. It is filled with stalls, each of which displays a different kind of merchandise. Many of the customers are Hispanic, since the Market is in "El Barrio" or Spanish Harlem, but the people who run the stalls come from all parts of the country and the world. It's a place where you get fresher produce for less money than you'd spend in the supermarket. On each block there is a separate building—sometimes they're connected to each other by a little plaza. Entering one you smell the mixture of fish, herbs, fruits, and spices. You pass from stall to stall, admiring the different ways people have found to display goods, trying to choose whose oranges look juiciest, whose lettuce is leafiest. The variety is overwhelming:

Fruits: not only piles of large oranges and grapefruits and bright apples, but mangoes, coconuts (which the stall-keeper will open for you with a machete so you can drink the coconut milk right there if you want), papayas, mameys, breadfruits, and bananas ranging from giant stalks of green *plátanos* down to bunches of tiny pinkish finger bananas.

Vegetables: all your ordinary supermarket varieties, plus squash, cactus leaves, enormous avocados, and stalks of sugar cane (which can be cut to order, and then should be peeled before you chew them).

Rice and grains: barrels and baskets are filled with grains like wheat, rice of all different lengths, and every kind of bean —navy, pinto, kidney, yellow-eyed peas, turtle beans.

Herbs: for cooking and for medicines.

Fish: you can tangle with live crabs and lobsters, buy fresh clams, mussels, and shrimp, or have a fish filleted.

Meats: every kind, from pig snouts to chickens to ox tails.

Dairy Products: butter and cheese and eggs.

You can also buy soap, pots and pans, clothes. In fact, just about anything you'd ordinarily need, and then many things you wouldn't know you wanted. You can touch, ask questions, and sometimes taste a sample of some fruit you have never tried. It's a find—a shopping trip and adventure combined.

Supermarket, Supermarket

(A CITY JUMP-ROPE RHYME)

EVE MERRIAM

Supermarket, supermarket,
shelves piled high
with brand-new products
for you to buy:

vegetable soapflakes,
filtertip milk,
frozen chicken wings ready to fly,
shreddable edible paper towels,
banana detergent,
deodorant pie.

The Magic No-Word

NORMA FARBER

The thieves that Ali Baba heard
had to say *Open, Sesame!*

I never have to say a word.

I brake my bike and neatly park it
beside the local supermarket.

And doors just open up for me.

HOW FOOD COMES TO THE CITY, OR WHAT TO DO WITH ALL THOSE BANANAS

CATHARINE EDMONDS

On your way to the supermarket, a restaurant, or home to your own table, all you see are cement, asphalt, tar, and bricks. Where does your food come from? Of course it comes from the farmer, but how does it get from the farmer to the city?

The growers' produce arrives by truck, train, and boat at outdoor wholesale markets, and then by truck at the grocery stores, supermarkets, and vegetable stands.

New York City's main market, the Hunts Point Terminal Market in the Bronx, is the largest fruit and vegetable distribution center in the *country*, covering 125 acres. The old Washington Market in downtown Manhattan, which was replaced by Hunts Point in 1967, had only 38 acres for its 267 fruit and vegetables stores, which were not only the same size as the ones at Hunts Point, but badly run-down and without offices or refrigeration facilities. All the produce was loaded and unloaded by hand in the narrow, cobblestone streets jammed with trucks. Hunts Point has four main buildings, six or seven blocks long, with loading docks on either side of each building. Enormous storage lofts—252 in all—lie in a row down the middle of each building. The volume of produce is immense. Every year, for example, more than *three hundred million pounds* of bananas are bought and sold at Hunts Point! (That's

about sixty pounds of bananas for every New Yorker.)

Around 3 in the morning, truck after truck, from huge tractor-trailers to panel vans, begins unloading its produce on one side of the building, and an hour or so later the railroad cars roll into unloading position on the other side. By 5 A.M. all the trucks, vans, and cars from the city—up to a thousand an hour—are let in to pick up the produce, which the grocery stores, retail markets, food coops, and so on buy from the middlemen stationed at Hunts Point. Soon the place is buzzing with activity—people buying and selling, engines and machinery humming.

Each middleman, known as a "receiver" or "merchandiser," specializes, mostly according to the season. There are tomato "repackers" and melon sellers, who buy their wares from California or Florida in the winter (transported by plane and then truck or rail) and from the tri-state area in the summer. Some specialize in more than one fruit or vegetable, though it may be particular kinds—for example, one type of melon only grown in the northeast in summer. Food comes to Hunts Point from South America, Puerto Rico, Mexico, and Europe too. There is one company that specializes exclusively in tropical fruits.

Everywhere, mountains of crates, bags and boxes, shadowed by open truck trailers. Fresh dill, purple eggplant, ripe strawberries: the colors and shapes are beautiful. Spiny artichokes; dark cherries; pink and tan new potatoes; rows and rows of lettuces. One feels a little closer to fields and earth and growing things.

Here's one good reason for all those millions of bananas:

BANANA CAKE

ESTHER HAUTZIG

You will need and use:

1   stick of butter or margarine (¼ lb.)
1¼ cups of sugar (or less)
2   eggs
¼   cup of sour cream
1   teaspoon baking soda
3   very ripe bananas
1½ cup of unbleached flour
1   teaspoon vanilla

medium-sized mixing bowl, small bowl
measuring spoons, fork
measuring cup
electric mixer
loaf baking pan
toothpick or skewer, oven mitt

Make it like this:

1. Preheat oven to 350 degrees.
2. Put one stick of butter or margarine into medium-sized mixing bowl. Add 1¼ cups of sugar to the bowl. Cream butter and sugar together for about five minutes on medium speed on your electric mixer.

3. Crack two eggs and add them to the butter-sugar mixture in mixing bowl. Beat for about 3 minutes on medium speed.

4. Put into a measuring cup enough sour cream to make ¼ full. Add 1 teaspoon of baking soda to the sour cream. Let it stand. Sour cream will "rise" in the cup.

5. With a fork mash three ripe bananas in small bowl. Add the bananas and 1¼ cups of flour to the mixture in the large mixing bowl. Do this a little at a time, using the mixer set on its lowest speed, alternating bananas and flour.

6. Add the sour cream and 1 teaspoon of vanilla. Mix for a minute or so on the mixer's lowest speed.

7. Grease a loaf pan with a little margarine or butter. Sprinkle a little flour over the butter in the loaf pan. Shake out excess flour from the pan. Pour in the batter from the mixing bowl. Bake in preheated, 350-degree oven for one hour. (To test whether the cake is done, insert a toothpick or skewer into the middle of the cake. If the toothpick or skewer comes out dry, cake is done.) Always use oven mitts when taking things out of a hot oven.

My mother's wedding lace was Mechlin lace . . . It was bought at Thomas Morton's, on William Street, and cost eight dollars a yard. It would seem funny to go down to William Street now to buy lace.

From *Diary of a Little Girl in Old New York*, 1849–50

POTPOURRI

Lights Out

On Wednesday, May 12, 1959, all of New York was hit by a massive power blackout. The electricity and the lights went out all over town. There were some, however, who weren't at all bothered by the sudden darkness. These people were the blind. On Broadway, in the four-story New York Guild for the Jewish Blind, two hundred blind workers, who knew the building backward and forward by touch, led seventy sighted workers down the stairs and safely out onto a darkened Broadway.

Where I Was When the @#$%¢&* Lights Went Out

OLGA LITOWINSKY

DATE: July 13, 1977
PLACE: Columbus Circle, New York
(part of the time)
TIME: 9:32 P.M. and thereafter

Well, there I was with my friend Bebe. We were on our way to the subway after dinner and a hot walk across Central Park South. Feeling hot and grubby and tired, I says to her I says: "I don't want to go down in the subway yet. Let's sit and talk some more." And there we were, sitting on a filthy stone bench, looking at the fountain through a yellow haze, when suddenly a street lamp near us expired. What, ho, I thought. And then another lamp pooped out. "Uh-oh," I said. Then it happened. ALL THE LIGHTS WENT OUT!

We were surrounded by junkies, cops, and ladies of the night, including one who was wearing a phosphorescent necklace. I looked toward the cops—did they know anything? No, they were in the street directing traffic. Quickly I dialed a friend. Had he heard anything? Yes, he had heard that it was a city-wide blackout, but nothing else had come over the radio. OMINOUS. I decided to spend the night with Bebe at her apartment uptown unless the lights came back in an hour.

All the electricity that should have filled all the wires leading to all the lights, air conditioners, subway trains, was in the air, loose! The atmosphere was galvanic. Even the junkies stopped nodding. SOMETHING WAS HAPPENING.

It was just too exciting to get into a cab or bus or anything like that. We walked up Broadway to Seventy-second Street. The picture got grimmer and grimmer. It stopped being fun. It was too dark. No moon, no stars, just hot haze.

At Seventy-second Street we decided to wait for a bus. All the buses were humping along, overcrowded. Nearby was a small candy store, and we walked in to get some ice cream. The owner of the store was

glinting ghastily in the lights of some votive candles. "I got them from the church,"
he said. "Churches always have candles."

At this point, I couldn't wait to get
home. For me, home meant a place that
was well lighted, air-conditioned, with a
TV blasting. Somehow I thought that just
because Bebe's apartment was uptown, she
would have all those electrical delights.

We stood on the corner, licking our ice
cream pops (which were half melted when
we bought them), hoping for a bus or taxi.
Nada, as they say on Columbus Avenue.
At one point a big black car full of men
came speeding by with a man shouting
from it. "We're going up to break windows," he yelled. I shuddered.

Finally, a woman in a small brown car
pulled up and asked: "Anyone for uptown?" "Us," we yelled and got in the car
with seven other people (one of them was
a kid). With springs bumping the Broadway pavement we rode slowly up the
Great (not-so) White Way. Past Ninety-
sixth Street we began to hear the sound of
breaking glass. "They're lootering," said
the driver in a West Indian accent. "We
just came from Brooklyn, and they're lootering all up and down Flatbush Avenue."
And so it was until about 110th Street. We
saw a car on the sidewalk outside a store
near 106th, the folding gate ripped down
from a window and just hanging there.
Groups of men stood outside. Three blocks
away a policeman was directing traffic. I
felt afraid and angry. Many citizens were
directing traffic too, but the looters kept on
looting, hitting the city when it was down
and people needed help.

At last we reached 114th Street. We got
out of the car and thanked our driver.
Then we made the long, dark walk, which

was dark for only a short while, for Columbia students were sitting on the stoops
with candles to light the way for travelers.
At Bebe's house a young man held the
flashlight so she could see her key and
lock. At last: home—hot and dark, just like
everywhere else.

Finally, after an uncomfortable sleep it
was daylight. News bulletins over the telephone told us to stay home. There were no
subways. At 9 A.M. the West Side got
power, and we went out for breakfast. After
breakfast, I decided to try to get home to
Brooklyn, and thought I'd take a bus as
far as I could since there are no buses from
Manhattan to Brooklyn.

The bus was crowded. The looted stores
looked tragic. We made good time on the
bus after Columbus Circle because there
was no power yet midtown and no traffic
lights.

I got off the bus at the Public Library
and into a cab. Fifth Avenue looked like
Sunday. Altman's was closed. People were
strolling. There was very little traffic.

We zipped down the FDR Drive past a
housing project. Kids were filling water
jugs at a hydrant. The news over the cab's
radio explained: no water in high rises because the electric water pumps weren't
working.

We crossed the Brooklyn Bridge. The
city and blue water gleamed in the sun-
shine. The driver was happy to visit Brooklyn. There was no traffic and he was in a
good mood.

I got out of the cab and walked into the
lobby of my apartment building. It had
just occurred to me that I lived nine floors
up and there was no elevator. A strange
man was sitting at the desk, surrounded by
candles. He gave me one for the long

OH THOSE POOR NEW YORKERS!

climb to nine. To my surprise, I didn't feel tired until I hit seven. I emerged from the incinerator/fire door onto my floor and frightened a neighbor with my candle-lit face. The neighbors were milling about, doors open to the apartments letting a little bit of light into the corridor.

At last I was HOME. There was light from the windows. It was wonderful. But there was no water. Aha! The refrigerator was defrosting, and I could use the defrosting water for washing. (Boy, did I feel dirty.) And then I waited. There was nothing to do. I was too nervous to read, the TV was out, I couldn't cook, take a bath, or use the toilet. Finally, I settled down with one ear on my transistor radio (the batteries were weak, naturally).

I heard that lights were coming on here and there around the city: the Lenox Hill area, the eastern part of Brooklyn, a spot in Queens. Mayor Beame was demanding an explanation from Con Edison. Con Edison was blaming God. Betty Furness was saying that people should send bills for spoiled food to the Public Service Commission. At four-thirty, the lamp in the living room lighted up. IT WAS OVER. One hour later the hot water started flowing. SHOWER. NORMAL. WHEW.

So, to those who ask where *I* was when the lights went out, I say, simply, "in the dark."

Manhattan Lullabye

NORMA FARBER

Lulled by rumble, babble, beep,
let these little children sleep,
let these city girls and boys
dream a music in the noise,
hear a tune their city plucks
up from buses, up from trucks
up from engines wailing *fire!*
up ten stories high, and higher,
up from hammers, rivets, drills,
up tall buildings, over sills,
up where city children sleep,
lulled by rumble, babble, beep.

The Last Venusian in New York

DANIEL MANUS PINKWATER

Mike Gershkowitz is an old Venusian, the only one in New York City. He runs a small candy store on Second Avenue between Twenty-third and Twenty-fourth streets, and lives alone, in the back of the store, drinking seltzer, eating pretzels, watching television—and remembering.

"Before 1900, this used to be a big Venusian neighborhood," Mike Gershkowitz says. "Most of the storekeepers around here were Venusians, with maybe a few Martians mixed in. You could get all sorts of Venusian delicacies, like aluminum pretzels—crunchier and saltier than the earth kind—hot seltzer in a lead cup, and candies made of copper wire. Those were the days."

Mike's eyes get moist when he talks about the old days when New York's interplanetary community bustled and thrived on the East Side. What happened to all the Venusians, Martians, and Plutonians who once enriched the life of our city? We asked Mike.

"Most of them went to live in New Jersey. Some went to California. All of a sudden, everybody left—but me. Around the turn of the century, it became fashionable to live like Earth people. Everybody stopped eating ferrous minerals, began to wear Earth-type clothing, and stopped using their native languages. By 1905 there wasn't a word of Venusian heard on the street. Also, people used to stare at folks from other planets because of them being

blue, or having eyes on stalks—little things like that. So, sure enough, the interplanetary ones started turning up in Earth-people colors, with eyes on both sides of a nose, and wearing derby hats, and neckties. It's a shame, if you ask me," Mike says, "losing a whole culture like that."

But Mike says that once in a long while, a person will come into his store, maybe buy a comic book—and eat it, or ask for some hot seltzer in a lead cup. "Then," Mike says, rubbing his old blue head, "I know it's one of the ones from Teaneck, New Jersey, or even Los Angeles, remembering the old days."

New York in the Twenty-first Century

STEPHEN MOOSER

Maybe this story should have been titled "Bo-Wash in the Twenty-first Century" because it's very possible that's where twenty-first-century New Yorkers will be living. You see Bo-Wash is the name of a giant megalopolis that futurologists predict will someday engulf all of New York City. Bo-Wash, a city that's already starting to form, will be the result of the cities of Boston, New York, and Washington, D.C., growing together to make a giant megalopolis stretching for hundreds of miles along the eastern seaboard.

Other megalopolises around the nation will grow up as well. There will be the city of Chi-Pitts stretching from Chicago to Pittsburgh, and on the West Coast there will most likely be a six-hundred-mile-long city called San-San which will sprawl all the way from San Francisco in the north to San Diego near the Mexican border. Of course, all of this need not come to pass, but a growing population and a scarcity of land makes it all very possible.

There are alternative futures for New York, however. Some futurologists envision a twenty-first-century New York as a city of five or six majestically tall buildings, three or four miles high, surrounded by large parks. Others say New York may spread out onto huge platforms anchored at sea. A few have predicted that some New Yorkers in the twenty-first century might find themselves living in domed, pressurized cities built on the floor of the ocean. For residents of this seabed city, life would be like living in an aquarium in reverse—with the people on the inside and the fish on the outside. Or, if gravity can be conquered, as some predict, all of New York may someday float high up among the clouds.

Other changes in transportation, schools, and communications will surely come to pass in the next hundred years. For one thing, the car and the bus will probably disappear from our streets. Already cars are causing too much pollution and congestion. Besides, we are running out of

oil and gas. Our new form of basic transportation may very well become teleportation. With teleportation you would enter a special chamber in, let's say, Grand Central Station. The machine would break you down into atoms and send you flying through a wire at the speed of light. Presto! In less than a second you would be sped across town or across the country to another teleportation chamber. There, you would be reconstructed, we hope, into your original shape. For shorter trips you might find yourself riding on round little scooter boards that zoom down the street suspended just above the pavement by a powerful magnetic field.

Like the automobile, traditional schools may also become extinct in the next hundred years. Before very long it appears as if every home will be equipped with a sophisticated computer. These computers will be tied into data centers around the city and around the world. By punching in a code you will be able to obtain a print-out of every book in the New York Public Library, or, for that matter, any book in any data center or library anywhere in the world. With access to that much information you will be able to take any course you desire. Anybody will be able to study to be a doctor or a lawyer or to take up one of the many new jobs of the next century such as space mining or robot repair.

Of course, from time to time you may want to talk directly to a teacher or fellow classmate. When that need arises you won't have to call them on anything as old-fashioned or clumsy as the telephone. Instead, all you'll have to do is slip on a special mind booster helmet. The helmet will boost your thoughts and send them directly into the mind of the person cross town you want to communicate with. Perhaps you'll want to tell your classmate to meet you for the special live hologram broadcast direct from the Mars Colony, which is being presented that afternoon in Central Park (no matter how many changes take place it would be hard to imagine New Yorkers ever giving up Central Park). A hologram is a type of 3-D television. It's all done with lasers and looks very realistic. Looking at hologram pictures from Mars would almost be like being there in person.

Hologram shows, of course, will not be the only forms of entertainment available to residents of future Fun City. If present predictions come to pass, we'll be able to entertain ourselves even as we sleep! Before going to sleep all we'll have to do is set a few dials on the Holo-Dream Maker kept just above our bed. While we sleep the dream maker will beam into our minds any dream we desire. We will be able to learn a foreign language, visit some faraway galaxy, or just relive the good old days of the twentieth century. Today we waste one third of our lives sleeping. In the next century we will put those hours to good use, thanks to our Holo-Dream Makers.

All the predictions for the future are not just idle dreams. But to make them realities we will all have to help. After all, the future just doesn't happen, it is made. As a futurologist once said, "I want to make the future the best place possible. After all, the future is where I'm going to be spending the rest of my life."

January 2, 1850

Yesterday was New Year's Day, and I had lovely presents. We had 139 callers, and I have an ivory tablet and I write all their names down in it . . .

Next January we shall be half through the nineteenth century. I hope I shall live to see the next century, but I don't want to be alive when the year 2000 comes, for my Bible teacher says the world is coming to an end then, and perhaps sooner.

From *Diary of a Little Girl in Old New York, 1849–50*

TEN QUESTIONS
ON THREE CENTURIES IN FIVE BOROUGHS:

A NEW YORKER'S QUIZ

(SOLUTION, PG. 377.)

RICHARD PECK

1. Curbside New York is enlivened by streets featuring the flavors of many national groups. Herewith the streets; you name the ethnic group that makes each street its showcase:
   a. Mulberry Street _____
   b. Eighty-sixth Street _____
   c. Mott Street _____
   d. Atlantic Avenue _____
   e. Orchard Street _____

2. America's most famous duel was waged across the Hudson in 1804, between two giants of our early history. Both men are remembered in their stately mansions restored and open to the public on the heights above Harlem. Who were the men? For extra credit, what are their homes named?
   _____ at home at _____
   _____ at home at _____

3. SoHo is the world's newest hotbed of the arts: a grid of galleries, bohemian cafes, and the new loft-lifestyles of the artists. What's the derivation of the place named *SoHo?*_____
   _____

4. The world's longest suspension bridge opened in 1964 to connect two New York City boroughs. What boroughs? _____ and _____

5. In *The Great Gatsby*, F. Scott Fitzgerald called it "the Valley of Ashes." Cleaned up later, it was the site of two World's Fairs and then a lasting park. What park? _____
   What borough? _____

6. Washington, D.C.'s Smithsonian Institution's newest museum opened recently in New York. What is this newest addition to the local culture scene? _____ Whose magnificent mansion houses it? _____

7. From Washington and Adams to Kennedy and Nixon, New York is a presidential city. But the childhood home of one President is restored and open to the public in Manhattan. Who's this native born and bred President? _____

8. New York's first Landmarks Preservation Historic District was designated in 1965 for its architecture that sparked a brownstone revival. What is this first landmark neighborhood? _____

9. When New York was the nation's capital, Washington took his oath of presidential office on the steps of Federal Hall, the site of the original Dutch town hall. In what street did Washington become President? _____

10. One borough contains the homes, still visible, of these three greats: John F. Kennedy, Mark Twain, and Edgar Allan Poe. Which borough? _____

"DRESS UP DAY" on the West Side

Don Freeman

APPENDIX

For DIRECTIONS to get to where you want to go, telephone the Transit Authority at 330-1234 before leaving the house. They will give you subway or bus travel information.

Call 755-4100 for special FREE EVENTS in the city every day.

Call 472-1003 for the locations of SKATING RINKS and SWIMMING POOLS around the city.

Visit the NEW YORK CONVENTION AND VISITORS BUREAU at forty-second Street and Park Avenue for maps and information about the city.

Children's Theaters

The variety of theatrical productions for children in New York City is great. However, the troupes keep changing, and players move from one home base to another (These below are a sampling of available productions, but by the time this book went to press, some could have changed and others replaced them.) Check your local newspaper listings and use the phone numbers below to be sure of the most current information.

Alice May's Puppets, Alice May Hall, Marien-Heim Tower, 870 Ocean Parkway, Brooklyn

Bill Baird Marionette Theater, 59 Barrow Street (989-7060)

Children's Improvisational Company, New Media Studio, 350 East 81 Street (249-9872)

Cottage Marionette Theater, Central Park West at 81 Street (988-9093)

Courtyard Playhouse, 39 Grove Street (765-9540)

Creative Theater for Children, 15 Gramercy Park South (475-3424)

Heights Players, 26 Willow Place, Brooklyn (237-2752)

Magic Towne House, 1026 Third Avenue (752-1165). Magic Shows every Saturday and Sunday, 1, 2:15, and 3:30.

Marble Hill Nursery School, 5470 Broadway (562-7055)

Meri Mini Players, Hotel Opera, downstairs, Broadway at 76 Street (697-0730)

Moofy Puppet, New Moravian Church, Lexington Avenue at 30 Street (691-8930)

Richard Morse Mime Theater, 302 East 45 Street (683-7584)

Off Center Theater, 436 West 18 Street (929-8299)

Paper Bag Players, 92nd Street Y, 1395 Lexington Avenue (427-6000)

Penny Jones & Company, 215 West 11 Street (924-4589)

Peoples Performing Company, Provincetown Playhouse, 133 MacDougal Street (730-9463)

The Proposition Circus, Hunter College Playhouse, 68 Street between Park and Lexington (535-5350)

Royal Playhouse, 219 Second Avenue (475-9647)

13th Street Theater, 50 West 13 Street (924-9785)

Shadow Box Theater, Riverside Church, Riverside Drive at 120
    Street
Time & Space Ltd., Universalist Church, 4 West 76 Street
TRG Repertory Company, Theater Club, 436 West 18 Street
We 3, Little Synagogue, 27 East 20 Street (255-0469)

Museums

Call before visiting for the latest hours and admission policies.
These change too frequently to list here.

American Museum of Immigration
Liberty Island, at the base of the Statue of
    Liberty, New York Bay
422-2150

American Museum of Natural History
Central Park West and 79 Street, Man-
    hattan
873-4225

American Numismatic Society
Broadway and 156 Street, Manhattan
286-3030

Anthology Film Archives
80 Wooster Street, Manhattan
226-0010

Aunt Len's Doll & Toy Museum
6 Hamilton Terrace, Manhattan
281-4143

Bronx Museum of the Arts
851 Grand Concourse, Bronx
681-6000

The Brooklyn Museum
188 Eastern Parkway, Brooklyn
638-5000

The Children's Museum
Brooklyn Avenue and Park Place, Brooklyn
735-4432

Chinatown Museum
7–9 Mott Street, Manhattan
964-1542

The Cloisters
Fort Tryon Park, Broadway and 190
    Street, Manhattan
923-3700

Federal Hall Memorial Museum
15 Pine Street, Manhattan
344-3830

The Fire Department Museum
104 Duane Street, Manhattan
744-1000

Fort Wadsworth Military Museum
School Road and Bay Street, Staten Island
447-5100

Fraunces Tavern Museum
54 Pearl Street, Manhattan
425-1776
(Continued)

The Frick Collection
1 East 70 Street, Manhattan
288-0700

The Gallery of Prehistoric Paintings
20 East 12 Street, Manhattan
By appointment only, 674-5389

The Guggenheim Museum
Fifth Avenue and 89 Street, Manhattan
860-1313

Guinness World Records Exhibit Hall
350 Fifth Avenue, Manhattan
947-2335

Hall of Science
Flushing Meadow Park, Queens
699-9400

The Hayden Planetarium
Central Park West and 81 Street,
   Manhattan
873-4225

Hispanic Society of America
Broadway and 155 Street, Manhattan
690-0743

International Center of Photography
1130 Fifth Avenue, Manhattan
860-1783

The Jacques Marchais Center of Tibetan
   Art
338 Lighthouse Avenue, Staten Island
987-3478

The Jewish Museum
Fifth Avenue and 92 Street, Manhattan
860-1860

Jumel Mansion
Edgecomb Avenue and West 161 Street,
   Manhattan
923-8008

Junior Museum
Metropolitan Museum of Art
Fifth Avenue and 92 Street, Manhattan
879-5500

Lincoln Center Library and Museum of
   the Performing Arts
Amsterdam Avenue and 64 Street,
   Manhattan
799-2200

The Metropolitan Museum of Art
Fifth Avenue and 82 Street, Manhattan
879-5500

Museo del Barrio
1945 Third Avenue, Manhattan
831-7272

Museum of American Folk Art
49 West 53 Street, Manhattan
581-2474

Museum of the American Indian/Heye
   Foundation
Broadway and 155 Street, Manhattan
283-2420

Museum of Archeology
631 Howard Avenue, Staten Island
273-3300

Museum of Broadcasting
1 East 53 Street, Manhattan
752-4690

Museum of Bronx History
3266 Bainbridge Avenue, Bronx

Museum of the City of New York
Fifth Avenue and 103 Street, Manhattan
534-1672

Museum of Contemporary Crafts
29 West 53 Street, Manhattan
977-8989

Museum of Holography
11 Mercer Street, Manhattan
925-0526

The Museum of Modern Art
11 West 53 Street, Manhattan
956-7070

The National Art Museum of Sport
Madison Square Garden
4 Penn Plaza, Manhattan
244-4127

The New York City Transit Exhibition
110 Livingston Street, Brooklyn

The New York Experience
McGraw-Hill Building
1221 Avenue of the Americas, Manhattan
869-0345

The New York Historical Society
170 Central Park West at 77 Street,
    Manhattan
873-3400

The New York Jazz Museum
236 West 54 Street, Manhattan
765-2150

The Police Museum
New York City Police Academy
235 East 20 Street, Manhattan
477-9753

Puerto Rican Center for the Arts
250 West 108 Street, Manhattan
222-2966

Queens Museum
New York City Building
Flushing Meadow Park, Queens
592-2406

Theodore Roosevelt Birthplace
28 East 20 Street, Manhattan
260-1616

Songwriters Hall of Fame
One Times Square, Manhattan
221-1252

South Street Seaport Museum
16 Fulton Street, Manhattan
766-9020/weekends 766-9049

Staten Island Historical Society
302 Center Street, Staten Island

Staten Island Museum
75 Stuyvesant Place, Staten Island

The Studio Museum in Harlem
2033 Fifth Avenue, Manhattan
427-5959

Ukrainian Museum
203 Second Avenue, between 12 and 13
    streets, Manhattan
228-0110

The Whitney Museum of American Art
75 Street and Madison Avenue, Manhattan
249-4100

Parks

Battery Park
Lower Broadway, Manhattan

Brooklyn Botanic Garden
Flatbush Avenue between Eastern Parkway and Empire Boulevard, Brooklyn

New York Botanical Garden
East 180 Street and Boston Post Road, Bronx

Canarsie Beach
Canarsie, Brooklyn

Carl Shurz Park
86 Street and East End Avenue, Manhattan

Central Park
59 Street to 110 Street, Fifth Avenue to Central Park West, Manhattan

City Hall Park
Broadway and Park Row, Manhattan

Clove Lakes Park
Victory Boulevard and Clove Road, Staten Island

Flushing Meadow Park
Grand Central Parkway and Long Island Expressway, Queens

Forest Park
Myrtle Avenue and Woodhaven Boulevard, Queens

Fort Tryon Park
between Broadway and Henry Hudson Pkwy at 190 Street and Dyckman Street, Manhattan

High Rock Park Conservation Center
200 Nevada Avenue, New Dorp, Staten Island

Inwood Hill Park
Dyckman Street, Hudson River

Kissena Park
158 Street and Booth Memorial Avenue, Flushing, Queens

New York Botanical Gardens
Bronx Park, Bronx

Pelham Bay Park
Pelham Bay, Bronx

Prospect Park
Flatbush Avenue and Empire Boulevard, Brooklyn

Jacob Riis Park
between Fort Tilden and Neponsit, Queens

Riverside Park
Hudson River and 72 Street to about 150 Street (where it runs into Fort Washington Park)

Silver Lake Park
Victory Boulevard and Forest Avenue, Staten Island

Van Cortlandt Park
West 242 Street and Broadway, Bronx

Ward's Island
Manhattan

Washington Square Park
foot of Fifth Avenue

Places of Interest

Brooklyn Bridge
Lower Manhattan/Brooklyn

Brooklyn Heights
Brooklyn, along the East River from Clark to Remsen streets

Brooklyn Public Library
Grand Army Plaza, Brooklyn

Carnegie Hall
57 Street and Seventh Avenue, Manhattan

Cathedral of St. John the Divine
112 Street and Amsterdam Avenue, Manhattan

Chinatown
Mott Street and surrounding area, Manhattan

City Hall
Broadway and Park Row, Manhattan

Columbia University
116 Street and Broadway, Manhattan

Coney Island
Brooklyn, on the Atlantic Ocean

Diamond Center
47 Street between Fifth and Sixth avenues, Manhattan

Donnell Library Center
20 West 53 Street, Manhattan

Empire State Building—Observatory
Fifth Avenue and 34 Street, Manhattan

Explorers Club
46 East 70 Street, near Fifth Avenue, Manhattan

Federal Hall
28 Wall Street, Manhattan

Flatiron Building
Fifth Avenue and 23 Street, Manhattan

Fraunces Tavern
Broad and Pearl streets, Manhattan

Fulton Fish Market
South and Fulton streets, Manhattan

George Washington Bridge
179 Street, Manhattan/Fort Lee, New Jersey

Grand Central Station
42 Street and Vanderbilt Avenue, Manhattan

Grant's Tomb
Riverside Drive and 122 Street, Manhattan

Greenwich Village
from Spring to 14 streets, from Greenwich Street to Broadway, approximately, Manhattan

Hall of Fame
New York University
West 181 Street and University Avenue, Bronx

Hunts Point Market
Hunts Point Avenue and East Bay Avenue, Bronx

Jamaica Bay Wildlife Refuge
Jamaica, Queens

J.F.K. International Airport
Jamaica, Queens

La Guardia Airport
Jackson Heights, Queens

(*Continued*)

La Marqueta (Park Avenue Market)
111 to 116 streets on Park Avenue, Manhattan

Lincoln Center
Amsterdam Avenue between 62 and 66 streets, Manhattan

Little Italy
Mulberry Street and surrounding area, Manhattan

Madison Square Garden
Seventh Avenue and 33 Street, Manhattan

Nathan's—Coney Island
Surf Avenue, Coney Island, Brooklyn

New York Public Library
Fifth Avenue at 42 Street, Manhattan

New York Stock Exchange
Broad and Wall streets, Manhattan

New York University—Uptown Campus
181 Street and University Avenue, Manhattan

Radio City Music Hall
Avenue of the Americas between 50 and 51 streets, Manhattan

Riverside Church
Riverside Drive between 120 and 122 streets, Manhattan

Rockefeller Center
Fifth Avenue between 48 and 51 streets, Manhattan

Roosevelt Island
East River, 50 to 86 streets, Manhattan

St. Mark's-in-the-Bowery
10 Street and Second Avenue, Manhattan

St. Patrick's Cathedral
Fifth Avenue and 51 Street, Manhattan

Sheepshead Bay
Shore Parkway and Ocean Avenue, Brooklyn

Staten Island Ferry
South Ferry Station, foot of Whitehall Street, Manhattan

Statue of Liberty
Liberty Island, Upper New York Bay
(Circle Line from Battery Park)

Temple Emanu-El
Fifth Avenue and 65 Street, Manhattan

Theater District
43 to 53 streets, between Broadway and Eighth Avenue, Manhattan

Times Square
Broadway and 42 Street

Trinity Church
Broadway, at the beginning of Wall Street, Manhattan

United Nations Headquarters
42 Street and East River, Manhattan

Verrazano-Narrows Bridge
Lower New York Bay, connecting Brooklyn (at Fort Hamilton) to Staten Island

World Trade Center—Observation Deck
Trinity Place between Vesey and Liberty streets, Manhattan

Sports Teams

To find out what's happening, check the listings of your daily newspaper, or call the numbers below. For tickets to sporting events, go to the stadium or look under "Theater and Sports Ticket Services" in the Yellow Pages for agencies around town where tickets are sold.

BASEBALL (April to October)
New York Mets   Shea Stadium   672-3000
                       Flushing Meadow, Queens
New York Yankees   Yankee Stadium   293-6000
                       East 161 St. and River Avenue
                       Bronx

FOOTBALL (September to December)
New York Giants   Giant Stadium   201-935-8111
                       East Rutherford, N.J.
New York Jets   Shea Stadium   421-6600
                       Flushing Meadow, Queens

BASKETBALL
New York Knicks   Madison Square Garden   563-8000
                       4 Pennsylvania Plaza
                       Manhattan

HOCKEY
New York Islanders   Nassau Coliseum   516-694-5522
                       Racket & Rink
                       1155 Conklin Street
                       Farmingdale, N.Y. 11735

New York Rangers   Madison Square Garden   563-8000
                       4 Pennsylvania Plaza
                       Manhattan

Zoos

Animal Nursery
West 15 Street, Brooklyn

Bronx Park
East 180 Street and Boston Post Road
Bronx

Central Park
Fifth Avenue and 64 Street, Manhattan

Children's Farm
111 Street and 46 Avenue
Flushing Meadows, Queens

Children's Zoo
Bronx Park, Bronx

Children's Zoo
Central Park
66 Street and Fifth Avenue, Manhattan

The New York Aquarium
Boardwalk and West 8 Street
Coney Island, Brooklyn

Prospect Park
Flatbush Avenue at Empire Boulevard
Brooklyn

Queens Zoo
111 Street and 46 Avenue
Flushing Meadows, Queens

Staten Island Zoological Society Zoo
Broadway and Clove Road, Staten Island

Solutions to Puzzles

NEW YORK,
HOW YOU'VE CHANGED!

(p. 10)

1. NIEUW AMSTERDAM

2. NIEUWAASTERDAA

3. NDEUWAASTERIAA

4. NDEUWAAKSTERIAA

5. NDEUWAAKTERIAAS

6. NDEUWAAOKTERIAAOS

7. NDEUWOKTERIOS

8. NDEUYWOKTEYRIOYS

9. NEUYWORTEYKIOYS

10. NEUWYORTEYKIOYS

11. NEUWYORTKIYS

12. NEWYORKITYS

13. NEW YORK CITY

SIGHTSEEING

(pg. 24)

SECRET LANGUAGE FOR NEW YORK KIDS

(pg. 63)

NEW YORK IS A GREAT CITY

THE BIG APPLE

(pg. 78)

LOST IN THE PARK

(pg. 115)

A FUNNY CROSSWORD FROM ENGLAND

(pg. 129)

P	U	N	C	H
P	U	N	C	H
P	U	N	C	H
P	U	N	C	H
P	U	N	C	H

ALL AROUND THE TOWN

(pg. 137)

BRIGHT LIGHTS

(pg. 164)

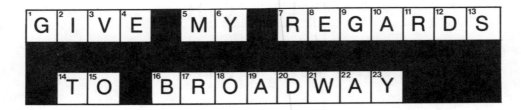

WHO'S AT THE GUGGENHEIM?

(pg. 186)

Answer: The Stewardess

Stewardess	Writer	Model	Actress
pizza	yogurt	hot dog	bagel
Guggenheim	Macy's	Zoo	Central Park
bicycle	bus	subway	motorcycle

ANSWERS TO
THE MYSTERY OF THE STOLEN PAINTING

(pg. 190)

Academy	Adrian	Albany	Allen	Ann	Arden
Attorney	Bank	Canal	Cathedral	Chambers	
Charles	Cherry	Church	Claremont	Depew	Dey
Dominick	Downing	East	Eighth	Eleventh	
Exchange	Exterior	Extra	Fiftieth	First	Front
Fulton	Grand*	Great Jones	Hall	Henry	Henshaw
Hester	Howard	Jackson	Jay	Jersey	John	Jones
King	Lincoln	Manhattan	Montgomery	Morningside	
Mott	Nagle	New	Ninth	Oliver	Park	Patchin
Pleasant	Post	Reade	Rector	Rivington	Rose
Second	Seventh	Seventy-seventh	Spring	Staff	
State	Stone	Tenth	Third	Vandam	Vestry
Walker	Wall	Washington	Worth	York	

See below to find out where in the story these street names are hidden.

* Grand Street at different points is one block north of both Howard and Hester streets.

THE MYSTERY OF THE STOLEN PAINTING

"Only the painting is missing," said *Charles Montgomery*, *rector* of St. *Dominick*'s in *Manhattan*. "It was here in the *vestry* an hour ago at nine thirty."

*Clare Montg*omery, his wife, said, "*Allen* Smith and *Howard Jones* were here when *Adrian York* brought it last night to be auctioned at the *Spring* Fair. They know we work for an hour in the office downstairs each morning from nine thirty to now with the *front* door open."

"The painting is *worth* a lot. York is a member of the *Academy* of Fine Painters. He would be better known if he didn't hate to sell his paintings," the rector said.

"But can Howard be a thief? *Can Al?* I'll call them and see if they can account for their time this *morning*." *Side* by side, he and his wife returned to the office.

"I've of*ten thought*," his wife said, "that we should keep that door locked when we're downstairs. We must be *extra* careful from now on."

The rector phoned Howard Jones. Jones had been *patching* the vestry *wall*s the night before. The rector hired him whenever he could talk him into doing some work but Howard never accepted much pay.

"Hello, Rector," Howard said. "Would

you believe I was *washing tons* of clothes at the laundromat from *eight thi*rty on? My wife *Hester* says she works *h*ard *en*ough at the *Post* Office without doing laundry. Just got back *seconds* ago and I'm *downing* a *cherry* soda when who pops by? My mother-in-law."

"That's *great, Jones,*" said the rector, ready to hang up.

Howard went on tal*king.* "Right away she's at me about getting a job so we can move to one of those nice brown*stones* a block uptown. She's always saying, 'If Howard and Hester moved north a block, wouldn't it be *grand!*'"

They *exchange*d a few more words and the rector hung up without having to explain why he called.

He got Allen Smith on the phone. "What's up?" said Smith. "Got some more legal work for me to do on the s*ide? You* know I'll help." The *attorney* did all the church's legal work free.

The rector explained about the missing painting.

"I have an alibi if that's why you called," Smith said. "Left at *seven thi*rty, for an appointment in *New Jersey,* smashed into a van on *Ninth* Avenue. The *van dam*age was slight but the driver was surprised when I admitted it was my fault. I told him I only fi*nagle* legally, that's my *motto.* Got back half an hour ago after stopping off at Judge *Jackson's chambers* and the *bank.* Just gave my *staff* instructions for tomorrow. I'm d*riving toni*ght to *Albany* on business."

"Thanks, Smith," the rector said. "I s*hall* see Adrian York now and tell him his painting is lost so he c*anno*t hear it elsewhere *first.*"

"He'd feel a*wful to n*early lose a nickel.

That guy is tight with a buck," Smith said before hanging up.

The rector's *church* was in the *east* Forties and York lived in the east Fifties. The rector, a good *walker,* went up *Third* Avenue. He missed the old *El even th*ough it had made the street below bleak.

In York's small but *pleasant* studio, the artist greeted him with, "I'm bushed. I went to *Fiftieth* Street to St. Patrick's *Cathedral* early to sketch the *exterior* and at nine thirty went downtown to *John Jay Park* at *Seventy-seventh* Street."

The rector told York about the stolen painting.

"That's terrible," the artist said. "That was one of my best."

"I'd planned on buying some wi*de pews* with the money," said the rector. He *rose* to look at the bookshelves. York was a *reade*r. On the top shelf were *Oliver* Twist, Life of *Lincoln,* Shakespeare's Plays, t*hen Shaw*'s Plays, a travel guide by *Henry* Kissinger, and a row of income tax guides.

"But I think I know who took the painting," the rector *state*d suddenly.

WHO WAS IT?

"Smith wouldn't risk his career by stealing and Jones isn't interested in money," the rector said. "You were in a hurry to give me an alibi that couldn't be proved but you said you went downtown from the Cathedral to the park when you should have said uptown. You did go downtown to take the painting which you had donated to give yourself a tax deduction."

The artist hung his head. "I did mean to give up the painting but I found I couldn't part with it and was too embarrassed to ask for it back."

FULTON FISH MARKET

(pg. 237)

faint	unfit	toast	safer	smith	harsh	aloft
faith	unite	tonal	saint	smoke	haste	alone
fakir	unlit	torah	salon	smolt	haunt	alter
false	untie	torte	satin	smote	heart	amino
fault	until	total	saute	snake	heath	amour
feast	urine	train	serif	snare	heron	amuse
feint	usher	trail	shaft	snarl	hiker	anise
fetus	utile	trait	shake	sneak	hoist	ankle
fifth	utter	trash	shale	snore	horse	arise
filth		treat	shank	snort	house	arson
final		trial	share	snout	human	aster
first	lathe	trite	shark	solar	humor	atone
flake	learn	troth	sheaf	sonar		
flank	leash	trout	shear	south		
flash	least	trunk	shelf	staff	maker	raise
flask	liken	trust	shift	stain	marsh	ratio
flint	liner	tuner	shine	stair	matte	realm
flirt	liter	tutor	shirk	stake	meant	refit
float	lithe		shirt	stale	melon	remit
flora	loris		shoal	stalk	merit	resin
flour	loser	oaken	shoer	stare	miner	rifle
flout	lotus	offer	shone	start	minor	rinse
fluke	louse	often	shore	state	miser	roast
flunk	lunar	onset	shorn	steak	miter	rosin
flush		orate	short	steal	moist	route
flute		other	shout	steam	molar	
forte	taint	otter	shunt	stein	moral	
forth	talon		siren	stele	morale	knelt
frail	taper		skate	stern	mores	knife
frank	tapir	noise	skein	stiff	motet	knish
freak	taste	north	skier	stile	motif	krona
fresh	taunt	nurse	skiff	stink	moult	
frisk	tenor		skirt	stint	mount	
front	tenth		skoal	stoat	mourn	earth
frost	thank	infer	slain	stoke	mouse	elfin
froth	their	inker	slant	stole	mouth	enter
fruit	theta	inkle	slate	stone	mufti	
	thief	inlet	slier	store		
	think	inset	slink	stork		
	thorn	inter	sloth	stout	afire	
	throe	inure	smart	strop	afoul	
	timer	irate	smear	strut	after	
	titan	islet	smelt	stuff	aisle	
	tithe		smile	stunt	alert	
	title		smirk	suite	alien	

ANSWERS TO
SKYLINE CROSSWORD

(pg. 232)

MISS LIBERTY MAZE

(pg. 235)

ANSWERS TO
A NEW YORKER'S QUIZ

(pg. 354)

1. a. Italian
    b. German
    c. Oriental
    d. Arab
    e. Jewish

2. Aaron Burr at home at the Morris-Jumel Mansion
    Alexander Hamilton at home at Hamilton Grange

3. SoHo means "South of Houston (Street)," the southern border of
    Greenwich Village

4. Brooklyn and Richmond (Staten Island)
    Verrazano-Narrows Bridge

5. Flushing Meadows in Queens

6. The Cooper-Hewitt Museum in the home of Andrew Carnegie

7. Theodore Roosevelt, whose home is at 28 East 20 Street

8. Brooklyn Heights

9. Wall

10. The Bronx

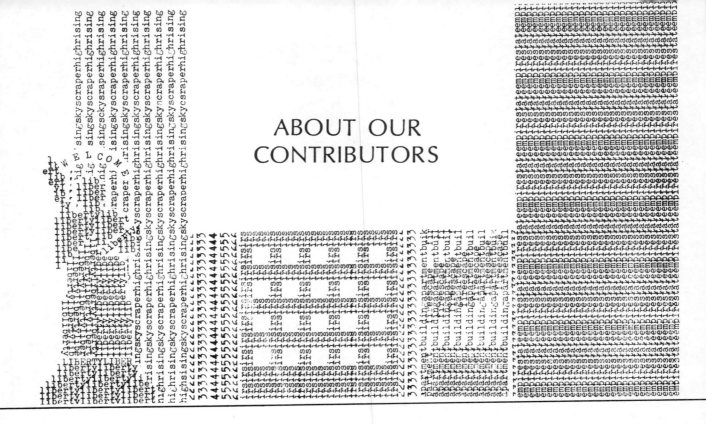

ABOUT OUR CONTRIBUTORS

ADRIENNE ADAMS: *The Easter Egg Artists*, Scribner, 1976; *Hansel and Gretel*, Scribner, 1975; *Jorinda and Joringel*, translated by Elizabeth Shuls, Scribner, 1968.

JOAN AIKEN: *Go Saddle the Sea*, Doubleday, 1977; *The Faithless Lollybird*, Doubleday, 1978; *Street*, Viking, 1978.

LLOYD ALEXANDER: *Black Cauldron*, Holt, Rinehart & Winston, 1965. *The Foundling and Other Tales of Prydain*, Holt, Rinehart & Winston, 1973; *The Cat Who Wished to Be a Man*, Dutton, 1973.

SUE ALEXANDER: *Peacocks Are Very Special*, Doubleday, 1976; *Witch, Goblin and Sometimes Ghost*, Pantheon, 1976; *Small Plays for Special Days*, Seabury, 1977.

ALIKI: *At Mary Bloom's*, Greenwillow, 1976; *Corn Is Maize: The Gift of the Indians*, Crowell, 1976; *The Many Lives of Benjamin Franklin*, Prentice-Hall, 1977.

GERALD AMES AND ROSE WYLER: *Secrets in Stones*, Four Winds Press, 1970; *Funny Number Tricks*, Parents' Magazine Press, 1976; *Spooky Tricks*, Harper & Row, 1968.

BERTHE AMOSS: *The Chalk Cross*, Seabury, 1976; *The Great Sea Monster or, a Book by You*, Parents' Magazine Press, 1975; *The Very Worst Thing*, Parents' Magazine Press, 1972.

MARY ANDERSON: *I'm Nobody! Who Are You?* Atheneum, 1974; *F°T°C° Superstar*, Atheneum, 1976; *Matilda's Masterpiece*, Atheneum, 1977.

LOUISE ARMSTRONG: *How to Turn Up into Down into Up, A Child's Guide to Inflation, Depression and Economic Recovery*, Harcourt Brace Jovanovich, 1978; *How to Turn Lemons into Money, A Child's Guide to Economics*, Harcourt Brace Jovanovich, 1977.

FRANK ASCH: *City Sandwich*, Greenwillow, 1978; *Moonbear*, Scribner, 1978; *Turtle Tale*, Dial, 1978.

PHIL AULT: *Wires West*, Dodd, Mead, 1974; *All Aboard*, Dodd, Mead, 1974; *Introduction to Mass Communications*, Harper & Row, 1976.

TOM AYLESWORTH: *Monsters from the Movies,* Lippincott, 1972; *Movie Monsters,* Lippincott, 1975; *The Story of Vampires,* McGraw-Hill, 1977.

NORMAN BAKER: *Thor Heyerdahl and the Reed Boat,* coauthored with Barbara Murphy, Lippincott, 1974.

RICHARD MERAN BARSAM: *A Peaceable Kingdom: The Shaker Abecedarius,* Viking, 1978; *In the Dark: A Primer for the Movies,* Viking, 1977; *Nonfiction Film: A Critical History,* Dutton, 1973.

BILL BASSO: *The Top of the Pizzas,* Dodd, Mead, 1977.

NATHANIEL BENCHLEY: *Beyond the Mists,* Harper & Row, 1975; *Bright Candles,* Harper & Row, 1974; *George the Drummer Boy,* Harper & Row, 1977.

MARVIN BILECK: *Rain Makes Applesauce,* by Julian Sheer, illustrated by Marvin Bileck, Holiday House, 1964; *The Penny That Rolled Away,* by Louis Mcneice, illustrated by Marvin Bileck, G. P. Putnam's Sons, 1954; *A Walker in the City,* by Alfred Kazin, illustrated by Marvin Bileck, Harcourt, Brace, 1951.

MARY BLOOM is the real-life subject of Aliki's *At Mary Bloom's.* She's a photographer, animal talent agent, and animal lover.

JUDY BLUME: *Are You There God, It's Me Margaret,* Bradbury, 1970; *Blubber,* Bradbury, 1974; *Deenie,* Bradbury, 1973.

BETTY BOEGEHOLD: *Here's Pippa Again,* Knopf, 1975; *What the Wind Told,* Parents' Magazine Press, 1976; *Small Deer's Magic Trick,* Coward, McCann & Geoghegan, 1977.

DON BOLOGNESE: *How to Draw Horses and Foals,* Franklin Watts, 1977; *Wagon Wheels,* by Barbara Brenner, illustrated by Don Bolognese, Harper & Row; *All Upon a Sidewalk,* by Jean George, illustrated by Don Bolognese, Dutton, 1974.

DEMETRE BOVE holds a master's degree in Museum Education from Bank Street College of Education. She is a staff member at the Museum of Modern Art in New York City.

FRANKLYN BRANLEY: *Color from Rainbows to Lasers,* Crowell, 1978; *Energy for the 21st Century,* Crowell, 1977; *Black Holes, Red Giants and Superstars,* Crowell, 1976.

STANLEE BRIMBERG: *Black Stars,* Dodd, Mead, 1974.

BARBARA BULLOCK develops programs on folk art and folkways. She has worked with the Museum of Contemporary Crafts, the Museum of American Indian, and UNICEF.

ROBERT BURCH: *The Whitman Kick,* Dutton, 1977; *Two That Were Tough,* Viking, 1976; *Skinny,* Viking, 1964.

BARBARA BURN: *The Penguin Book of Pets,* Penguin, 1978; *The Whole Horse Catalog,* Simon & Schuster, 1977; *Horseless Rider,* St. Martin's, 1979.

MALCOLM CARRICK: *Tramp,* Harper & Row, 1977; *To-day Is Shrew's Day,* Harper & Row, 1978; *I Can Squash Elephants,* Viking Penguin, 1978.

IDA CHITTUM: *Farmer Hoo and the Baboons,* Delacorte, 1971; *Tales of Terror,* Rand McNally, 1975; *The Ghost Boy of El Toro,* Independence Press, 1978.

JOSEPH CIARDIELLO: *Buffalo Bill,* G. P. Putnam's Sons, 1976; *The Great Houdini,* G. P. Putnam's Sons, 1977; *Theodore Roosevelt,* G. P. Putnam's Sons, 1978.

DANIEL COHEN: *The World of UFOs,* Lippincott, 1978; *What Really Happened to the Dinosaurs,* Dutton, 1977; *Young Ghosts,* Dutton, 1978.

CHRIS CONOVER: *Six Little Ducks,* Crowell, 1976; *The School Mouse,* Frederick Warne, 1977; *Where Did My Mother Go?* Four Winds Press, 1978.

BARBARA COONEY: *Squawk to the Moon, Little Goose,* Viking, 1974; *When the Sky Is Like Lace,* Lippincott, 1975; *The Donkey Prince,* Doubleday, 1977.

SCOTT CORBETT: *The Baseball Bargain,* Atlantic Monthly Press, 1970; *The Baseball Trick,* Atlantic Monthly Press, 1965; *The Black Mask Trick,* Atlantic Monthly Press, 1976.

RACHEL COWAN: *Growing Up Yanqui,* Viking, 1974.

JULIA CUNNINGHAM: *Come to the Edge,* Pantheon, 1977; *Maybe, a Mole,* Pantheon, 1974; *Onion Journey,* Pantheon, 1967.

ROALD DAHL: *Charlie and the Chocolate Factory*, Knopf, 1976; *Danny: The Champion of the World*, Knopf, 1975; *Magic Finger*, Harper & Row, 1966.

BEATRICE SCHENCK DE REGNIERS: *A Bunch of Poems and Verses*, Seabury, 1977; *The Enchanted Forest*, Atheneum, 1974; *It Does Not Say Meow*, Seabury, 1972.

EMIL P. DOLENSEK is a veterinarian at the Central Park and Bronx zoos.

JUDY DONNELLY is a children's book editor at Hastings House.

MICHAEL DORMAN: *Witch Hunt: The Underside of American Democracy*, Delacorte, 1976; *The Making of a Slum*, Delacorte, 1972; *Under 21: A Young People's Guide to Legal Rights*, Delacorte, 1970.

ROGER DUVOISIN: *Crocodile in the Tree*, Knopf, 1973; *Donkey-Donkey*, Parents' Magazine Press, 1968; *Missing Milkman*, Knopf, 1966.

EDWARD EDELSON: *The Book of Prophecy*, Doubleday, 1974; *The Funny Men of the Movies*, Doubleday, 1976; *Visions of Tomorrow*, Doubleday, 1975.

CATHARINE EDMONDS has almost always lived in New York, is living there still, married with two children, and writing a children's novel.

ELEANOR ESTES: *The Moffats*, Harcourt, Brace, 1941; *Ginger Pye*, Harcourt, Brace, 1951; *The Witch Family*, Harcourt, Brace, 1960.

NORMA FARBER: *As I Was Crossing Boston Common*, Dutton, 1975; *Six Impossible Things Before Breakfast*, Addison-Wesley, 1977; *A Ship in a Storm on the Way to Tarshish*, Greenwillow, 1978.

MARGO FEIDEN has been an art dealer, a chemist, a Broadway playwright, producer, and director, a talk-show host, and the author of two books for adults.

EDITH BING FIRESTONE lives in Queens, New York, with her husband and son.

DON FREEMAN: *The Chalk Box Story*, Lippincott, 1976; *Bearymore*, Viking, 1976; *Corduroy*, Viking, 1968.

JEAN FRITZ: *And Then What Happened, Paul Revere?* Coward, McCann & Geoghegan, 1973;

The Cabin Faced West, Coward, McCann & Geoghegan, 1958; *Who's That Stepping on Plymouth Rock?* Coward, McCann & Geoghegan, 1975.

BURTON FRYE: *St. Nicholas: The Early Years*, Meredith, 1969; continuous weekly book column in the *Regional News*, Lake Geneva, Wisconsin, and the *RFD News*, Bellevue, Ohio.

NANCY GARDEN: *The Loners*, Viking, 1972; *Vampires*, Lippincott, 1973; *Witches*, Lippincott, 1975.

JAMES CROSS GIBLIN is editor in chief of Clarion Books for Young People at the Seabury Press, and the author of numerous articles about the writing and publishing of children's books.

WINNETTE GLASGOW is a potter, photographer, musician, writer, model airplane maker, and full-time teacher in the New York City public schools. She also enjoys dabbling in electricity, cabinetmaking, and needlepoint.

A. D. GOLDSTEIN is a writer who lives in New York City.

CONSTANCE C. GREENE: *Beat the Turtle Drum*, Viking, 1976; *Isabelle the Itch*, Viking, 1973; *Getting Nowhere*, Viking, 1977.

SHEILA GREENWALD: *The Secret in Miranda's Closet*, Houghton Mifflin, 1977; *The Hot Day*, Bobbs-Merrill, 1972; *The Secret Museum*, Lippincott, 1974.

JOAN GROSS is a native New Yorker and works as an assistant to a publisher's scout. She is currently finishing her first children's novel, is married, and has one child.

IRENE HAAS: *The Maggie B*, Atheneum, 1976; *Carrie Hepple's Garden*, Atheneum, 1977; *Come Away*, Atheneum, 1976.

MARYLIN HAFNER: *It's Halloween*, Greenwillow, 1977; *Jenny and the Tennis Nut*, Greenwillow, 1978; *Robbers, Bones and Mean Dogs*, Addison-Wesley, 1978.

PAUL HAGERMAN: *It's an Odd World*, Sterling, 1977; *It's a Mad Mad World*, Sterling, 1978; Contributor to *The Book of Lists*, William Morrow, 1977.

SUZANNE HALDANE is a book designer and photographer. Her book on stone carving will be published soon.

OLE HAMANN is the chief of the United Nations Postal Administration, he is also a graphic designer and a painter.

JAMES HASKINS: *Adam Clayton Powell*, Dial, 1974; *Barbara Jordan! Speaking Out*, Dial, 1977; *Fighting Shirley Chisolm*, Dial, 1975.

ESTHER HAUTZIG: *The Endless Steppe*, Crowell, 1968; *The Case Against the Wind*, Macmillan, 1975; *Life with Working Parents*, Macmillan, 1979.

BARBARA SHOOK HAZEN: *Amelia's Flying Machine*, Doubleday, 1977; *The Gorilla Did It*, Atheneum, 1974; *Ups and Downs of Marvin*, Atheneum, 1977.

BARBARA HENNESSY is art director for the Viking Press. She lives in Brooklyn, New York.

TOM HUFFMAN is an artist who lives in New York. He illustrated *Wrapped for Eternity*.

BERNICE KOHN HUNT is a children's book editor and the author of more than sixty books including *The Beachcomber's Book, Great Bread!* and *What a Funny Thing to Say!*

JOHANNA HURWITZ: *Busybody Nora*, William Morrow, 1976; *Nora and Mrs. Mind-Your-Own-Business*, William Morrow, 1977; *The Law of Gravity*, William Morrow.

PYKE JOHNSON, JR., is the managing editor for Doubleday & Company.

X. J. KENNEDY is the author of several collections of verse for adults. For children he has written two collections of nonsense jingles, *One Winter Night in August* and *The Phantom Ice-Cream Man*.

M. E. KERR: *Gentlehands*, Harper & Row, 1978; *Dinky Hocker Shoots Smack*, Harper & Row, 1972; *Is That You, Miss Blue?* Harper & Row, 1976.

BARRIE KLAITS: *When You Find a Rock*, Macmillan, 1976.

FERNANDO KRAHN: *April Fools*, Dutton, 1974; *The Family Minus*, Parents' Magazine Press, 1977; *A Funny Friend from Heaven*, Lippincott, 1977.

RUTH KRAUSS: *Hole Is to Dig: A First Book of First Definitions*, Harper & Row, 1952; *The Happy Egg*, Scholastic Book Services, 1972.

NANCY LARRICK: *More Poetry for the Holidays*, Scholastic Book Services, 1977; *A Parent's Guide to Children's Reading*, Doubleday, 1975; *Piping Down the Valleys Wild*, Dell, 1970.

MADELEINE L'ENGLE: *A Wrinkle in Time*, Farrar, Straus & Giroux, 1962; *A Wind in the Door*, Farrar, Straus & Giroux, 1973; *A Swiftly Tilting Planet*, Farrar, Straus & Giroux, 1978.

ELIZABETH LEVINE has been an art teacher for the Museum of Modern Art and a contributor to *School Arts Magazine*. She is an art consultant and a member of the Board of Trustees of the National Association of Artist-run Galleries.

JOAN LEXAU: *Olaf Reads*, Dial, 1961; *Archimedes Takes a Bath*, Crowell, 1969; *Emily and the Klunky Baby and the Next-door Dog*, Dial, 1972.

HOWARD LISS: *They Changed the Game* (*Football's Great Coaches, Players and Games*), Lippincott, 1975; *Record Breakers of the NFL*, Random House, 1975; *Football Talk for Beginners*, Julian Messner, 1970.

OLGA LITOWINSKY: *The High Voyage*, Viking, 1977; *The Dream Book*, coauthored with Bebe Willoughby, Coward, McCann & Geoghegan, 1978.

JEAN LITTLE: *Listen to the Singing*, Dutton, 1977; *From Anna*, Harper & Row, 1973; *Kate*, Harper & Row, 1971.

MYRA COHN LIVINGSTON: *Come Away*, Atheneum, 1974; *Four Way Step and Other Poems*, Atheneum, 1976; *One Little Room*, Atheneum, 1975.

JOSEPH LOW: *Boo to a Goose*, Atheneum, 1975; *The Christmas Grump*, Atheneum, 1977; *Little Though I Be*, McGraw-Hill, 1976.

DAVID MACAULEY: *Great Moments in Architecture*, Houghton Mifflin, 1978; *Castle*, Houghton Mifflin, 1977; *Underground*, Houghton Mifflin, 1976.

ANN MCGOVERN: *Mr. Skinner's Skinny House*, Four Winds Press, 1979; *Half a Kingdom*, Frederick Warne, 1977; *The Underwater World of the Coral Reef*, Four Winds Press, 1976.

GEORGESS MCHARGUE: *Stoneflight*, Viking, 1975; *The Impossible People*, Holt, Rinehart & Winston, 1972; *The Talking Table Mystery*, Doubleday, 1977.

ROBERT MAKLA is an attorney and an active member of the Friends of Central Park.

EVE MERRIAM: *Ab to Zogg*, Atheneum, 1977; *Boys & Girls, Girls & Boys*, Holt, Rinehart & Winston, 1972; *Finding a Poem*, Atheneum, 1970.

SHEILA MOON: *A Magic Dwells*, Wesleyan University Press, 1970; *Braver Than That*, Golden Quill Press, 1975; *Scarlet Incantations*, Guild for Psychic Studies, 1977.

STEPHEN MOOSER is president of the Society of Children's Book Writers and the author of: *101 Black Cats*, Scholastic Book Services, 1976; *The Ghost with the Halloween Hiccups*, Franklin Watts, 1977; *The Woman Who Could See Through Walls and 13 Other Amazing Stories*, Lippincott, 1979.

GISELA MORIARTY frequently writes on child care and safety topics.

LILLIAN MORRISON: *Best Wishes, Amen*, Crowell, 1974; *The Sidewalk Racer and Other Poems of Sports and Motion*, Lothrop, Lee & Shepard; *Would You Marry a Mineral?* Lothrop, Lee & Shepard, 1978.

PAMELA MORTON lives in New York at the Cathedral of St. John the Divine with her husband and four daughters. She writes and illustrates picture books.

BARBARA MURPHY: *Home Free*, Delacorte, 1970; *Thor Heyerdahl & the Reed Boat RA*, Lippincott, 1974; *No Place to Run*, Bradbury, 1977.

WALTER DEAN MYERS: *Mojo and the Russians*, Viking, 1977; *Fast Sam, Cool Clyde and Stuff*, Viking, 1975; *The Dragon Takes a Wife*, Bobbs-Merrill, 1972.

LAURIE NORRIS is press agent at John Springer Associates in New York. She designs and makes greeting card clothes, and she is fascinated by the human and animal forms that are often apparent in cloud formations.

ANDRE NORTON contributed "Diary of a Young Girl in Old New York," by Catherine Elizabeth Havens, from his personal collection.

MARGARET O'CONNELL: *The Magic Cauldron: Witchcraft for Good and Evil*, S. G. Phillips, 1975.

SIDNEY OFFITT: *What Kind of Guy Do You Think I Am?* Lippincott, 1977; *Not All Girls Have Million Dollar Smiles*, Coward, McCann & Geoghegan, 1971; *The Adventures of Homer Fink*, St. Martin's, 1966.

RICHARD PECK: *Monster Night at Grandma's House*, Viking, 1977; *The Ghost Belonged to Me*, Viking, 1975; *Ghosts I Have Been*, Viking, 1977.

DANIEL MANUS PINKWATER: *The Big Orange Splot*, Scholastic Book Service, 1977; *The Blue Thing*, Prentice-Hall, 1977; *Fat Men from Space*, Dodd, Mead, 1977.

MARIANA PRIETO: *The Panther's Fleas/ Las Pulgas de la Pantera*, Prentice-Hall, 1976; *Johnny Lost*, John Day, 1969; *When the Monkeys Wore Sombreros*, E. M. Hale Co., 1969.

PENELOPE PRODDOW is a staff lecturer at the Metropolitan Museum of Art in New York City and author of: *Art Tells a Story: Greek and Roman Myths*, Doubleday, 1979; *Art Tells a Story: The Bible*, Doubleday, 1979.

ROBERT QUACKENBUSH: *The Holiday Song Book*, Lothrop, Lee & Shepard, 1977; *Mr. Snow Bunting's Secret*, Lothrop, Lee & Shepard, 1978; *Along Came the Model T: How Henry Ford Put the World on Wheels*, Parents' Magazine Press, 1978.

ELAINE RAPHAEL: *Donkey and Carlos*, Harper & Row; *Sam Baker Gone West*, Viking, 1977; *Letters to Horseface*, by F. N. Monjo, illustrated by Elaine Raphael, 1975.

SAM REAVIN: *I Wish I Had a Pony*, Grosset & Dunlap; *The Hunters Are Coming*, Grosset & Dunlap; *Hurray for Captain Jane*, Parents' Magazine Press.

JOHANNA REISS: *The Upstairs Room*, Crowell, 1972; *The Journey Back*, Crowell, 1976.

KEN RINCIARI has illustrated several books, including Joan Aiken's *Skin Spinners, Poems*, and his work has appeared frequently in the New York *Times Book Review*. Born in New York, he is living in the Netherlands.

JERRY ROBINSON is an illustrator, an author, and a political cartoonist.

BARBARA ROLLOCK is the director of Children's Services at the New York Public Library, and the moderator of "The World of Children's Literature" on WNYC radio.

RICHARD ROSENBLUM: *Tugboats*, written and illustrated by Richard Rosenblum, Holt, Rinehart & Winston, 1976; *Bridges*, by Scott Corbett, illustrated by Richard Rosenblum, Four Winds Press, 1978.

LAVINIA RUSS: *Over the Hills and Far Away,* Harcourt, Brace, 1968; *Alec's Sand Castle,* Harper & Row, 1972; *The April Age,* Atheneum, 1975.

ALICE SHICK AND JOEL SHICK: *Zoo Year,* by Alice Schick and Sara Ann Friedman; illustrated by Joel Schick, Lippincott, 1978; *Serengeti Cats,* by Alice Schick, illustrated by Joel Schick, Lippincott, 1977; *Just This Once,* written and illustrated by Alice and Joel Schick, Lippincott, 1978; *Joel Schick's Christmas Present,* by Joel Schick, Lippincott, 1977.

GEORGE SELDEN: *The Cricket in Times Square,* Farrar, Straus & Giroux, 1960; *Tucker's Countryside,* Farrar, Straus & Giroux, 1969; *Harry Cat's Pet Puppy,* Farrar, Straus & Giroux, 1977.

BARBARA SEULING: *The Last Cow on the White House Lawn and Other Little-known Facts About the Presidency,* Doubleday, 1978; *You Can't Eat Peanuts in Church and Other Little-known Laws,* Doubleday, 1975; *The Great Big Elephant and the Very Small Elephant,* Crown, 1977.

DENNIS SEULING, a native New Yorker, teaches film and speech at John F. Kennedy High School in Riverdale, New York. He has appeared in several films (crowd scenes) shot on location in New York City.

PHIL SEULING is an avid comic book fan and collector, as well as a noted authority on the subject. He lives in Brooklyn, where he was born, and where he taught English at Lafayette High School for many years.

ANNE ZANE SHANKS: *About Garbage and Stuff,* Viking, 1973; *Old Is What You Get,* Viking.

DOROTHY SHUTTLESWORTH: *To Find a Dinosaur,* Doubleday, 1973; *How Wild Animals Fight,* Doubleday, 1976; *Zoos in the Making,* Dutton, 1977.

ALVIN AND VIRGINIA SILVERSTEIN: *Gerbils: All About Them,* Lippincott, 1976; *The Left-hander's World,* Follett, 1977; *Cats: All About Them,* Lothrop, Lee & Shepard, 1978.

ALFRED SLOTE: *Jake,* J. B. Lippincott, 1971; *Hang Tough, Paul Mather,* Lippincott, 1973; *A Trip to Alpha,* Lippincott, 1978.

NORAH SMARIDGE: *School Is Not a Missile Range,* Abingdon Press, 1977; *The World of Chocolate,* Julian Messner, 1969; *Famous Literary Teams for Young People,* Dodd, Mead, 1977.

SUSAN TRENTACOSTE is a free-lance photographer. She lives in New York City.

JUDITH TURNER is a photographer who has exhibited her works both in this country and abroad.

KAREN SHAW WIDMAN is a former editorial assistant at the Viking Press and a student of library science. Born in Brooklyn, she lives in Queens with her husband and daughter.

JAY WILLIAMS: *The Danny Dunn Books,* McGraw-Hill; *The Practical Princess,* Parents' Magazine Press, 1969; *The Hero from Otherwhere,* Walck, 1972.

BEBE WILLOUGHBY: *The Dream Book,* coauthored with Olga Litowinsky, Coward, McCann & Geoghegan, 1978.

LAUREN L. WOHL works for Harper & Row/ T. Y. Crowell in their library promotion department.

JUDIE WOLKOFF: *Wally,* Bradbury, 1977.

JANE YOLEN: *The Girl Who Cried Flowers,* Crowell, 1974; *The Seeing Stick,* Crowell, 1977; *The Mermaid's Three Wisdoms,* Collins-World, 1978.

GEORG ZAPPLER: *Behind the Scenes at the Zoo,* Doubleday, 1977; *Snakes,* Grosset and Dunlap, 1976.

MARGOT ZEMACH: *The Judge,* by Harve Zemach, illustrated by Margot Zemach, Farrar, Straus & Giroux, 1969; *A Penny a Look,* by Harve Zemach, illustrated by Margot Zemach, Farrar, Straus & Giroux, 1971; *It Could Always Be Worse,* Farrar, Straus & Giroux, 1977.

CHARLOTTE ZOLOTOW: *The Beautiful Christmas Tree,* Parnassus, 1972; *A Father Like That,* Harper & Row, 1971; *It's Not Fair,* Harper & Row, 1976.

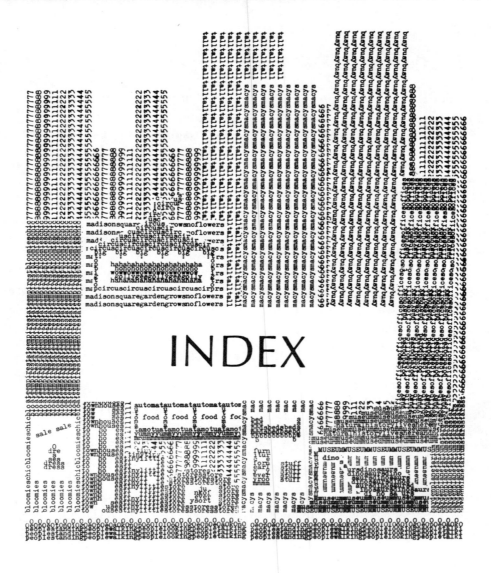

INDEX